A MARVEL COMICS EVENT

CIVIL WAR

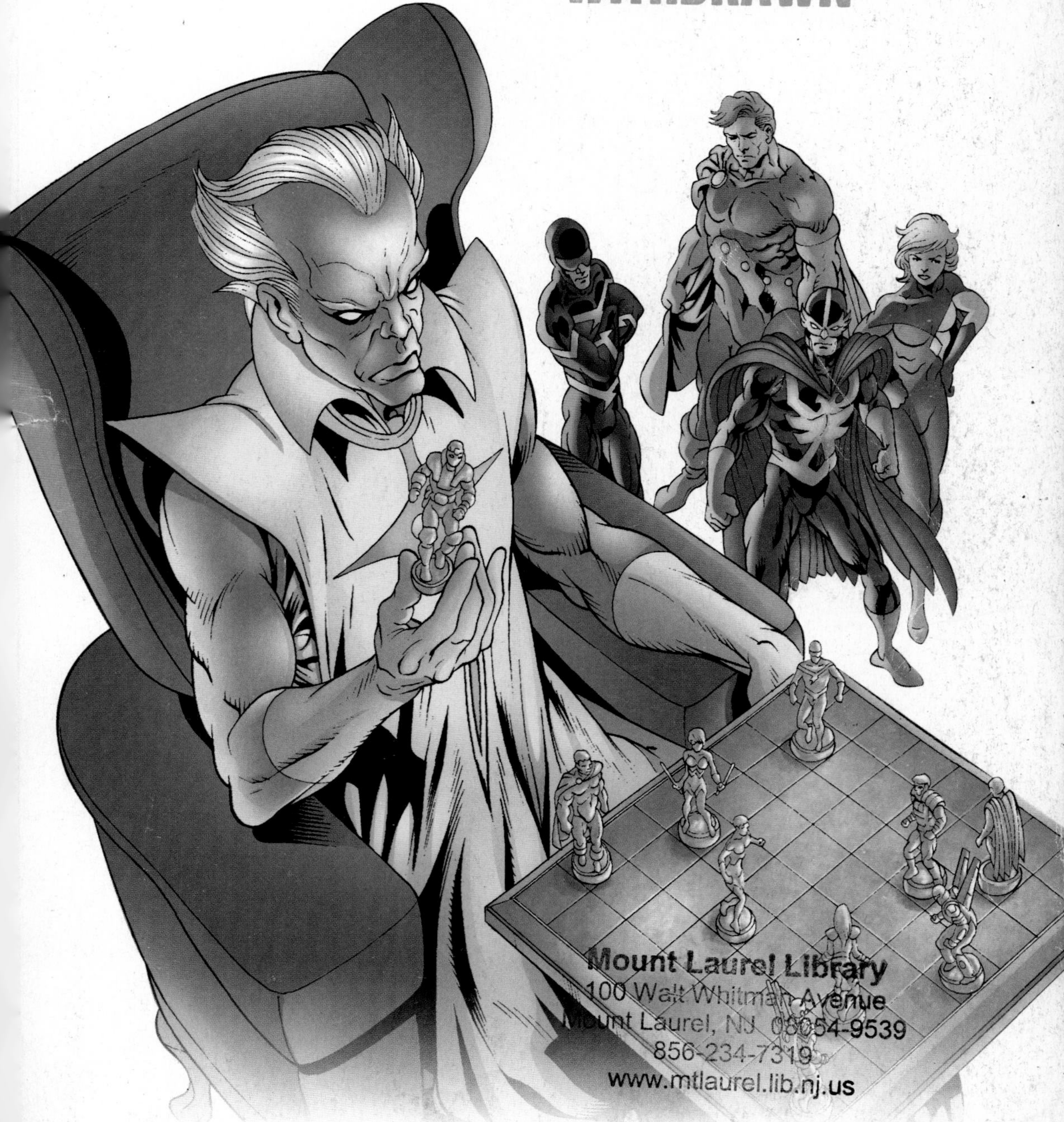

THUNDERBOLTS

A

MARVEL COMICS

PRESENTATION

CIVIL

T

WRITER
FABIAN NICIEZA

PENCILERS
TOM GRUMMETT
WITH DAVE ROSS (ISSUE #101)

INKERS
GARY ERSKINE
WITH CAM SMITH (ISSUE #101)

COLORIST
SOTOCOLOR'S J. BROWN
WITH A. STREET (ISSUE #101)

LETTERER
RS & COMICRAFT'S
ALBERT DESCHESNE

EDITOR
MOLLY LAZER

CONSULTING EDITOR
TOM BREVOORT

COLLECTION EDITOR
JENNIFER GRÜNWALD

ASSISTANT EDITORS
MICHAEL SHORT &
CORY LEVINE

ASSOCIATE EDITOR
MARK D. BEAZLEY

SENIOR EDITOR, SPECIAL PROJECTS
JEFF YOUNGQUIST

SENIOR VICE PRESIDENT OF SALES
DAVID GABRIEL

PRODUCTION
JERRY KALINOWSKI

BOOK DESIGNER
DAYLE CHESLER

VICE PRESIDENT OF CREATIVE
TOM MARVELLI

EDITOR IN CHIEF
JOE QUESADA

PUBLISHER
DAN BUCKLEY

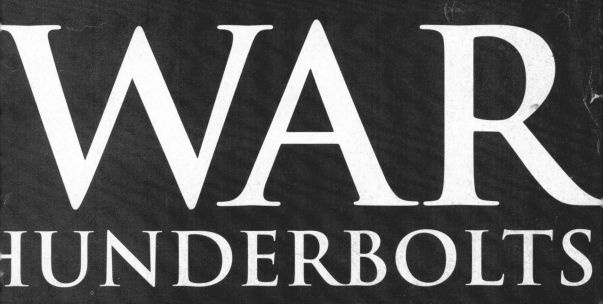

WAR
HUNDERBOLTS

TG
GE 05
¡SOTO!

THUNDERBOLTS #101

THEY WERE THE MASTERS OF EVIL. THEY WERE SUPER-VILLAINS. THEY HAD A PLAN. THEY PRETENDED TO BE HEROES. SLOWLY, THEY REALIZED THEY REALLY WANTED TO BE HEROES. SOME HAVE FAILED. SOME HAVE SUCCEEDED. MOST ARE STILL TRYING...

THUNDERBOLTS

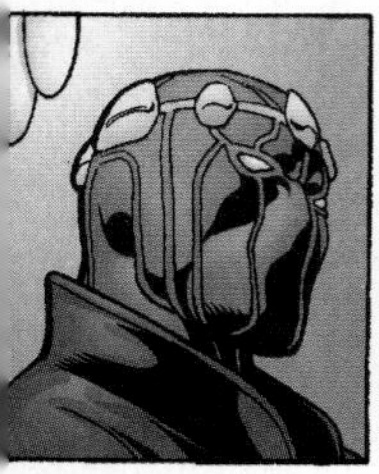

ARON HELMUT ZEMO

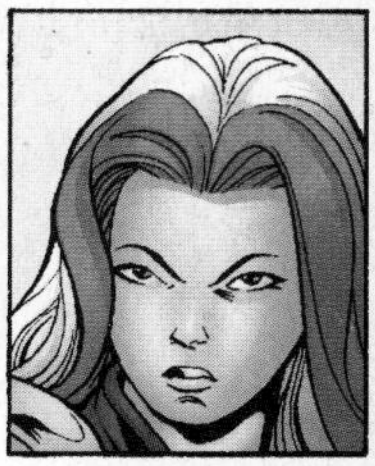

MELISSA GOLD
SONGBIRD

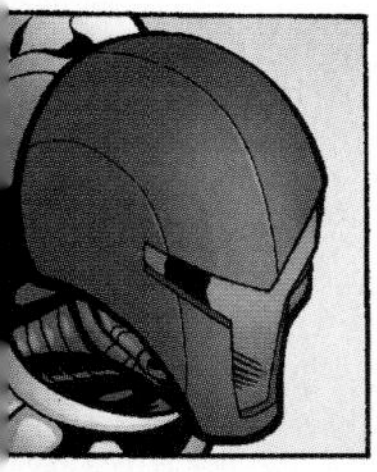

ABE JENKINS
M.A.C.H. IV

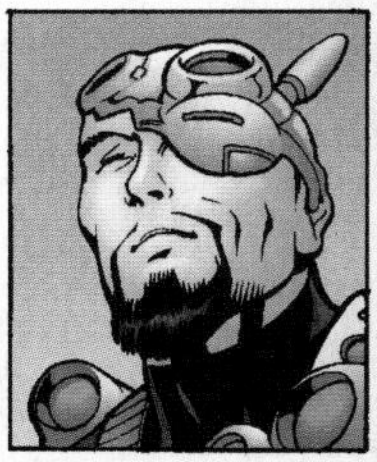

P. NORBERT EBERSOL
FIXER

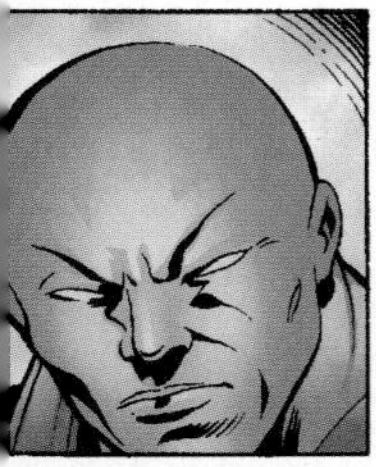

DR. CHEN LU
E RADIOACTIVE MAN

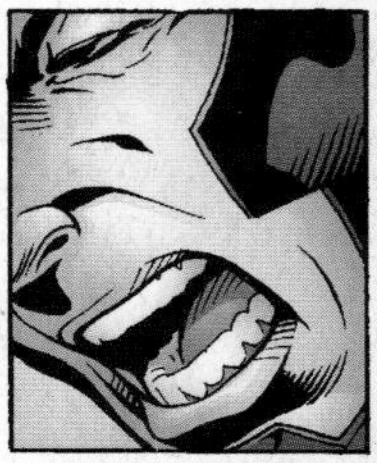

ERIK JOSTEN
ATLAS

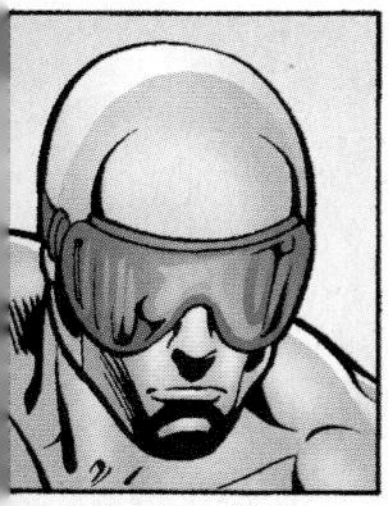

DONNIE GILL
BLIZZARD

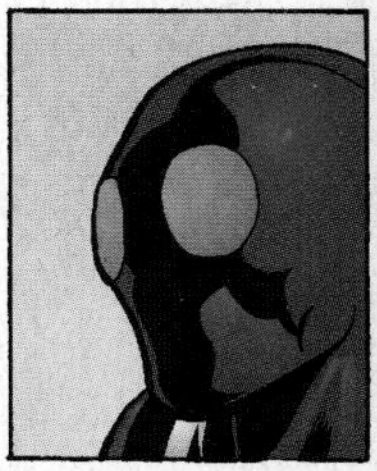

CONRAD JOSTEN
SMUGGLER

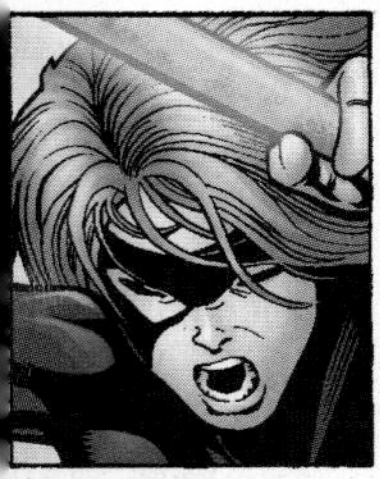

NICE OLIVIA YANIZESKI
JOYSTICK

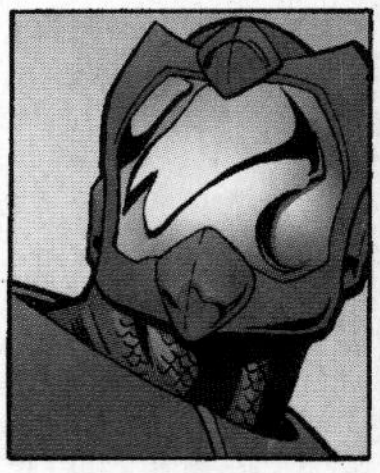

ANDREAS STRUCKER
SWORDSMAN

IT DOESN'T ALWAYS GO THE WAY WE PLANNED. THE WAY WE WANT. IT'S GETTING TO THE POINT WHERE I ALMOST DON'T WANT TO BOTHER ASKING WHY ANYMORE. IN ORDER TO SAVE THE UNIVERSE, WE HAD TO KILL ONE OF OUR TEAMMATES. RIDICULOUS. ***GENIS-VELL*** WAS ONCE KNOWN AS ***LEGACY,*** THEN HE ACCEPTED HIS FATHER'S MANTLE, CALLING HIMSELF ***CAPTAIN MARVEL.*** THEN, FEELING HE'D FAILED LIVING UP TO THAT, HE CHANGED HIS NAME TO ***PHOTON.***

I THINK HE DID THAT BECAUSE A PART OF HIM *KNEW* HE WAS GOING TO HAVE TO DIE AND HE DIDN'T WANT TO FAIL AGAIN AS CAPTAIN MARVEL. I WAS TEAM LEADER, AND I AGREED WITH THE DECISION TO KILL HIM BECAUSE HE'D BECOME LIKE SOME WALKING ***HOLE*** IN ***TIME*** AND ***SPACE*** AND THOSE HOLES WERE *SPREADING.* EVENTUALLY, THEY WOULD HAVE SWALLOWED UP ALL OF EXISTENCE.

SO WITH GENIS BURIED, WE'VE DONE WHAT WE ALWAYS DO: WE'VE MOVED ON (*ACTUALLY, SINCE HIS BODY WAS BISECTED AND SPREAD ACROSS TIME AND SPACE, THERE WASN'T MUCH TO BURY*).

ZEMO HAD GATHERED A GROUP OF FORMER T-BOLTS TO KILL PHOTON. HE WAS RESPONSIBLE FOR THE PROBLEMS GENIS WAS HAVING AND WANTED TO SOLVE THE MATTER--AND TAKE THE RESPONSIBILITY OUT OF OUR HANDS.

AFTER THE FIGHT, THERE WERE SOME LOOSE ENDS. OUR OLD TEAMMATE, ***MOONSTONE,*** WHO HAD ATTACKED US, TURNED OUT TO STILL BE IN A ***VEGETATIVE STATE*** *(PUPPET STRINGS PULLED COURTESY OF ZEMO'S CONTROL OVER HER TWIN ALIEN GEMSTONES).*

AND ***BLACKOUT,*** WHO WE *KNEW* HAD ***DIED*** BATTLING THE ***AVENGERS*** YEARS AGO, TURNED OUT TO HAVE BEEN DEAD ALL ALONG. HIS CORPSE HAD BEEN SUCKED INTO THE DARKFORCE DIMENSION, WHICH SEEMS TO CALL BACK ITS OWN, AND THAT PROVED TO BE THE HIDING PLACE FOR ATLAS'S BROTHER, THE ***SMUGGLER,*** WHO HAD BEEN LOST IN BATTLE OVER A YEAR AGO.

OH, YEAH, ***MAN-KILLER*** PULLED A DISAPPEARING ACT LIKE SHE ALWAYS DOES WHEN IT'S TIME TO MAKE HARD CHOICES.

SO THAT LEAVES US WITH ***TEN THUNDERBOLTS,*** EVERY SINGLE ONE OF THEM AFRAID TO ASK THE HARDEST QUESTION: *AFTER EVERYTHING THAT'S HAPPENED, WHY ARE WE DOING THIS?*

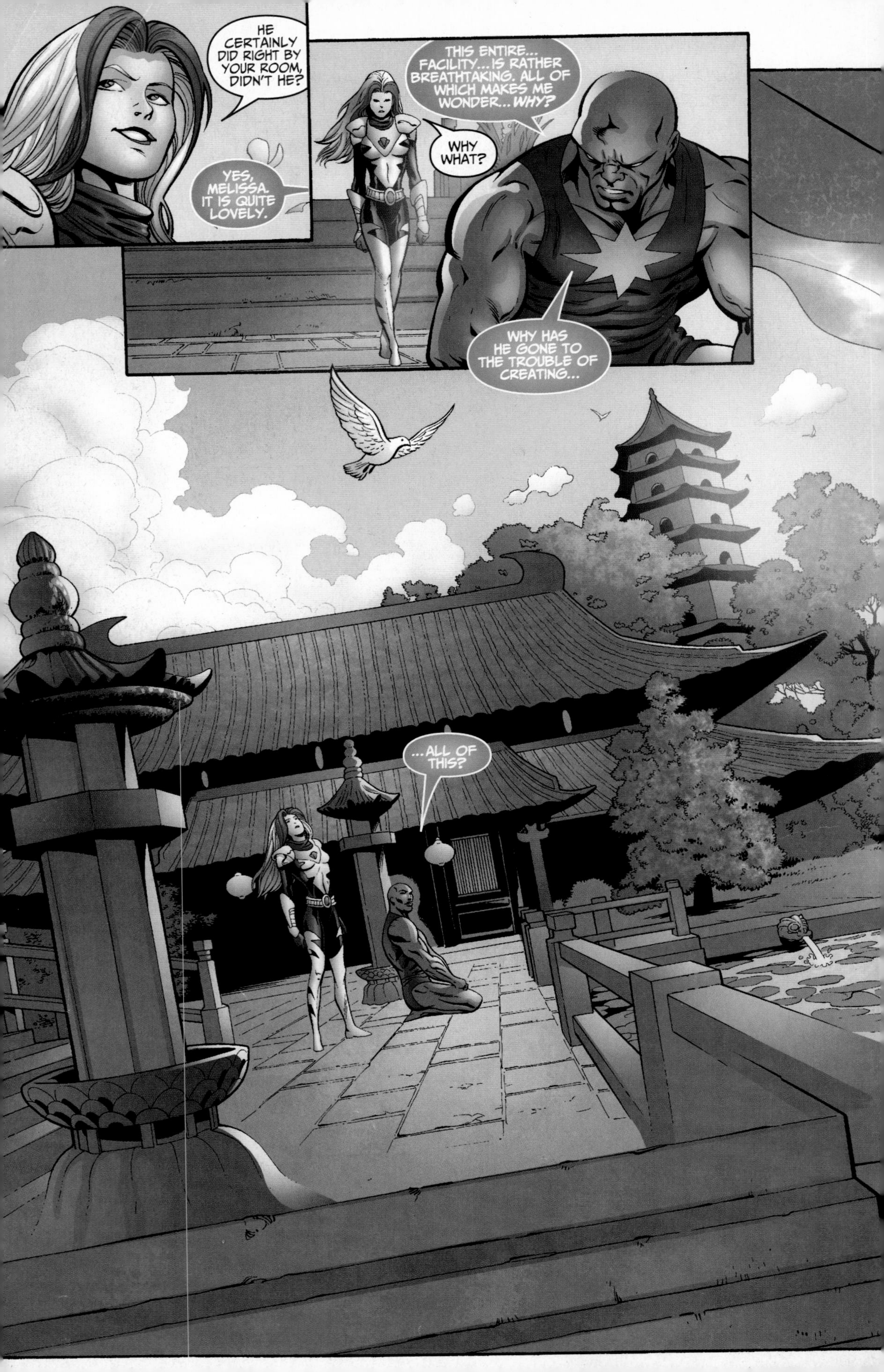
HE CERTAINLY DID RIGHT BY YOUR ROOM, DIDN'T HE?
YES, MELISSA. IT IS QUITE LOVELY.
THIS ENTIRE... FACILITY... IS RATHER BREATHTAKING. ALL OF WHICH MAKES ME WONDER... WHY?
WHY WHAT?
WHY HAS HE GONE TO THE TROUBLE OF CREATING...
...ALL OF THIS?

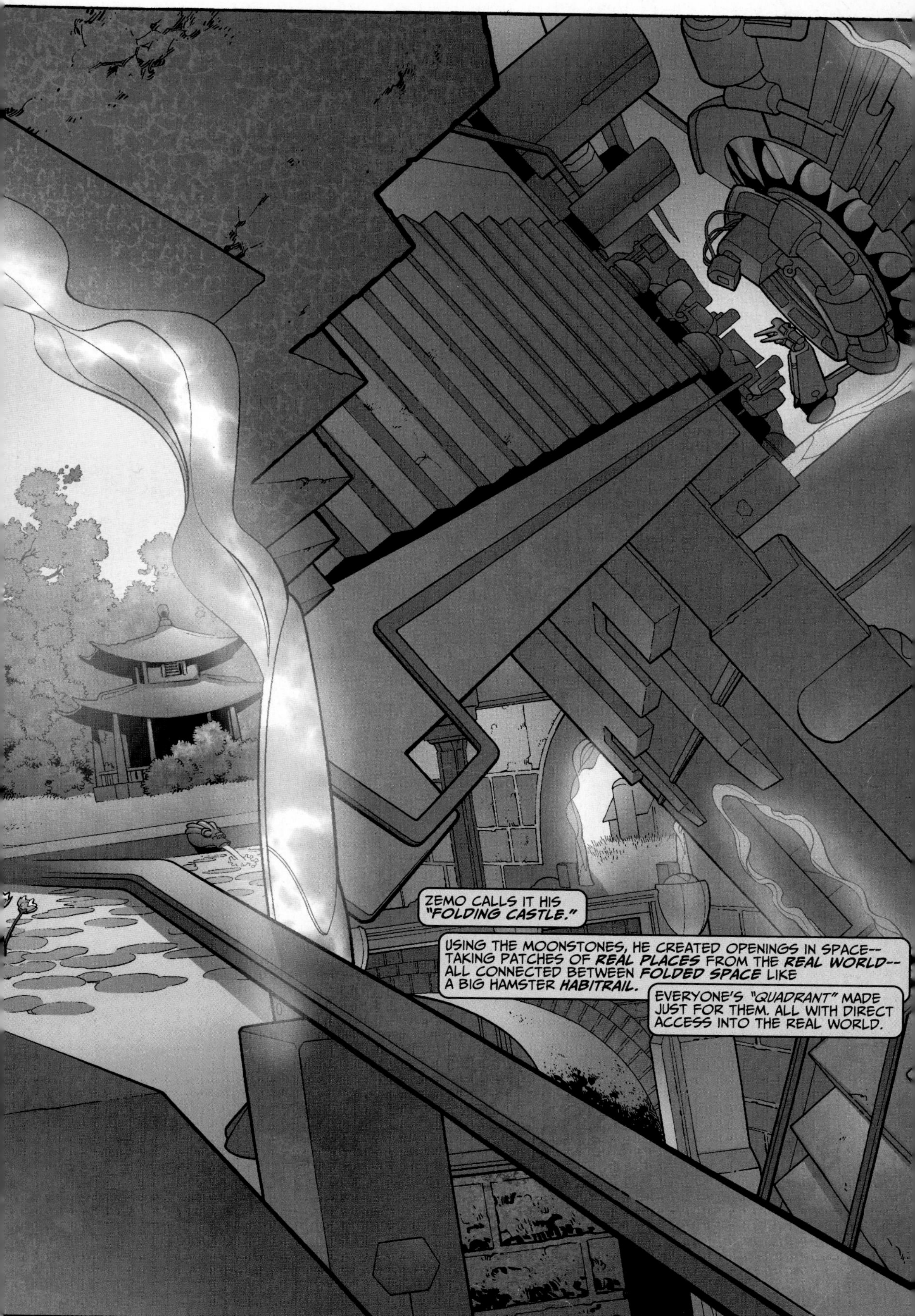
ZEMO CALLS IT HIS "FOLDING CASTLE."
USING THE MOONSTONES, HE CREATED OPENINGS IN SPACE-- TAKING PATCHES OF REAL PLACES FROM THE REAL WORLD-- ALL CONNECTED BETWEEN FOLDED SPACE LIKE A BIG HAMSTER HABITRAIL.
EVERYONE'S "QUADRANT" MADE JUST FOR THEM. ALL WITH DIRECT ACCESS INTO THE REAL WORLD.

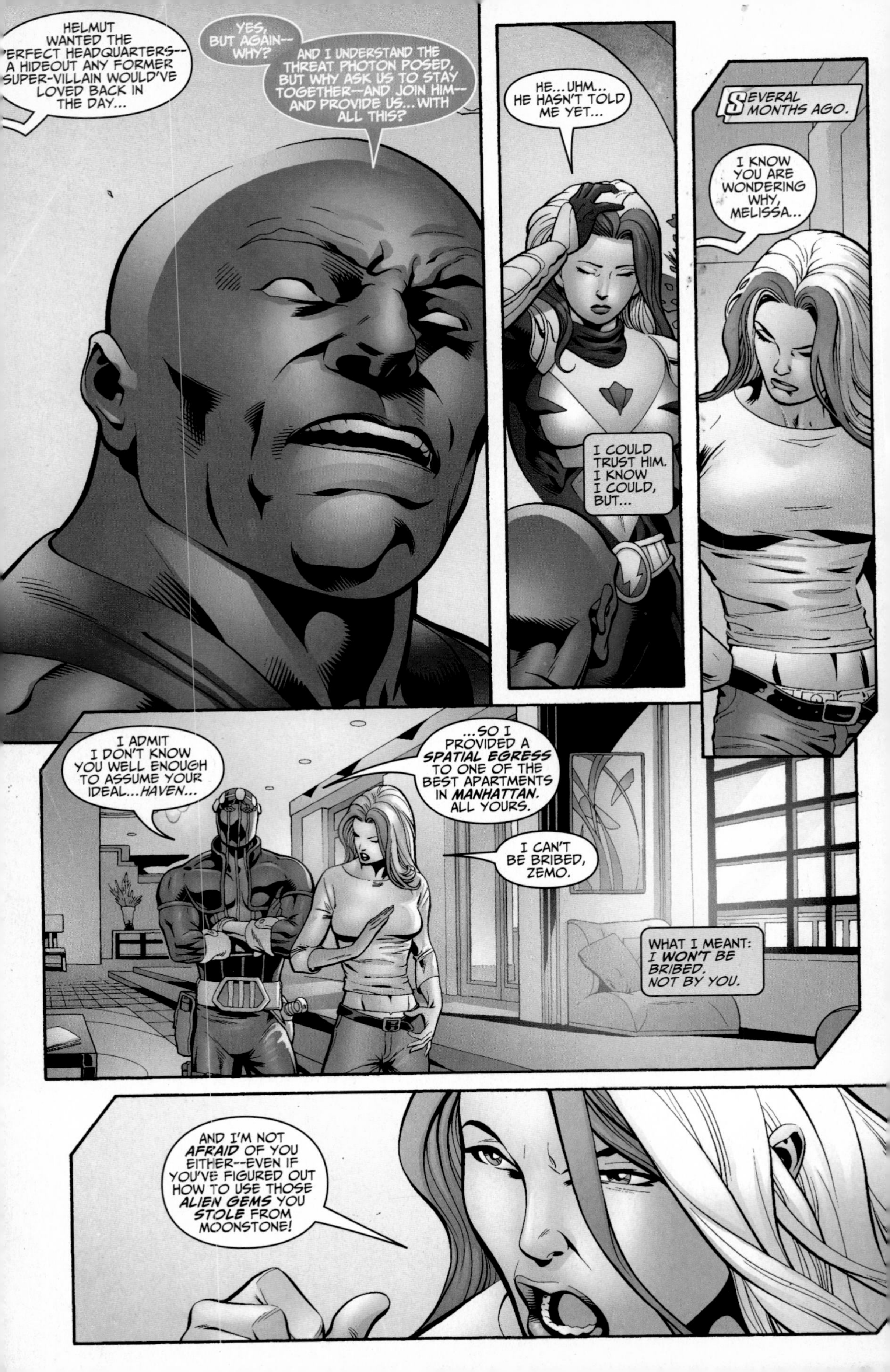
HELMUT WANTED THE PERFECT HEADQUARTERS-- A HIDEOUT ANY FORMER SUPER-VILLAIN WOULD'VE LOVED BACK IN THE DAY...
YES, BUT AGAIN-- WHY?
AND I UNDERSTAND THE THREAT PHOTON POSED, BUT WHY ASK US TO STAY TOGETHER--AND JOIN HIM-- AND PROVIDE US... WITH ALL THIS?
HE...UHM... HE HASN'T TOLD ME YET...
I COULD TRUST HIM. I KNOW I COULD, BUT...
SEVERAL MONTHS AGO.
I KNOW YOU ARE WONDERING WHY, MELISSA...
I ADMIT I DON'T KNOW YOU WELL ENOUGH TO ASSUME YOUR IDEAL...HAVEN...
...SO I PROVIDED A SPATIAL EGRESS TO ONE OF THE BEST APARTMENTS IN MANHATTAN. ALL YOURS.
I CAN'T BE BRIBED, ZEMO.
WHAT I MEANT: I WON'T BE BRIBED. NOT BY YOU.
AND I'M NOT AFRAID OF YOU EITHER--EVEN IF YOU'VE FIGURED OUT HOW TO USE THOSE ALIEN GEMS YOU STOLE FROM MOONSTONE!

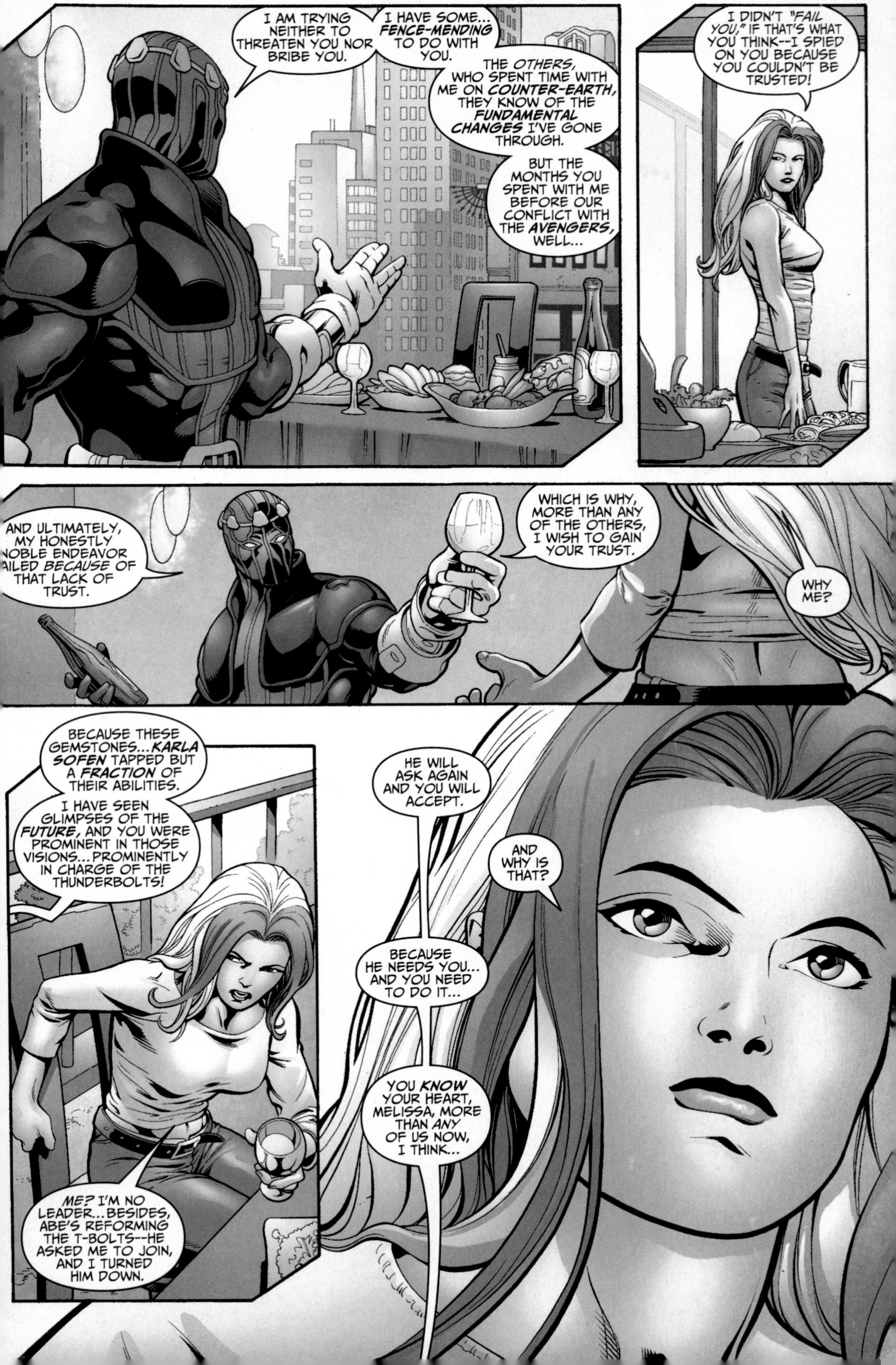

I AM TRYING NEITHER TO THREATEN YOU NOR BRIBE YOU.
I HAVE SOME... FENCE-MENDING TO DO WITH YOU.
THE OTHERS, WHO SPENT TIME WITH ME ON COUNTER-EARTH, THEY KNOW OF THE FUNDAMENTAL CHANGES I'VE GONE THROUGH.
BUT THE MONTHS YOU SPENT WITH ME BEFORE OUR CONFLICT WITH THE AVENGERS, WELL...
I DIDN'T "FAIL YOU," IF THAT'S WHAT YOU THINK--I SPIED ON YOU BECAUSE YOU COULDN'T BE TRUSTED!
AND ULTIMATELY, MY HONESTLY NOBLE ENDEAVOR FAILED BECAUSE OF THAT LACK OF TRUST.
WHICH IS WHY, MORE THAN ANY OF THE OTHERS, I WISH TO GAIN YOUR TRUST.
WHY ME?
BECAUSE THESE GEMSTONES... KARLA SOFEN TAPPED BUT A FRACTION OF THEIR ABILITIES.
I HAVE SEEN GLIMPSES OF THE FUTURE, AND YOU WERE PROMINENT IN THOSE VISIONS... PROMINENTLY IN CHARGE OF THE THUNDERBOLTS!
ME? I'M NO LEADER... BESIDES, ABE'S REFORMING THE T-BOLTS--HE ASKED ME TO JOIN, AND I TURNED HIM DOWN.
HE WILL ASK AGAIN AND YOU WILL ACCEPT.
AND WHY IS THAT?
BECAUSE HE NEEDS YOU... AND YOU NEED TO DO IT...
YOU KNOW YOUR HEART, MELISSA, MORE THAN ANY OF US NOW, I THINK...

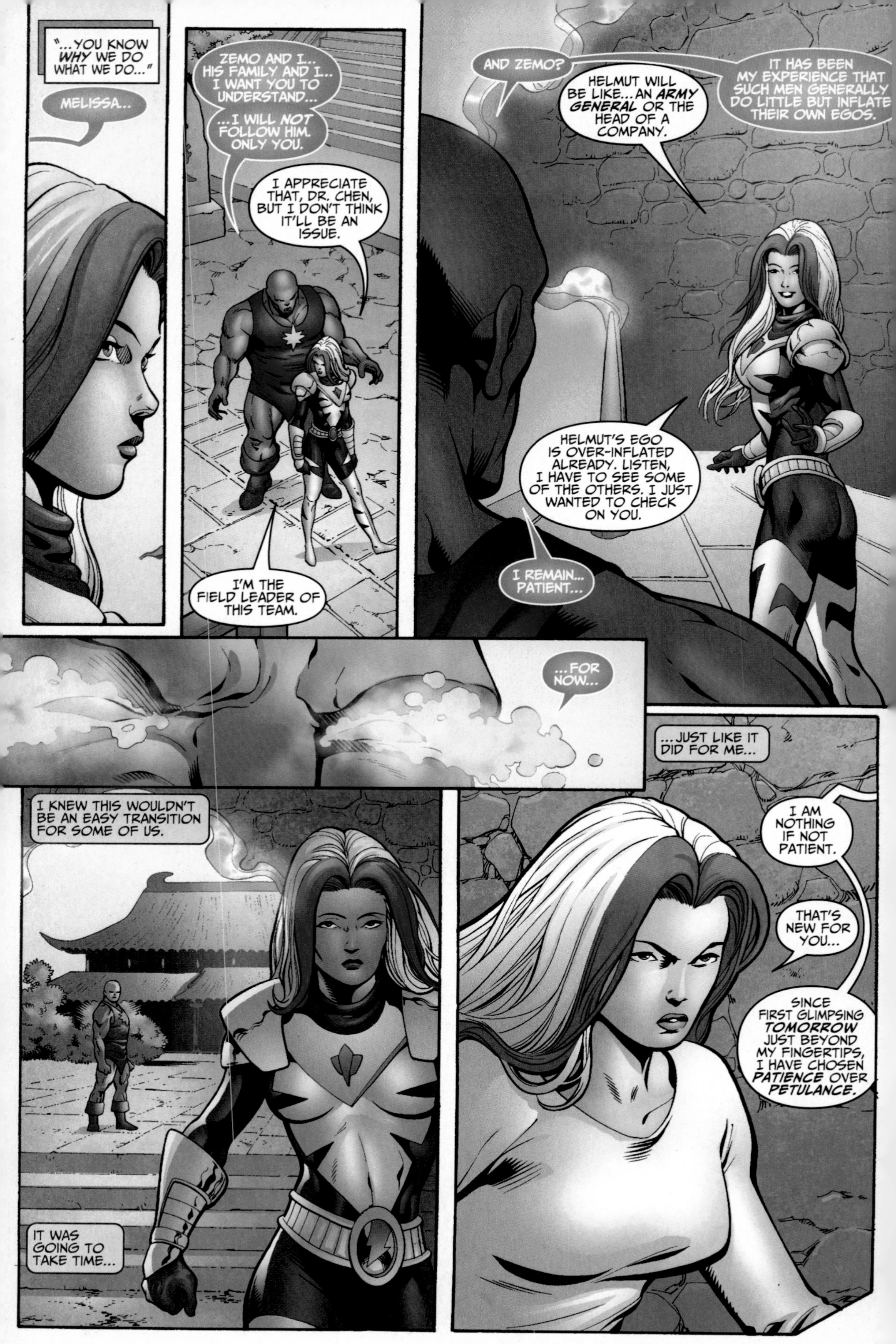

"...YOU KNOW WHY WE DO WHAT WE DO..."
MELISSA..
ZEMO AND I... HIS FAMILY AND I.. I WANT YOU TO UNDERSTAND...
...I WILL NOT FOLLOW HIM. ONLY YOU.
I APPRECIATE THAT, DR. CHEN, BUT I DON'T THINK IT'LL BE AN ISSUE.
I'M THE FIELD LEADER OF THIS TEAM.
AND ZEMO?
HELMUT WILL BE LIKE... AN ARMY GENERAL OR THE HEAD OF A COMPANY.
IT HAS BEEN MY EXPERIENCE THAT SUCH MEN GENERALLY DO LITTLE BUT INFLATE THEIR OWN EGOS.
HELMUT'S EGO IS OVER-INFLATED ALREADY. LISTEN, I HAVE TO SEE SOME OF THE OTHERS. I JUST WANTED TO CHECK ON YOU.
I REMAIN... PATIENT...
...FOR NOW...
...JUST LIKE IT DID FOR ME...
I KNEW THIS WOULDN'T BE AN EASY TRANSITION FOR SOME OF US.
IT WAS GOING TO TAKE TIME...
I AM NOTHING IF NOT PATIENT.
THAT'S NEW FOR YOU...
SINCE FIRST GLIMPSING TOMORROW JUST BEYOND MY FINGERTIPS, I HAVE CHOSEN PATIENCE OVER PETULANCE.

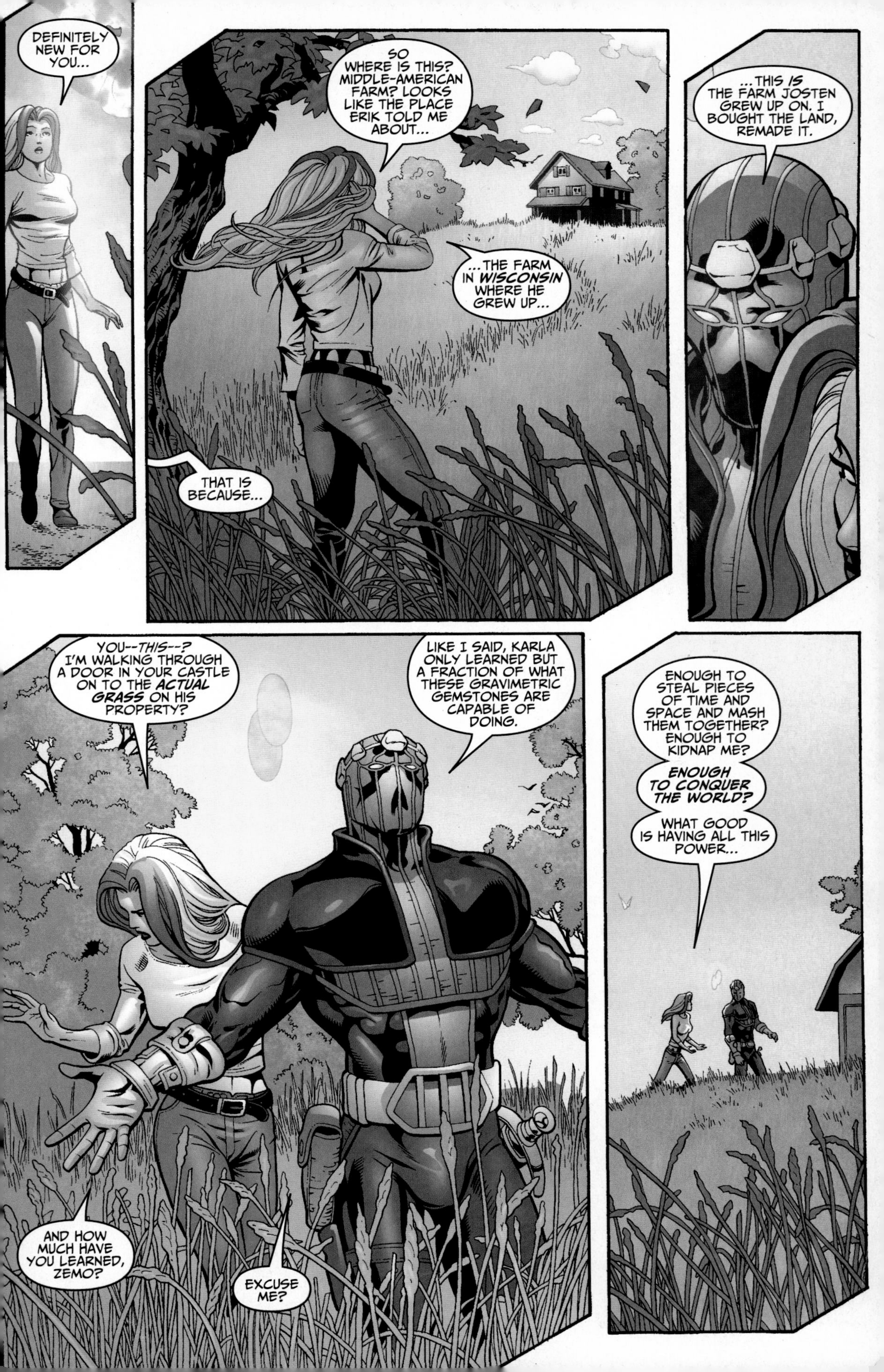
DEFINITELY NEW FOR YOU...
SO WHERE IS THIS? MIDDLE-AMERICAN FARM? LOOKS LIKE THE PLACE ERIK TOLD ME ABOUT...
...THE FARM IN *WISCONSIN* WHERE HE GREW UP...
THAT IS BECAUSE...
...THIS *IS* THE FARM JOSTEN GREW UP ON. I BOUGHT THE LAND, REMADE IT.
YOU--*THIS*--? I'M WALKING THROUGH A DOOR IN YOUR CASTLE ON TO THE *ACTUAL GRASS* ON HIS PROPERTY?
LIKE I SAID, KARLA ONLY LEARNED BUT A FRACTION OF WHAT THESE GRAVIMETRIC GEMSTONES ARE CAPABLE OF DOING.
AND HOW MUCH HAVE YOU LEARNED, ZEMO?
EXCUSE ME?
ENOUGH TO STEAL PIECES OF TIME AND SPACE AND MASH THEM TOGETHER? ENOUGH TO KIDNAP ME?
ENOUGH TO CONQUER THE WORLD?
WHAT GOOD IS HAVING ALL THIS POWER...

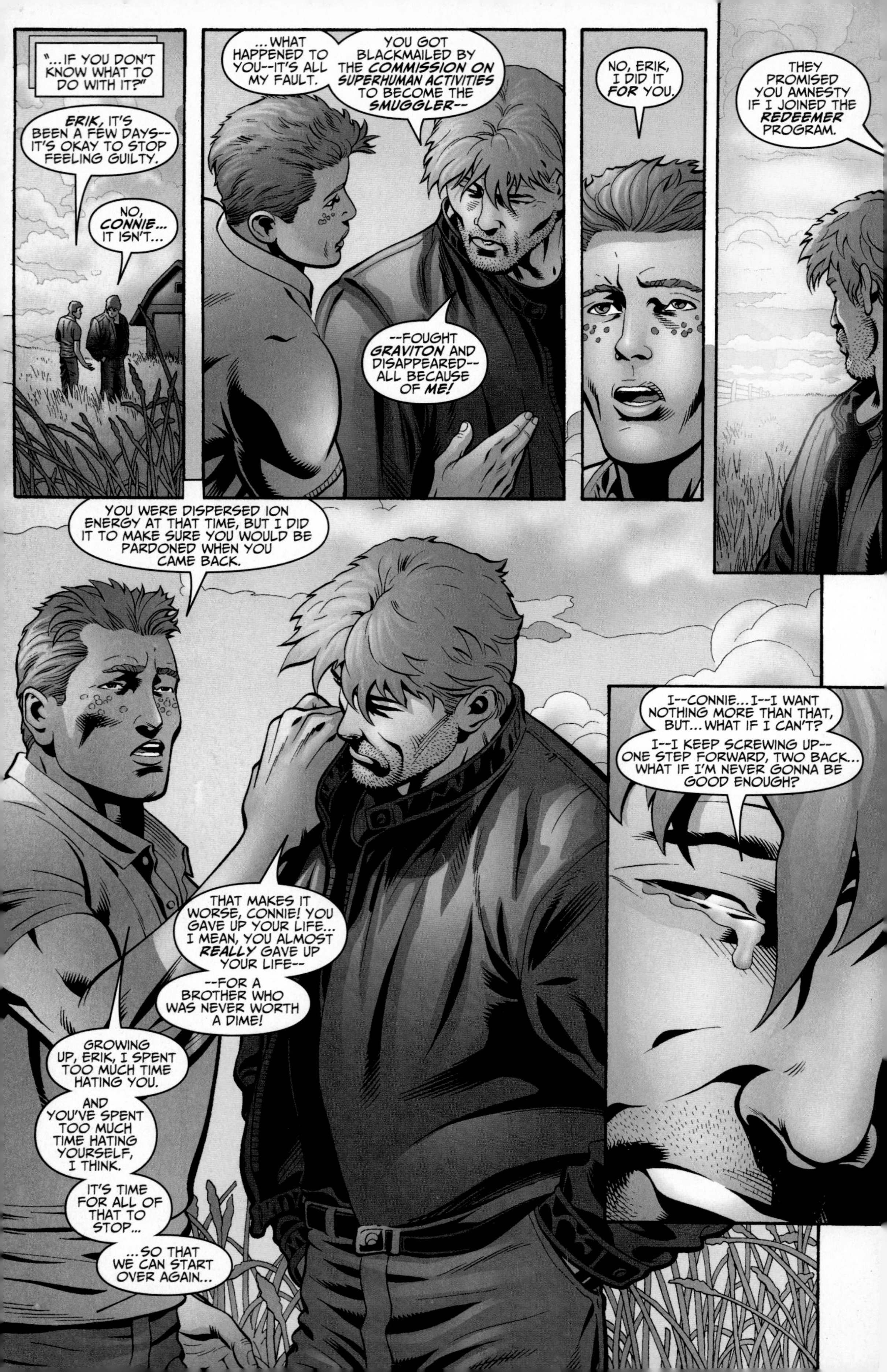
"...IF YOU DON'T KNOW WHAT TO DO WITH IT?"
ERIK, IT'S BEEN A FEW DAYS--IT'S OKAY TO STOP FEELING GUILTY.
NO, CONNIE... IT ISN'T...
...WHAT HAPPENED TO YOU--IT'S ALL MY FAULT.
YOU GOT BLACKMAILED BY THE COMMISSION ON SUPERHUMAN ACTIVITIES TO BECOME THE SMUGGLER--
--FOUGHT GRAVITON AND DISAPPEARED--ALL BECAUSE OF ME!
NO, ERIK, I DID IT FOR YOU.
THEY PROMISED YOU AMNESTY IF I JOINED THE REDEEMER PROGRAM.
YOU WERE DISPERSED ION ENERGY AT THAT TIME, BUT I DID IT TO MAKE SURE YOU WOULD BE PARDONED WHEN YOU CAME BACK.
THAT MAKES IT WORSE, CONNIE! YOU GAVE UP YOUR LIFE... I MEAN, YOU ALMOST REALLY GAVE UP YOUR LIFE--
--FOR A BROTHER WHO WAS NEVER WORTH A DIME!
GROWING UP, ERIK, I SPENT TOO MUCH TIME HATING YOU.
AND YOU'VE SPENT TOO MUCH TIME HATING YOURSELF, I THINK.
IT'S TIME FOR ALL OF THAT TO STOP...
...SO THAT WE CAN START OVER AGAIN...
I--CONNIE...I--I WANT NOTHING MORE THAN THAT, BUT...WHAT IF I CAN'T?
I--I KEEP SCREWING UP--ONE STEP FORWARD, TWO BACK... WHAT IF I'M NEVER GONNA BE GOOD ENOUGH?

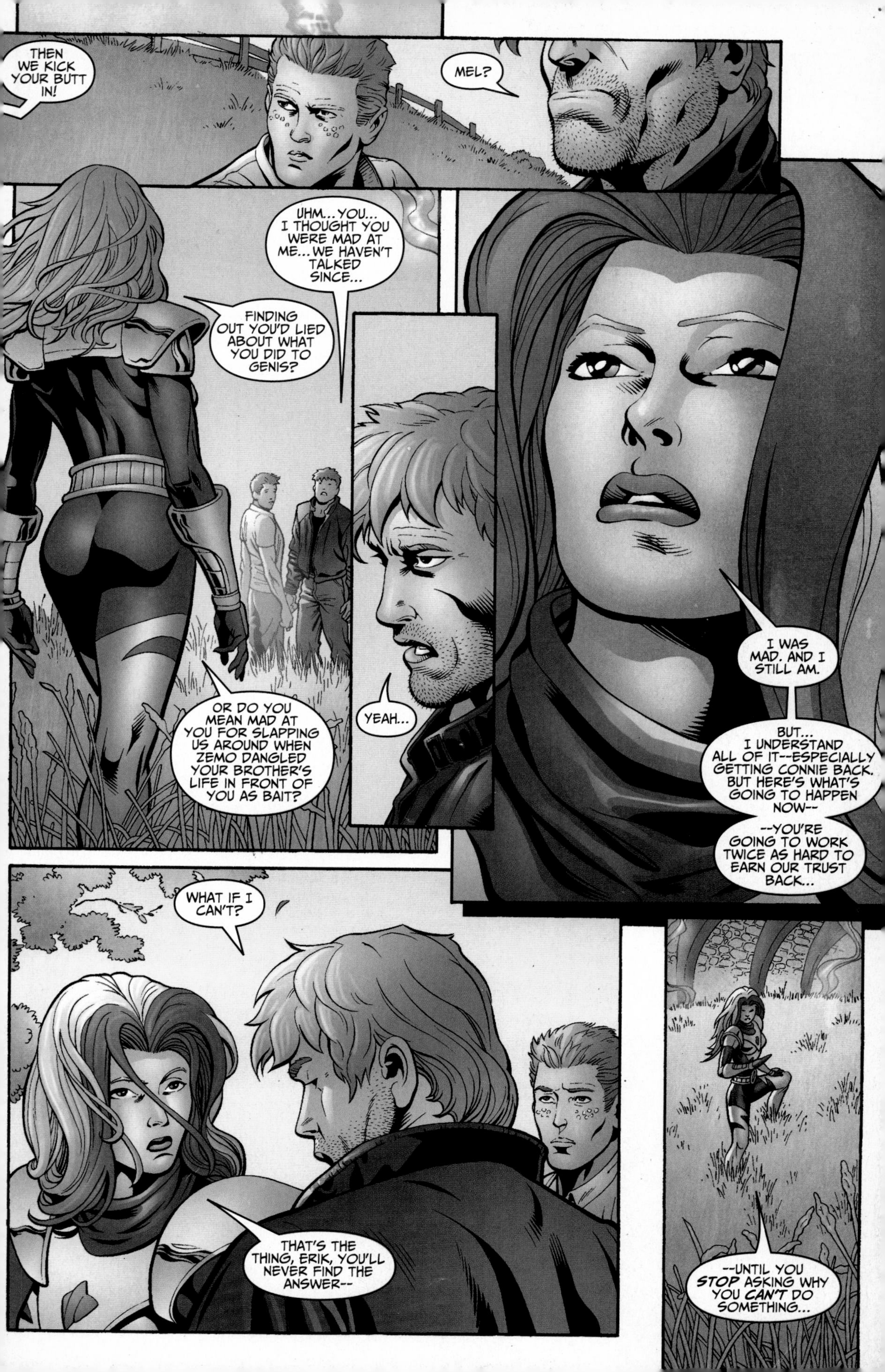
THEN WE KICK YOUR BUTT IN!
MEL?
UHM...YOU... I THOUGHT YOU WERE MAD AT ME...WE HAVEN'T TALKED SINCE...
FINDING OUT YOU'D LIED ABOUT WHAT YOU DID TO GENIS?
OR DO YOU MEAN MAD AT YOU FOR SLAPPING US AROUND WHEN ZEMO DANGLED YOUR BROTHER'S LIFE IN FRONT OF YOU AS BAIT?
YEAH...
I WAS MAD. AND I STILL AM.
BUT... I UNDERSTAND ALL OF IT--ESPECIALLY GETTING CONNIE BACK. BUT HERE'S WHAT'S GOING TO HAPPEN NOW--
--YOU'RE GOING TO WORK TWICE AS HARD TO EARN OUR TRUST BACK...
WHAT IF I CAN'T?
THAT'S THE THING, ERIK, YOU'LL NEVER FIND THE ANSWER--
--UNTIL YOU STOP ASKING WHY YOU CAN'T DO SOMETHING...

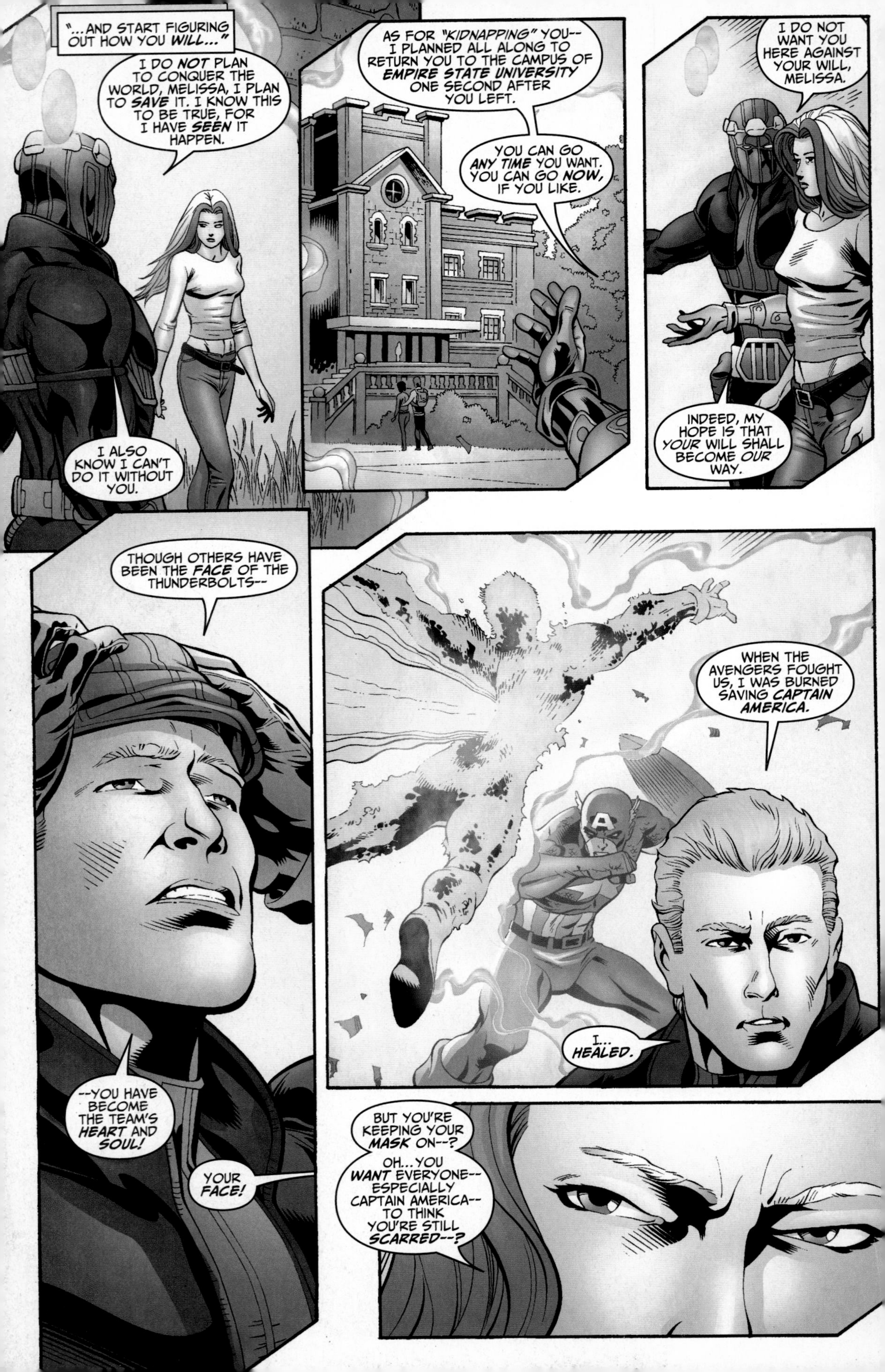
"...AND START FIGURING OUT HOW YOU WILL..."
I DO NOT PLAN TO CONQUER THE WORLD, MELISSA, I PLAN TO SAVE IT. I KNOW THIS TO BE TRUE, FOR I HAVE SEEN IT HAPPEN.
I ALSO KNOW I CAN'T DO IT WITHOUT YOU.
AS FOR "KIDNAPPING" YOU-- I PLANNED ALL ALONG TO RETURN YOU TO THE CAMPUS OF EMPIRE STATE UNIVERSITY ONE SECOND AFTER YOU LEFT.
YOU CAN GO ANY TIME YOU WANT. YOU CAN GO NOW, IF YOU LIKE.
I DO NOT WANT YOU HERE AGAINST YOUR WILL, MELISSA.
INDEED, MY HOPE IS THAT YOUR WILL SHALL BECOME OUR WAY.
THOUGH OTHERS HAVE BEEN THE FACE OF THE THUNDERBOLTS--
--YOU HAVE BECOME THE TEAM'S HEART AND SOUL!
YOUR FACE!
WHEN THE AVENGERS FOUGHT US, I WAS BURNED SAVING CAPTAIN AMERICA.
I... HEALED.
BUT YOU'RE KEEPING YOUR MASK ON--?
OH...YOU WANT EVERYONE-- ESPECIALLY CAPTAIN AMERICA-- TO THINK YOU'RE STILL SCARRED--?

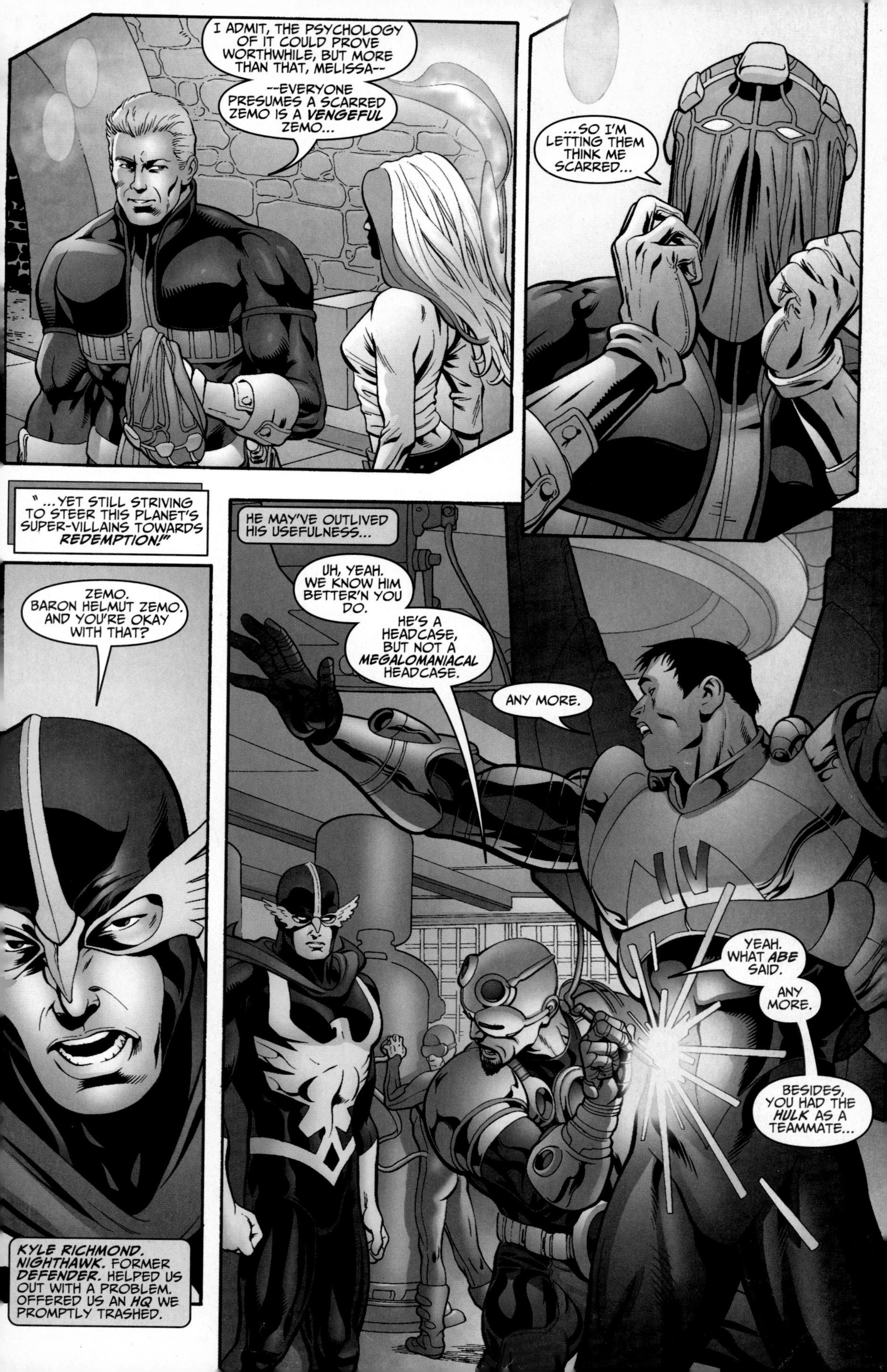
I ADMIT, THE PSYCHOLOGY OF IT COULD PROVE WORTHWHILE, BUT MORE THAN THAT, MELISSA--
--EVERYONE PRESUMES A SCARRED ZEMO IS A *VENGEFUL* ZEMO...
...SO I'M LETTING THEM THINK ME SCARRED...
"...YET STILL STRIVING TO STEER THIS PLANET'S SUPER-VILLAINS TOWARDS *REDEMPTION!*"
ZEMO. BARON HELMUT ZEMO. AND YOU'RE OKAY WITH THAT?
KYLE RICHMOND. NIGHTHAWK. FORMER *DEFENDER.* HELPED US OUT WITH A PROBLEM. OFFERED US AN *HQ* WE PROMPTLY TRASHED.
HE MAY'VE OUTLIVED HIS USEFULNESS...
UH, YEAH. WE KNOW HIM BETTER'N YOU DO.
HE'S A HEADCASE, BUT NOT A *MEGALOMANIACAL* HEADCASE.
ANY MORE.
YEAH. WHAT *ABE* SAID.
ANY MORE.
BESIDES, YOU HAD THE *HULK* AS A TEAMMATE...

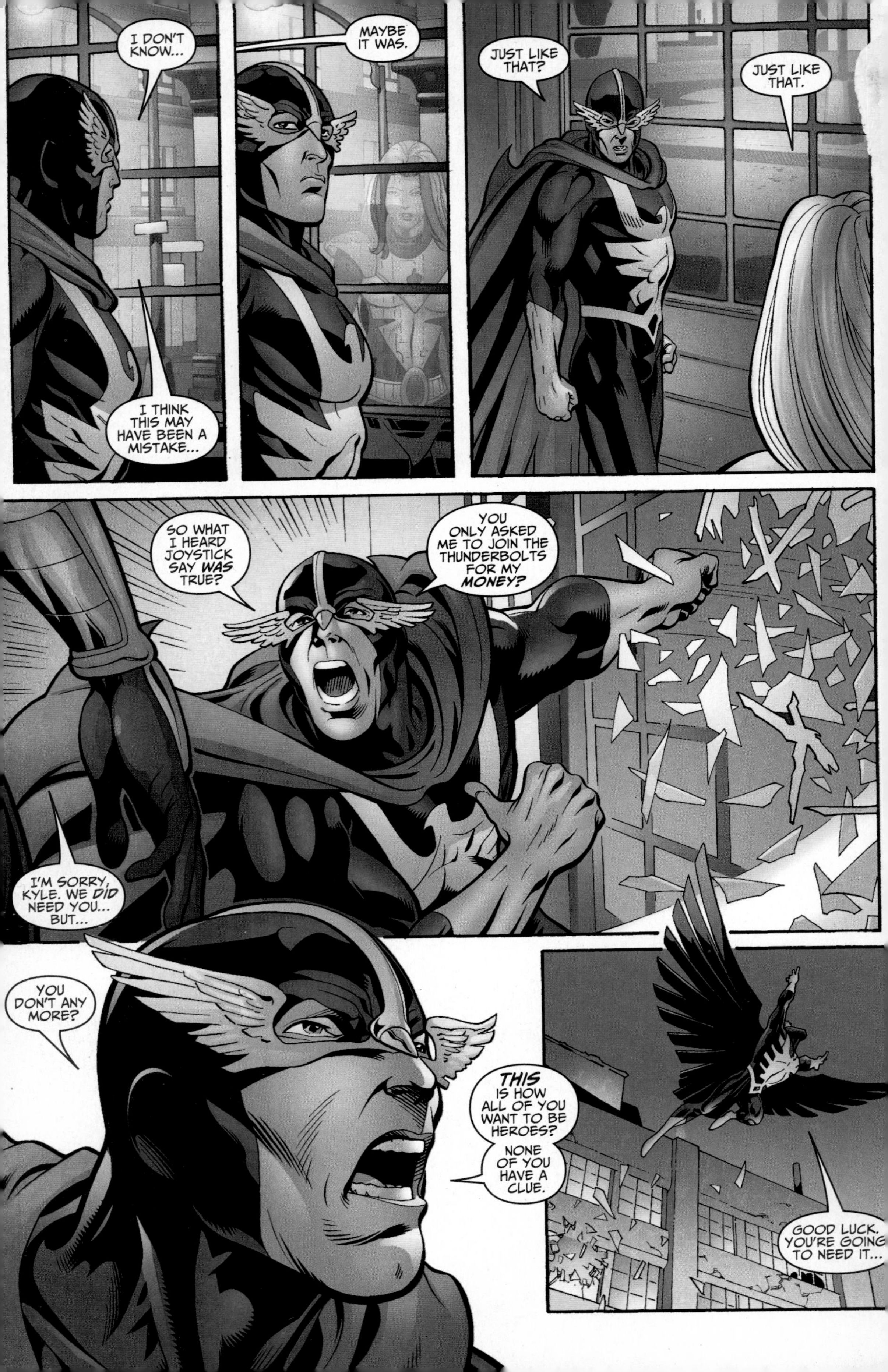
I DON'T KNOW...
MAYBE IT WAS.
JUST LIKE THAT?
JUST LIKE THAT.
I THINK THIS MAY HAVE BEEN A MISTAKE...
SO WHAT I HEARD JOYSTICK SAY *WAS* TRUE?
YOU ONLY ASKED ME TO JOIN THE THUNDERBOLTS FOR MY ***MONEY?***
I'M SORRY, KYLE. WE *DID* NEED YOU... BUT...
YOU DON'T ANY MORE?
THIS IS HOW ALL OF YOU WANT TO BE HEROES?
NONE OF YOU HAVE A CLUE.
GOOD LUCK. YOU'RE GOING TO NEED IT...

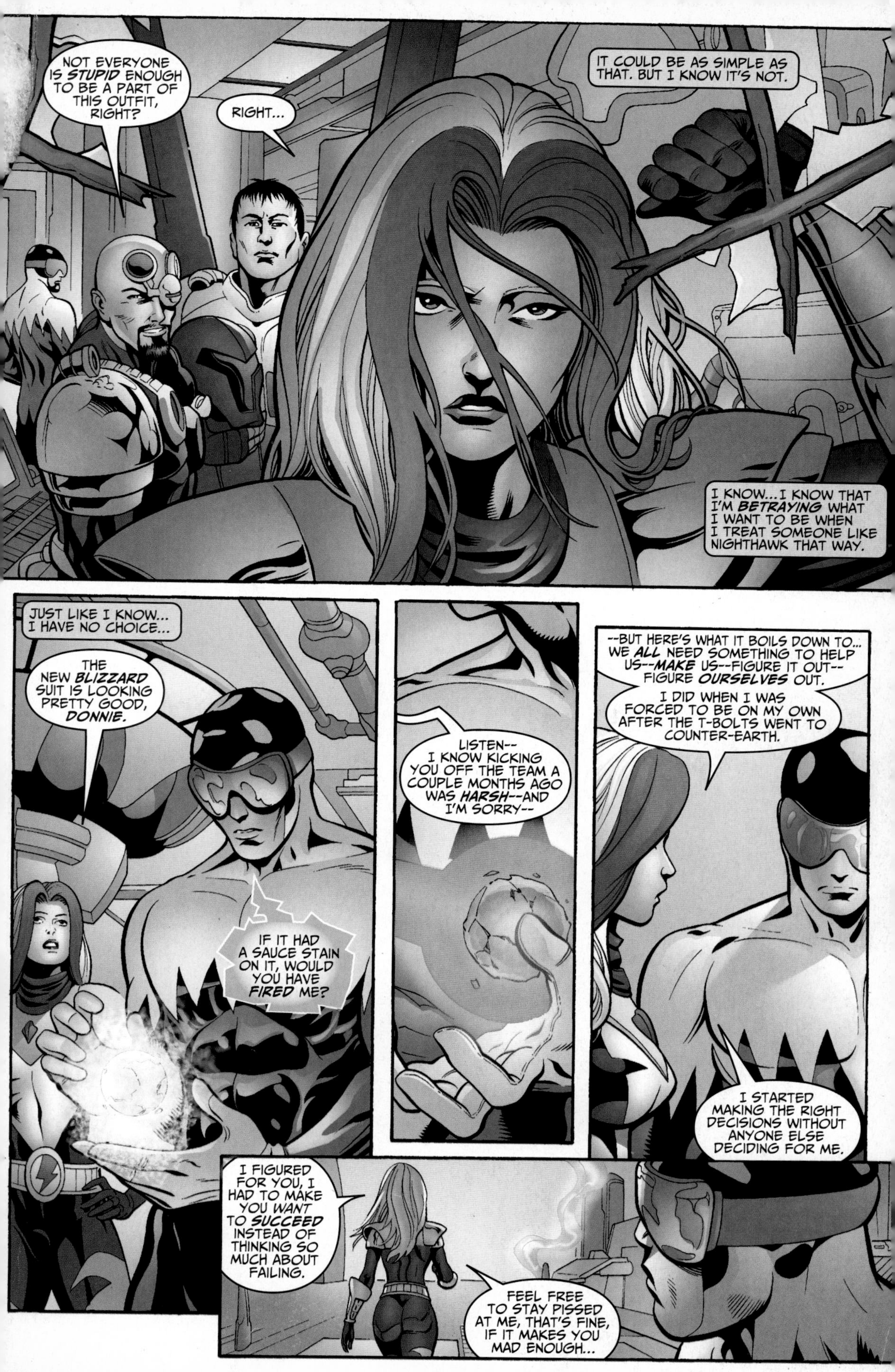

NOT EVERYONE IS STUPID ENOUGH TO BE A PART OF THIS OUTFIT, RIGHT?
RIGHT...
IT COULD BE AS SIMPLE AS THAT. BUT I KNOW IT'S NOT.
I KNOW...I KNOW THAT I'M BETRAYING WHAT I WANT TO BE WHEN I TREAT SOMEONE LIKE NIGHTHAWK THAT WAY.
JUST LIKE I KNOW... I HAVE NO CHOICE...
THE NEW BLIZZARD SUIT IS LOOKING PRETTY GOOD, DONNIE.
IF IT HAD A SAUCE STAIN ON IT, WOULD YOU HAVE FIRED ME?
LISTEN-- I KNOW KICKING YOU OFF THE TEAM A COUPLE MONTHS AGO WAS HARSH--AND I'M SORRY--
--BUT HERE'S WHAT IT BOILS DOWN TO... WE ALL NEED SOMETHING TO HELP US--MAKE US--FIGURE IT OUT-- FIGURE OURSELVES OUT.
I DID WHEN I WAS FORCED TO BE ON MY OWN AFTER THE T-BOLTS WENT TO COUNTER-EARTH.
I STARTED MAKING THE RIGHT DECISIONS WITHOUT ANYONE ELSE DECIDING FOR ME.
I FIGURED FOR YOU, I HAD TO MAKE YOU WANT TO SUCCEED INSTEAD OF THINKING SO MUCH ABOUT FAILING.
FEEL FREE TO STAY PISSED AT ME, THAT'S FINE, IF IT MAKES YOU MAD ENOUGH...

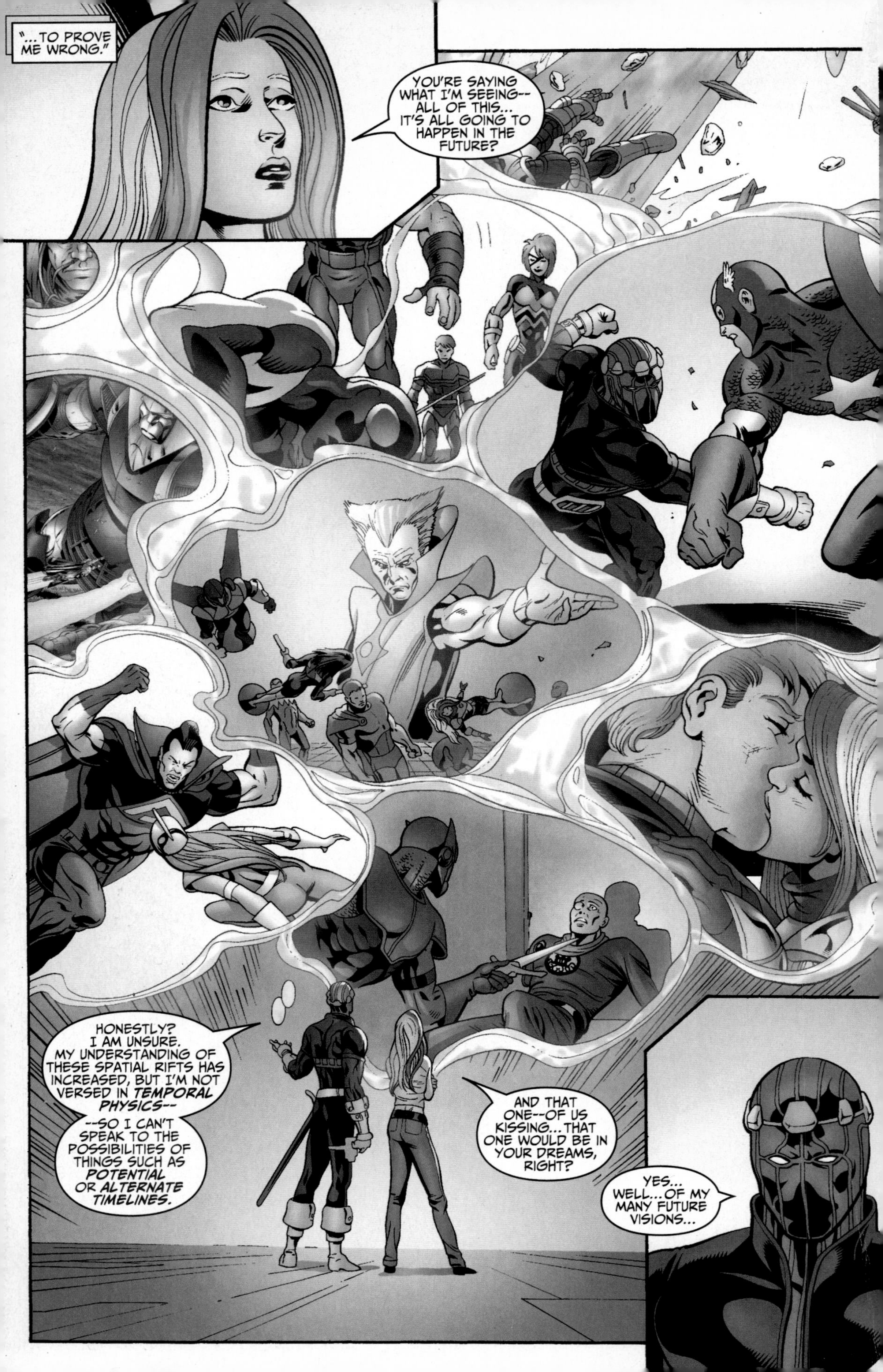
"...TO PROVE ME WRONG."
YOU'RE SAYING WHAT I'M SEEING-- ALL OF THIS... IT'S ALL GOING TO HAPPEN IN THE FUTURE?
HONESTLY? I AM UNSURE. MY UNDERSTANDING OF THESE SPATIAL RIFTS HAS INCREASED, BUT I'M NOT VERSED IN TEMPORAL PHYSICS--
--SO I CAN'T SPEAK TO THE POSSIBILITIES OF THINGS SUCH AS POTENTIAL OR ALTERNATE TIMELINES.
AND THAT ONE--OF US KISSING...THAT ONE WOULD BE IN YOUR DREAMS, RIGHT?
YES... WELL...OF MY MANY FUTURE VISIONS...

"...THAT ONE INTRIGUED ME THE MOST..."

GOTTA TELL YA, SOCK-HEAD--

--YOU'RE A LOT BETTER THAN I EXPECTED!

I DO ADMIT, JOYSTICK, THAT SINCE FOUNDING THE THUNDERBOLTS--

--THE PHYSICAL ASPECTS OF THIS "JOB"--

--HAVE BECOME MUCH MORE ENJOYABLE...

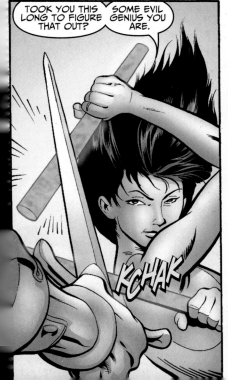

TOOK YOU THIS LONG TO FIGURE THAT OUT? SOME EVIL GENIUS YOU ARE.

KCHAK

YOU WANT SOME REAL PHYSICAL FUN, WHAT SAY WE END THIS NOW AND PICK UP IN THE SHOWER...?

A VERY TEMPTING OFFER, OF COURSE, BUT I DON'T THINK IT WOULD BE APPROPRIATE FOR US TO--

ZZZOHZZZT

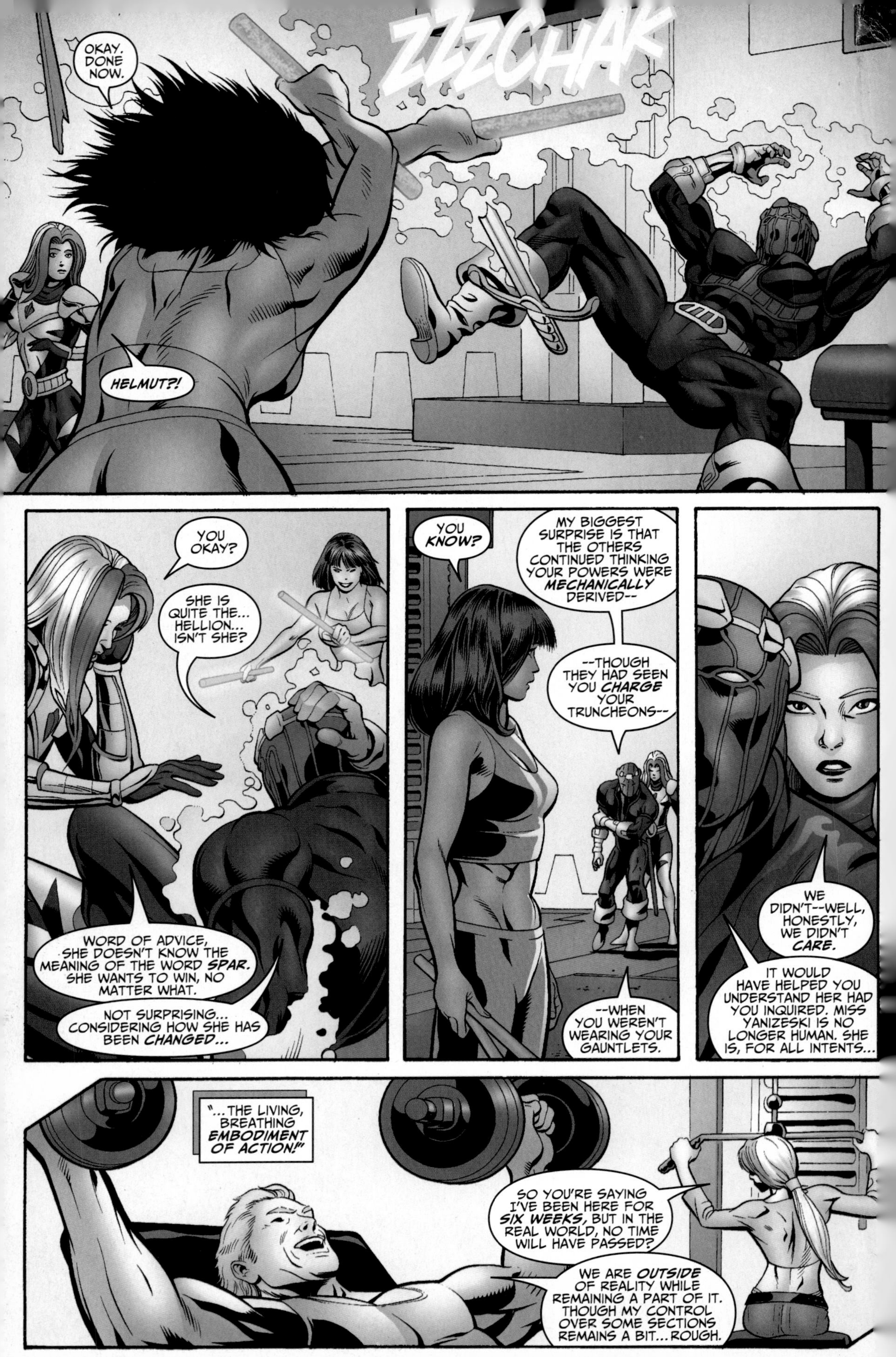

ZZZCHAK
OKAY. DONE NOW.
HELMUT?!
YOU OKAY?
SHE IS QUITE THE... HELLION... ISN'T SHE?
WORD OF ADVICE, SHE DOESN'T KNOW THE MEANING OF THE WORD SPAR. SHE WANTS TO WIN, NO MATTER WHAT.
NOT SURPRISING... CONSIDERING HOW SHE HAS BEEN CHANGED...
YOU KNOW?
MY BIGGEST SURPRISE IS THAT THE OTHERS CONTINUED THINKING YOUR POWERS WERE MECHANICALLY DERIVED--
--THOUGH THEY HAD SEEN YOU CHARGE YOUR TRUNCHEONS--
--WHEN YOU WEREN'T WEARING YOUR GAUNTLETS.
WE DIDN'T--WELL, HONESTLY, WE DIDN'T CARE.
IT WOULD HAVE HELPED YOU UNDERSTAND HER HAD YOU INQUIRED. MISS YANIZESKI IS NO LONGER HUMAN. SHE IS, FOR ALL INTENTS...
"...THE LIVING, BREATHING EMBODIMENT OF ACTION!"
SO YOU'RE SAYING I'VE BEEN HERE FOR SIX WEEKS, BUT IN THE REAL WORLD, NO TIME WILL HAVE PASSED?
WE ARE OUTSIDE OF REALITY WHILE REMAINING A PART OF IT. THOUGH MY CONTROL OVER SOME SECTIONS REMAINS A BIT... ROUGH.

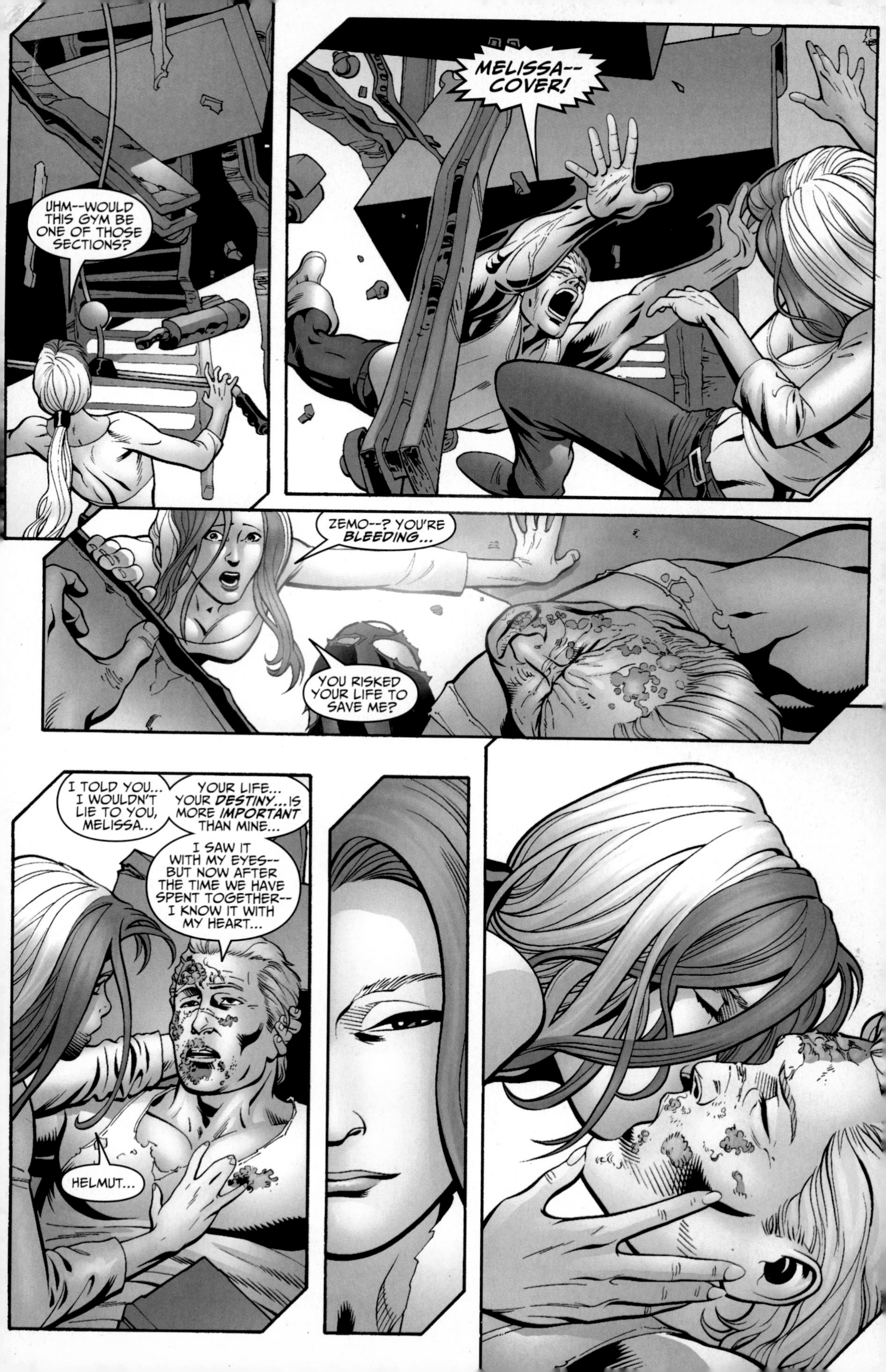
UHM--WOULD THIS GYM BE ONE OF THOSE SECTIONS?
MELISSA-- COVER!
ZEMO--? YOU'RE BLEEDING...
YOU RISKED YOUR LIFE TO SAVE ME?
I TOLD YOU... I WOULDN'T LIE TO YOU, MELISSA...
YOUR LIFE... YOUR DESTINY...IS MORE IMPORTANT THAN MINE...
I SAW IT WITH MY EYES-- BUT NOW AFTER THE TIME WE HAVE SPENT TOGETHER-- I KNOW IT WITH MY HEART...
HELMUT...

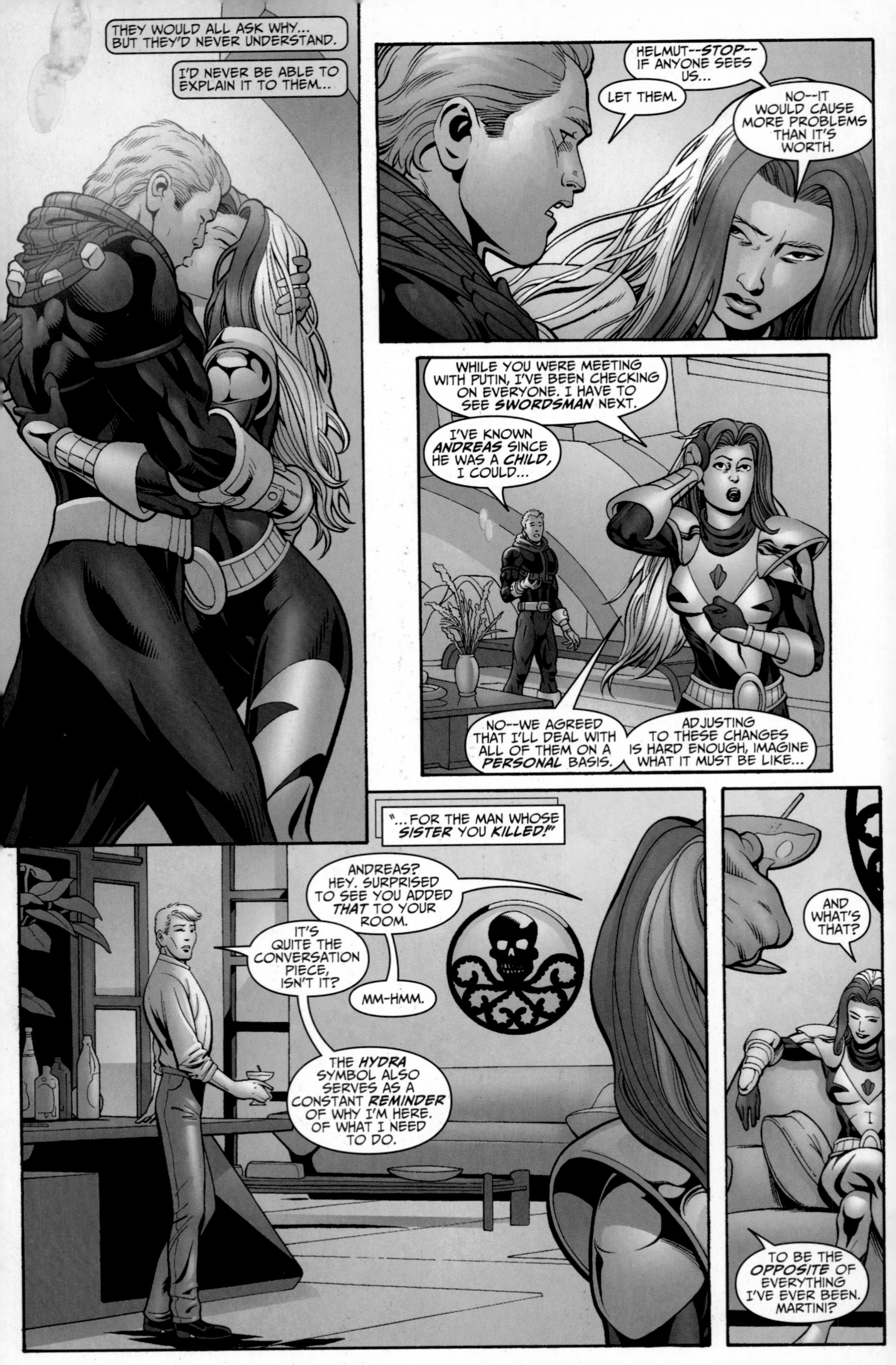

THEY WOULD ALL ASK WHY... BUT THEY'D NEVER UNDERSTAND.
I'D NEVER BE ABLE TO EXPLAIN IT TO THEM...
HELMUT--*STOP*--IF ANYONE SEES US...
LET THEM.
NO--IT WOULD CAUSE MORE PROBLEMS THAN IT'S WORTH.
WHILE YOU WERE MEETING WITH PUTIN, I'VE BEEN CHECKING ON EVERYONE. I HAVE TO SEE *SWORDSMAN* NEXT.
I'VE KNOWN *ANDREAS* SINCE HE WAS A *CHILD,* I COULD...
NO--WE AGREED THAT I'LL DEAL WITH ALL OF THEM ON A *PERSONAL* BASIS.
ADJUSTING TO THESE CHANGES IS HARD ENOUGH, IMAGINE WHAT IT MUST BE LIKE...
"...FOR THE MAN WHOSE *SISTER* YOU *KILLED!*"
ANDREAS? HEY. SURPRISED TO SEE YOU ADDED *THAT* TO YOUR ROOM.
IT'S QUITE THE CONVERSATION PIECE, ISN'T IT?
MM-HMM.
THE *HYDRA* SYMBOL ALSO SERVES AS A CONSTANT *REMINDER* OF WHY I'M HERE. OF WHAT I NEED TO DO.
AND WHAT'S THAT?
TO BE THE *OPPOSITE* OF EVERYTHING I'VE EVER BEEN. MARTINI?

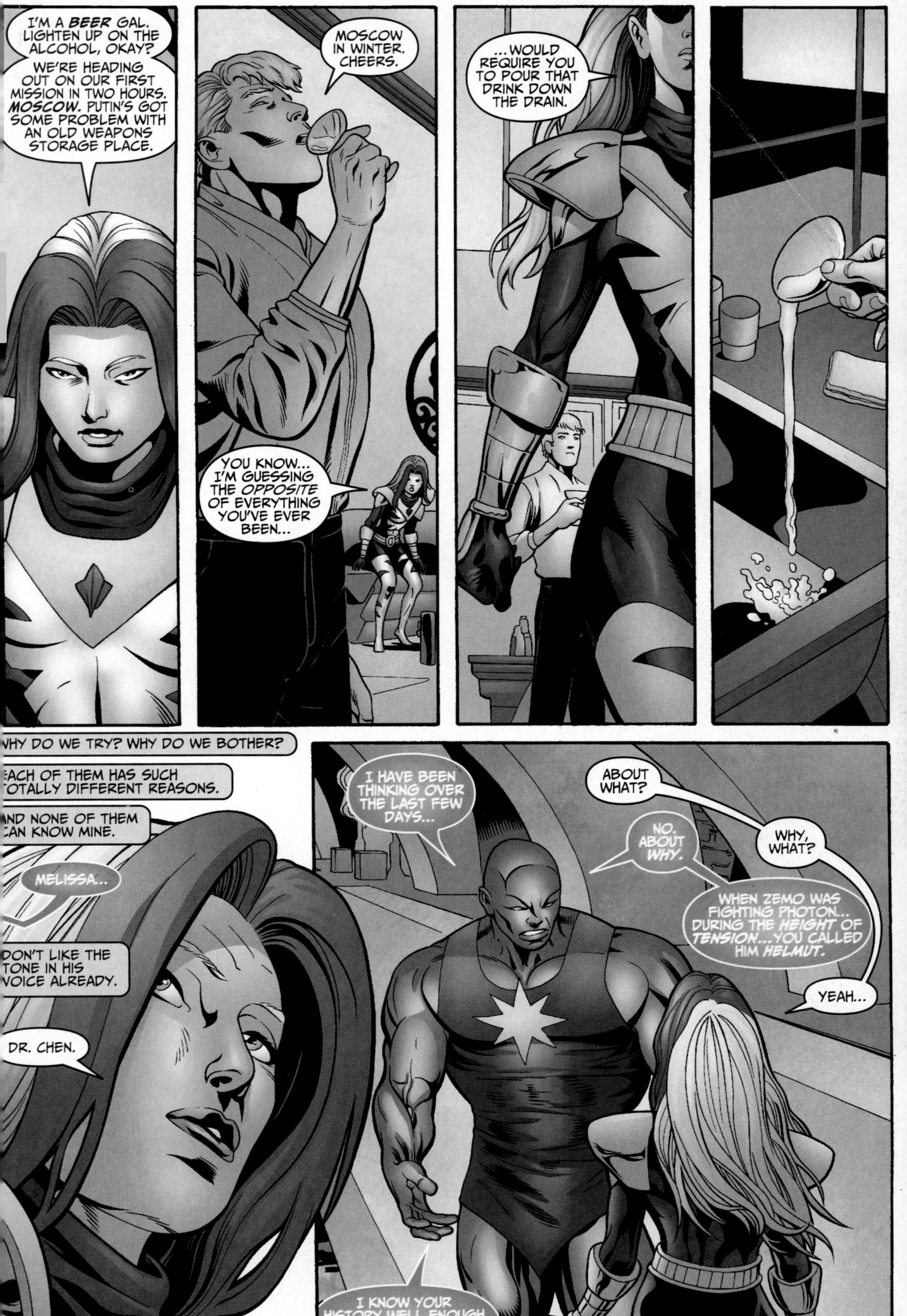
I'M A BEER GAL. LIGHTEN UP ON THE ALCOHOL, OKAY?
WE'RE HEADING OUT ON OUR FIRST MISSION IN TWO HOURS. MOSCOW. PUTIN'S GOT SOME PROBLEM WITH AN OLD WEAPONS STORAGE PLACE.
MOSCOW IN WINTER. CHEERS.
YOU KNOW... I'M GUESSING THE OPPOSITE OF EVERYTHING YOU'VE EVER BEEN...
...WOULD REQUIRE YOU TO POUR THAT DRINK DOWN THE DRAIN.
WHY DO WE TRY? WHY DO WE BOTHER?
EACH OF THEM HAS SUCH TOTALLY DIFFERENT REASONS.
AND NONE OF THEM CAN KNOW MINE.
MELISSA...
I DON'T LIKE THE TONE IN HIS VOICE ALREADY.
DR. CHEN.
I HAVE BEEN THINKING OVER THE LAST FEW DAYS...
ABOUT WHAT?
NO. ABOUT WHY.
WHY, WHAT?
WHEN ZEMO WAS FIGHTING PHOTON... DURING THE HEIGHT OF TENSION...YOU CALLED HIM HELMUT.
YEAH...
I KNOW YOUR HISTORY WELL ENOUGH TO KNOW YOU WERE NEVER PARTICULARLY FRIENDLY WITH ZEMO.

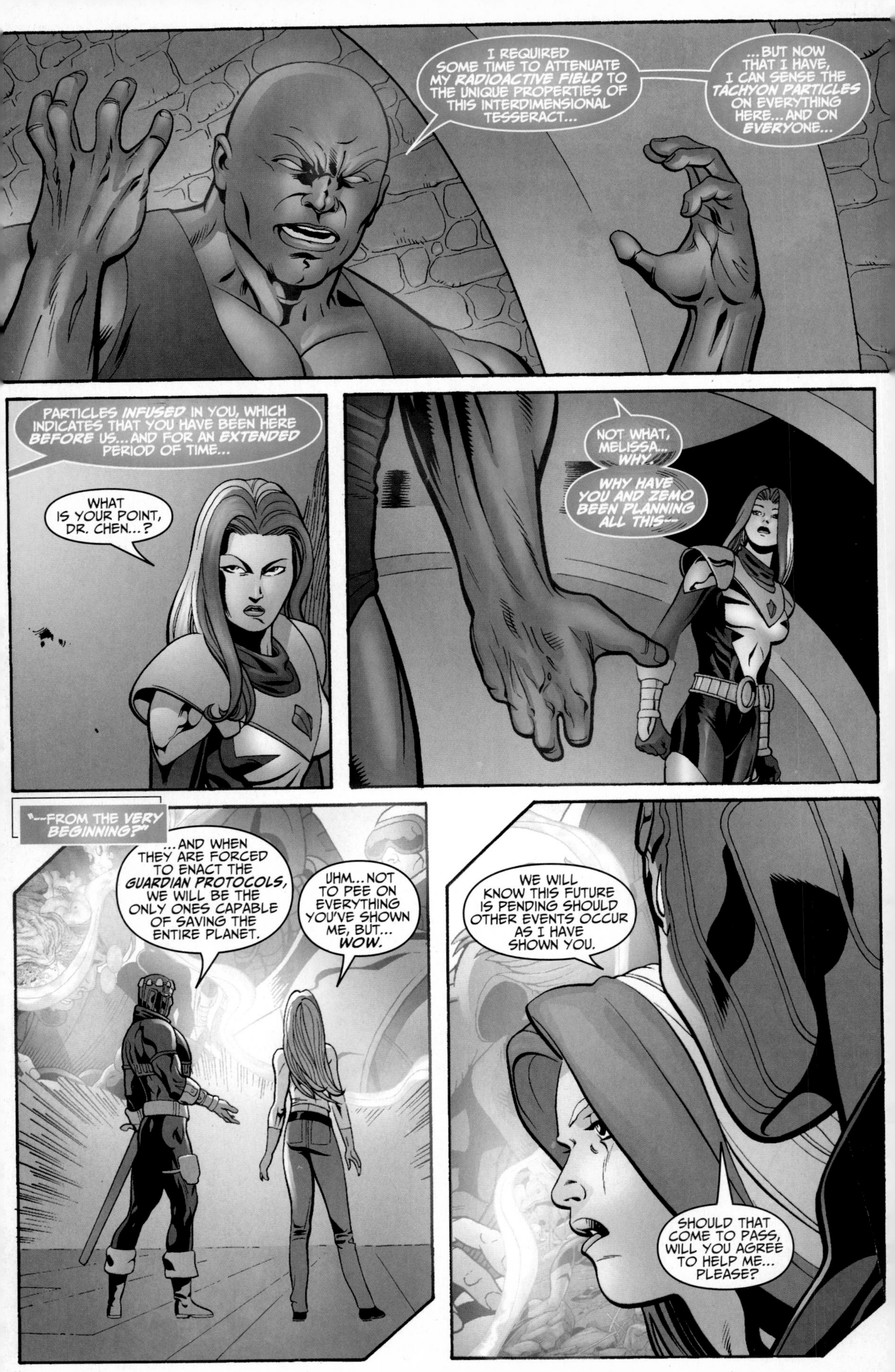
I REQUIRED SOME TIME TO ATTENUATE MY RADIOACTIVE FIELD TO THE UNIQUE PROPERTIES OF THIS INTERDIMENSIONAL TESSERACT...
...BUT NOW THAT I HAVE, I CAN SENSE THE TACHYON PARTICLES ON EVERYTHING HERE...AND ON EVERYONE...
PARTICLES INFUSED IN YOU, WHICH INDICATES THAT YOU HAVE BEEN HERE BEFORE US...AND FOR AN EXTENDED PERIOD OF TIME...
WHAT IS YOUR POINT, DR. CHEN...?
NOT WHAT, MELISSA... WHY.
WHY HAVE YOU AND ZEMO BEEN PLANNING ALL THIS--
"--FROM THE VERY BEGINNING?"
...AND WHEN THEY ARE FORCED TO ENACT THE GUARDIAN PROTOCOLS, WE WILL BE THE ONLY ONES CAPABLE OF SAVING THE ENTIRE PLANET.
UHM...NOT TO PEE ON EVERYTHING YOU'VE SHOWN ME, BUT... WOW.
WE WILL KNOW THIS FUTURE IS PENDING SHOULD OTHER EVENTS OCCUR AS I HAVE SHOWN YOU.
SHOULD THAT COME TO PASS, WILL YOU AGREE TO HELP ME... PLEASE?

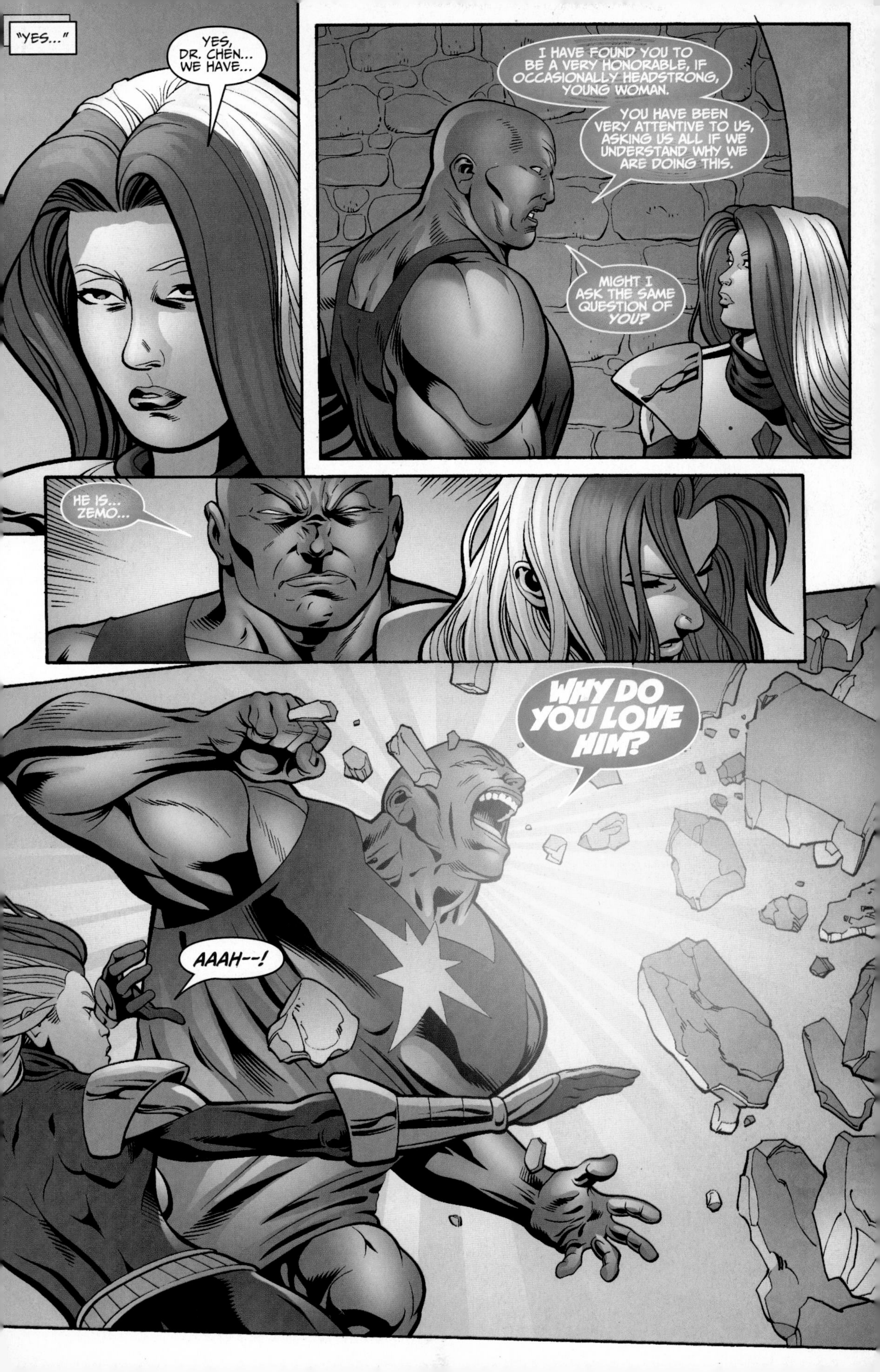
"YES..."
YES, DR. CHEN... WE HAVE...
I HAVE FOUND YOU TO BE A VERY HONORABLE, IF OCCASIONALLY HEADSTRONG, YOUNG WOMAN.
YOU HAVE BEEN VERY ATTENTIVE TO US, ASKING US ALL IF WE UNDERSTAND WHY WE ARE DOING THIS.
MIGHT I ASK THE SAME QUESTION OF YOU?
HE IS... ZEMO...
WHY DO YOU LOVE HIM?
AAAH--!

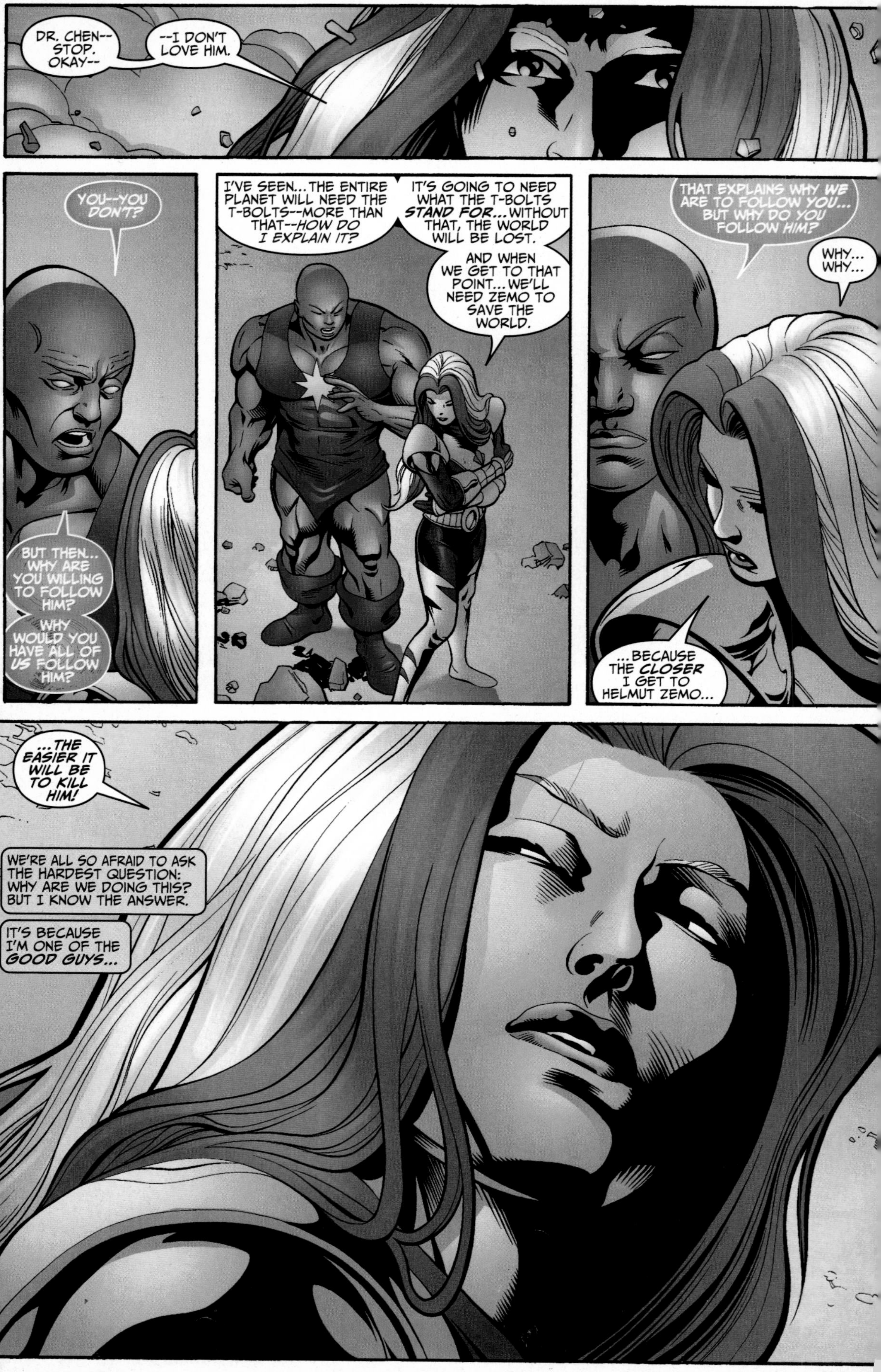
DR. CHEN-- STOP. OKAY--
--I DON'T LOVE HIM.
YOU--YOU DON'T?
BUT THEN... WHY ARE YOU WILLING TO FOLLOW HIM?
WHY WOULD YOU HAVE ALL OF US FOLLOW HIM?
I'VE SEEN... THE ENTIRE PLANET WILL NEED THE T-BOLTS--MORE THAN THAT--HOW DO I EXPLAIN IT?
IT'S GOING TO NEED WHAT THE T-BOLTS STAND FOR... WITHOUT THAT, THE WORLD WILL BE LOST.
AND WHEN WE GET TO THAT POINT... WE'LL NEED ZEMO TO SAVE THE WORLD.
THAT EXPLAINS WHY WE ARE TO FOLLOW YOU... BUT WHY DO YOU FOLLOW HIM?
WHY... WHY...
...BECAUSE THE CLOSER I GET TO HELMUT ZEMO...
...THE EASIER IT WILL BE TO KILL HIM!
WE'RE ALL SO AFRAID TO ASK THE HARDEST QUESTION: WHY ARE WE DOING THIS? BUT I KNOW THE ANSWER.
IT'S BECAUSE I'M ONE OF THE GOOD GUYS...

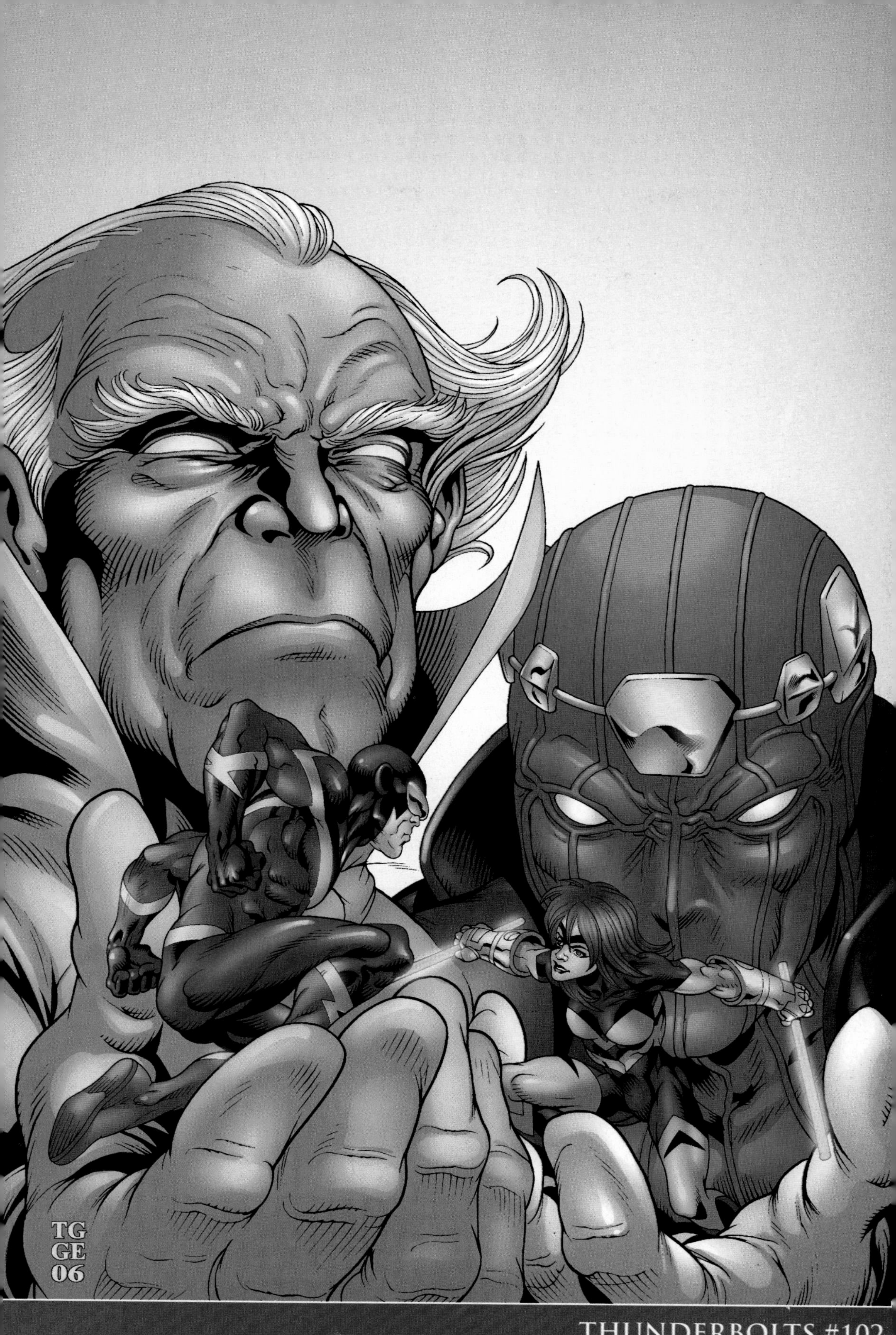
TG
GE
06

THUNDERBOLTS #102

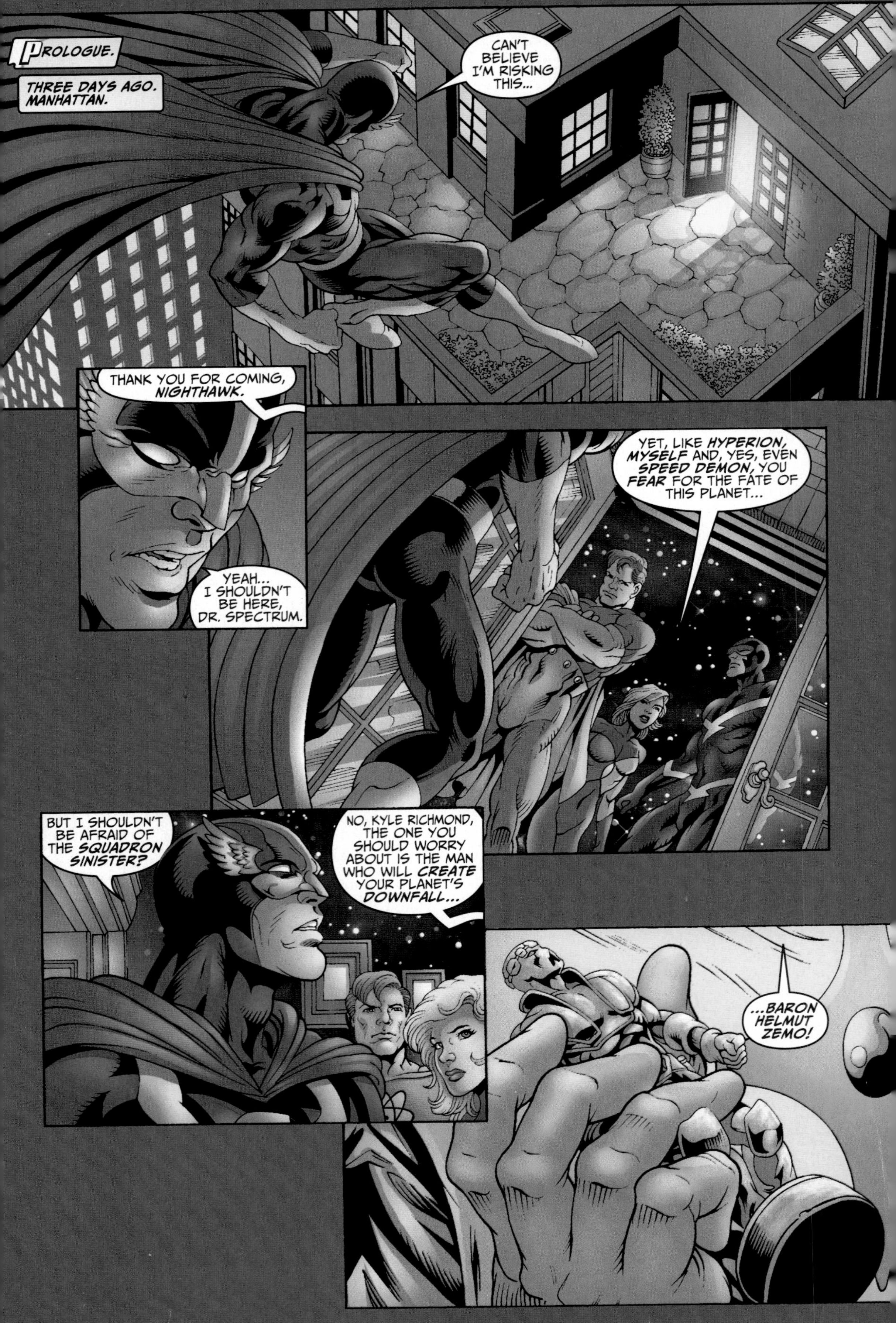
PROLOGUE.
THREE DAYS AGO. MANHATTAN.
CAN'T BELIEVE I'M RISKING THIS...
THANK YOU FOR COMING, NIGHTHAWK.
YEAH... I SHOULDN'T BE HERE, DR. SPECTRUM.
YET, LIKE HYPERION, MYSELF AND, YES, EVEN SPEED DEMON, YOU FEAR FOR THE FATE OF THIS PLANET...
BUT I SHOULDN'T BE AFRAID OF THE SQUADRON SINISTER?
NO, KYLE RICHMOND, THE ONE YOU SHOULD WORRY ABOUT IS THE MAN WHO WILL CREATE YOUR PLANET'S DOWNFALL...
...BARON HELMUT ZEMO!

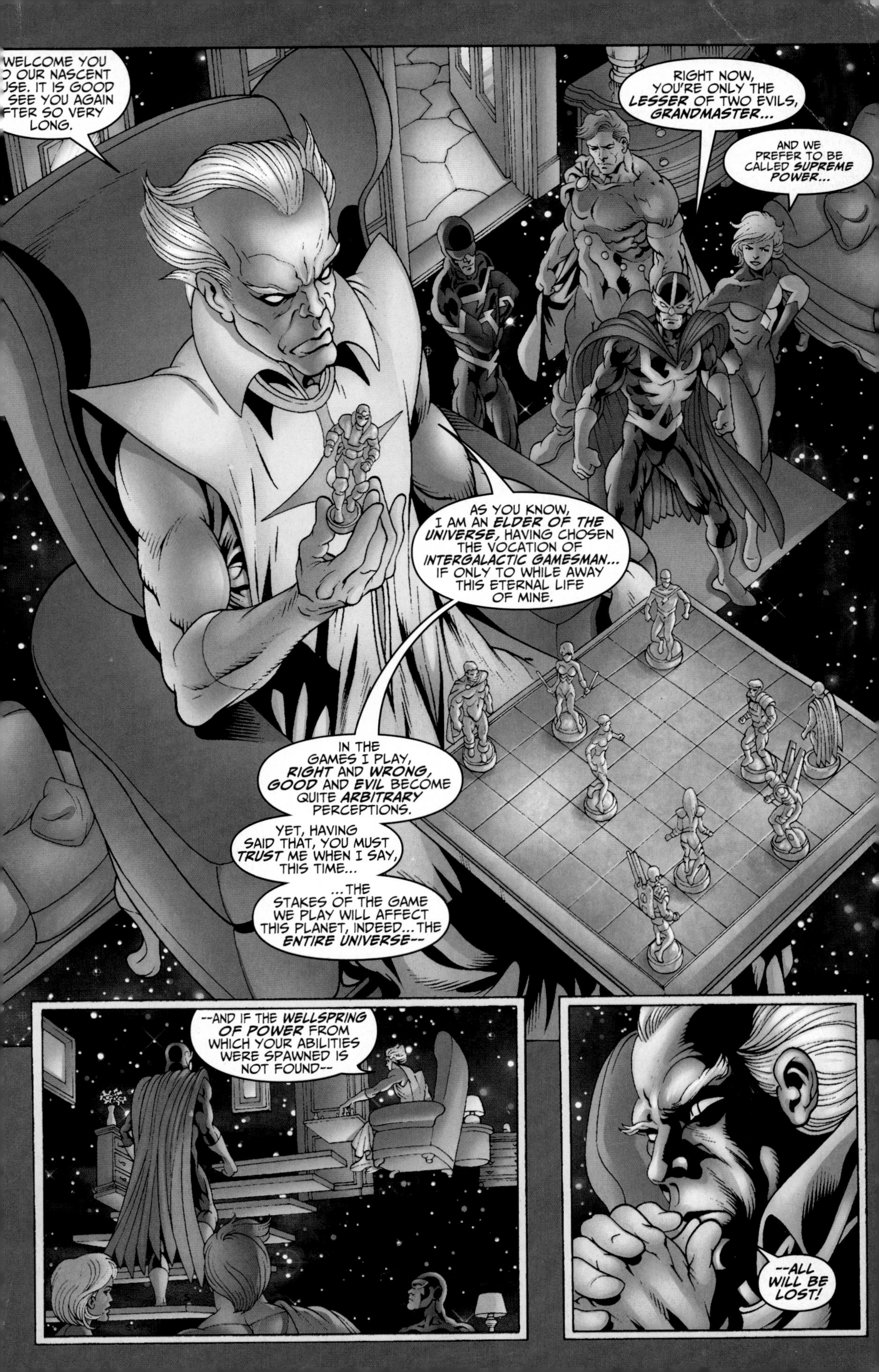
WELCOME YOU
O OUR NASCENT
USE. IT IS GOOD
SEE YOU AGAIN
FTER SO VERY
LONG.
RIGHT NOW, YOU'RE ONLY THE LESSER OF TWO EVILS, GRANDMASTER...
AND WE PREFER TO BE CALLED SUPREME POWER...
AS YOU KNOW, I AM AN ELDER OF THE UNIVERSE, HAVING CHOSEN THE VOCATION OF INTERGALACTIC GAMESMAN... IF ONLY TO WHILE AWAY THIS ETERNAL LIFE OF MINE.
IN THE GAMES I PLAY, RIGHT AND WRONG, GOOD AND EVIL BECOME QUITE ARBITRARY PERCEPTIONS.
YET, HAVING SAID THAT, YOU MUST TRUST ME WHEN I SAY, THIS TIME...
...THE STAKES OF THE GAME WE PLAY WILL AFFECT THIS PLANET, INDEED...THE ENTIRE UNIVERSE--
--AND IF THE WELLSPRING OF POWER FROM WHICH YOUR ABILITIES WERE SPAWNED IS NOT FOUND--
--ALL WILL BE LOST!

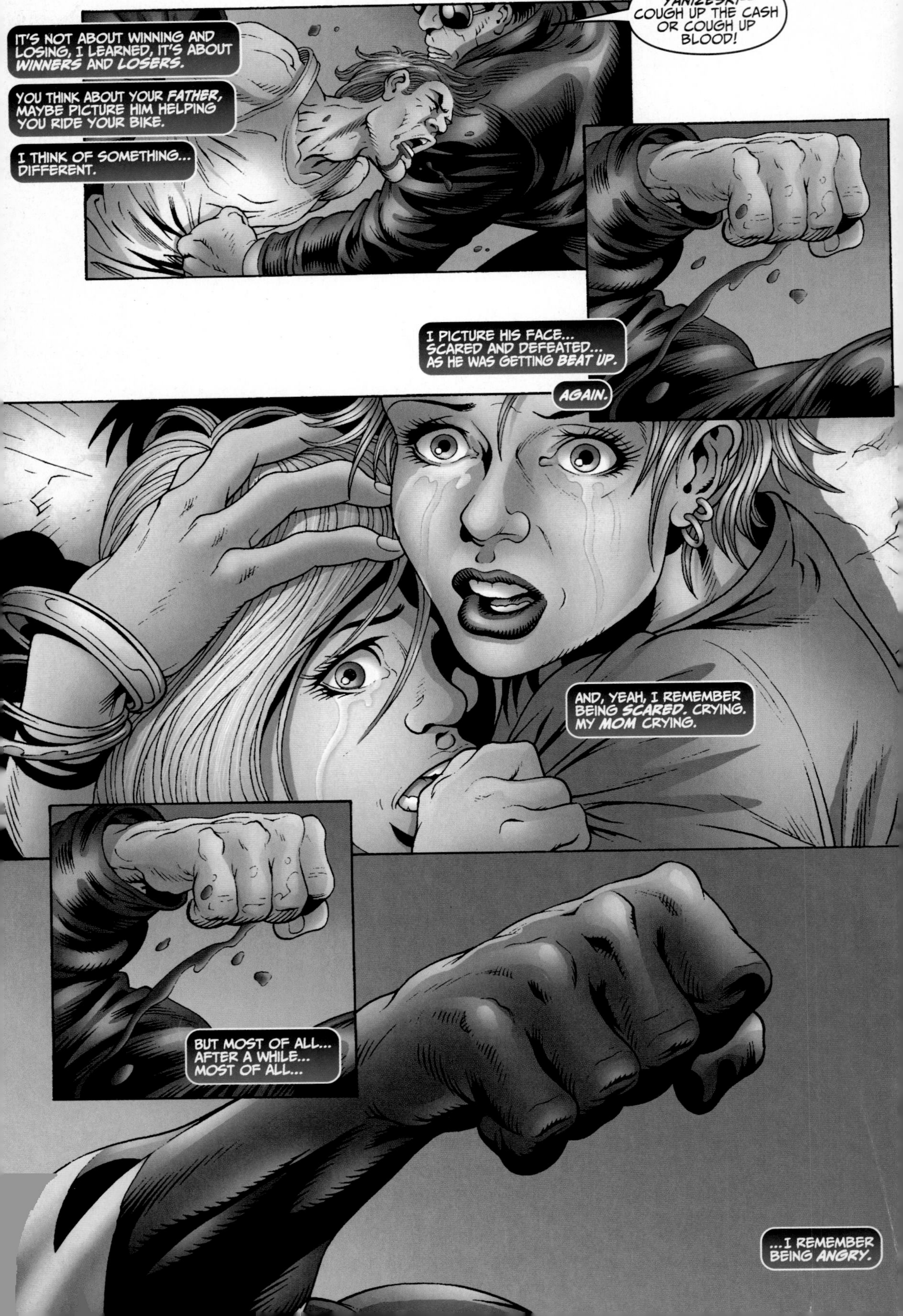
C'MON, YANIZESKI-- COUGH UP THE CASH OR COUGH UP BLOOD!
IT'S NOT ABOUT WINNING AND LOSING, I LEARNED, IT'S ABOUT WINNERS AND LOSERS.
YOU THINK ABOUT YOUR FATHER, MAYBE PICTURE HIM HELPING YOU RIDE YOUR BIKE.
I THINK OF SOMETHING... DIFFERENT.
I PICTURE HIS FACE... SCARED AND DEFEATED... AS HE WAS GETTING BEAT UP.
AGAIN.
AND, YEAH, I REMEMBER BEING SCARED. CRYING. MY MOM CRYING.
BUT MOST OF ALL... AFTER A WHILE... MOST OF ALL...
...I REMEMBER BEING ANGRY.

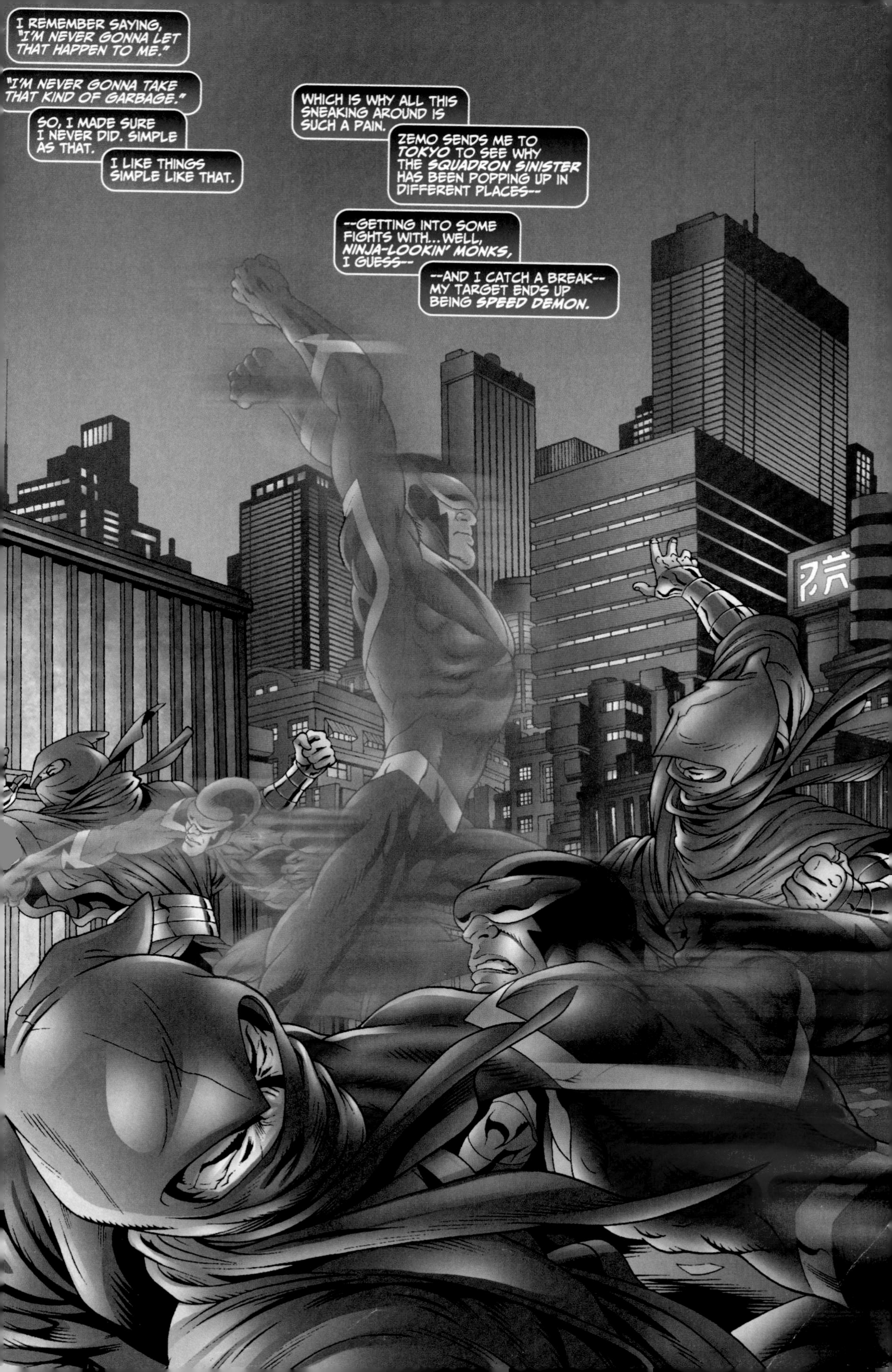
I REMEMBER SAYING, "I'M NEVER GONNA LET THAT HAPPEN TO ME."
"I'M NEVER GONNA TAKE THAT KIND OF GARBAGE."
SO, I MADE SURE I NEVER DID. SIMPLE AS THAT.
I LIKE THINGS SIMPLE LIKE THAT.
WHICH IS WHY ALL THIS SNEAKING AROUND IS SUCH A PAIN.
ZEMO SENDS ME TO TOKYO TO SEE WHY THE SQUADRON SINISTER HAS BEEN POPPING UP IN DIFFERENT PLACES--
--GETTING INTO SOME FIGHTS WITH... WELL, NINJA-LOOKIN' MONKS, I GUESS--
--AND I CATCH A BREAK-- MY TARGET ENDS UP BEING SPEED DEMON.

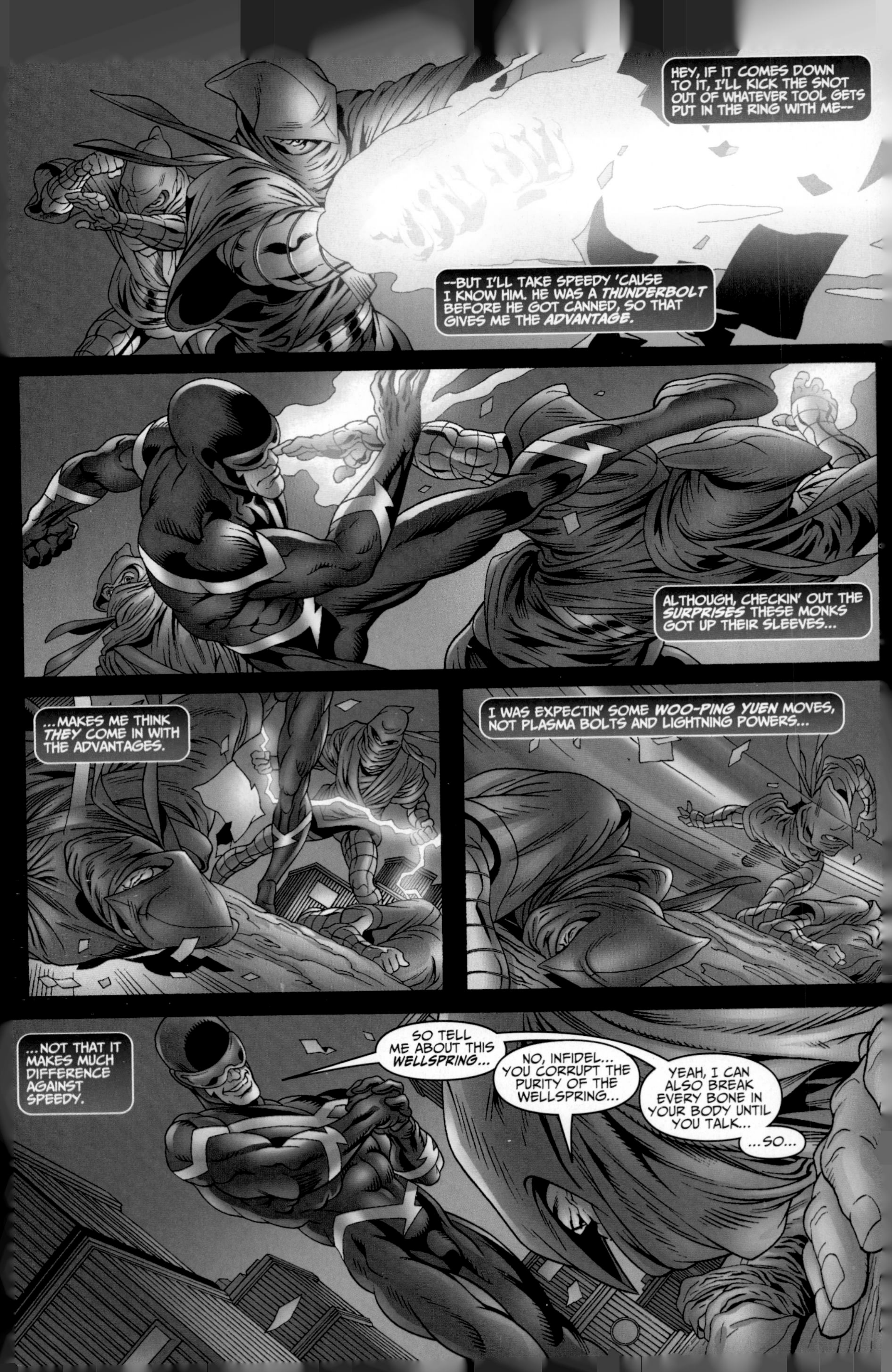
HEY, IF IT COMES DOWN TO IT, I'LL KICK THE SNOT OUT OF WHATEVER TOOL GETS PUT IN THE RING WITH ME--
--BUT I'LL TAKE SPEEDY 'CAUSE I KNOW HIM. HE WAS A *THUNDERBOLT* BEFORE HE GOT CANNED, SO THAT GIVES ME THE *ADVANTAGE*.
ALTHOUGH, CHECKIN' OUT THE *SURPRISES* THESE MONKS GOT UP THEIR SLEEVES...
...MAKES ME THINK *THEY* COME IN WITH THE ADVANTAGES.
I WAS EXPECTIN' SOME *WOO-PING YUEN* MOVES, NOT PLASMA BOLTS AND LIGHTNING POWERS...
...NOT THAT IT MAKES MUCH DIFFERENCE AGAINST SPEEDY.
SO TELL ME ABOUT THIS *WELLSPRING*...
NO, INFIDEL... YOU CORRUPT THE PURITY OF THE WELLSPRING...
YEAH, I CAN ALSO BREAK EVERY BONE IN YOUR BODY UNTIL YOU TALK...
...SO...

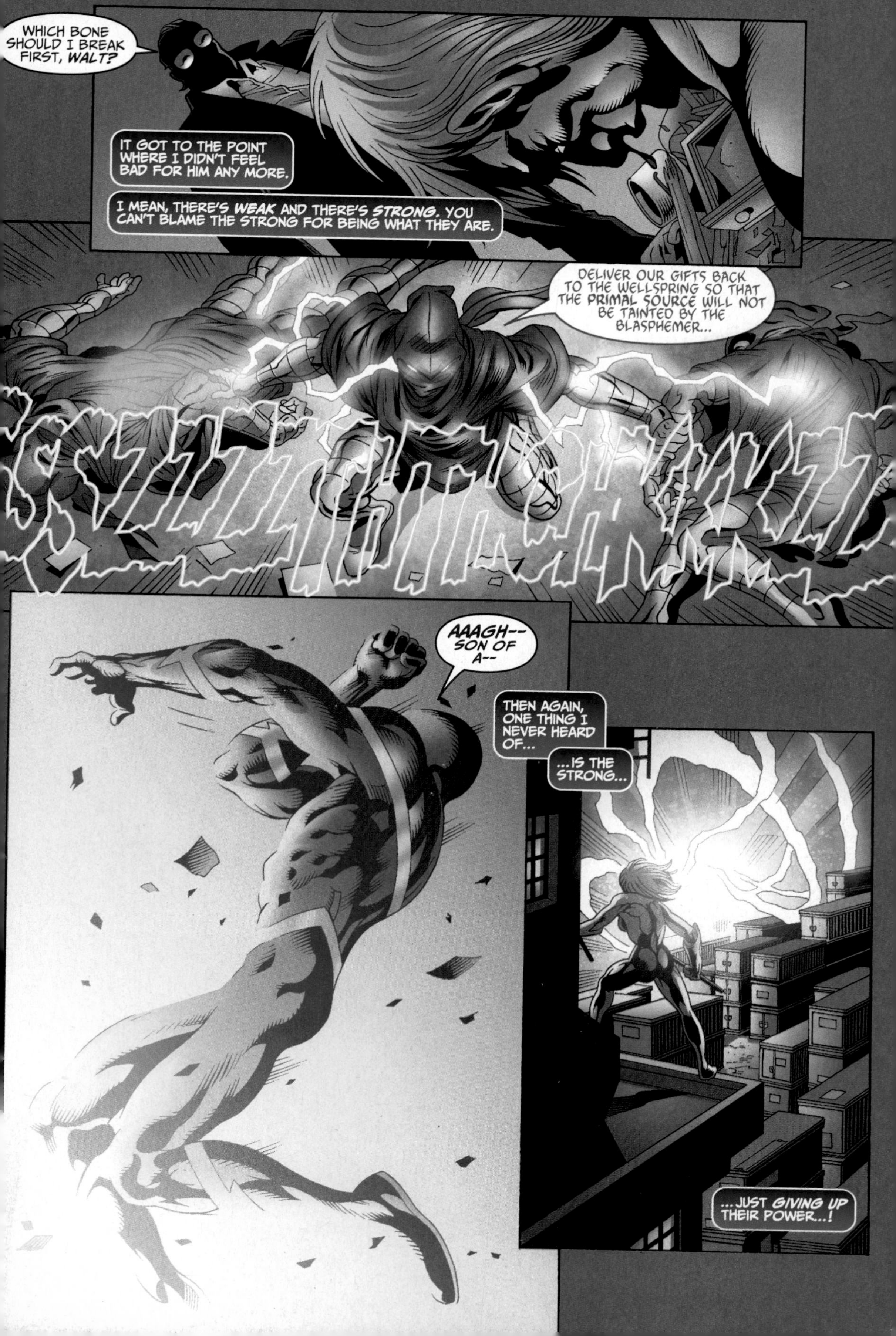
WHICH BONE SHOULD I BREAK FIRST, WALT?
IT GOT TO THE POINT WHERE I DIDN'T FEEL BAD FOR HIM ANY MORE.
I MEAN, THERE'S WEAK AND THERE'S STRONG. YOU CAN'T BLAME THE STRONG FOR BEING WHAT THEY ARE.
DELIVER OUR GIFTS BACK TO THE WELLSPRING SO THAT THE PRIMAL SOURCE WILL NOT BE TAINTED BY THE BLASPHEMER...
AAAGH-- SON OF A--
THEN AGAIN, ONE THING I NEVER HEARD OF...
...IS THE STRONG...
...JUST GIVING UP THEIR POWER...!

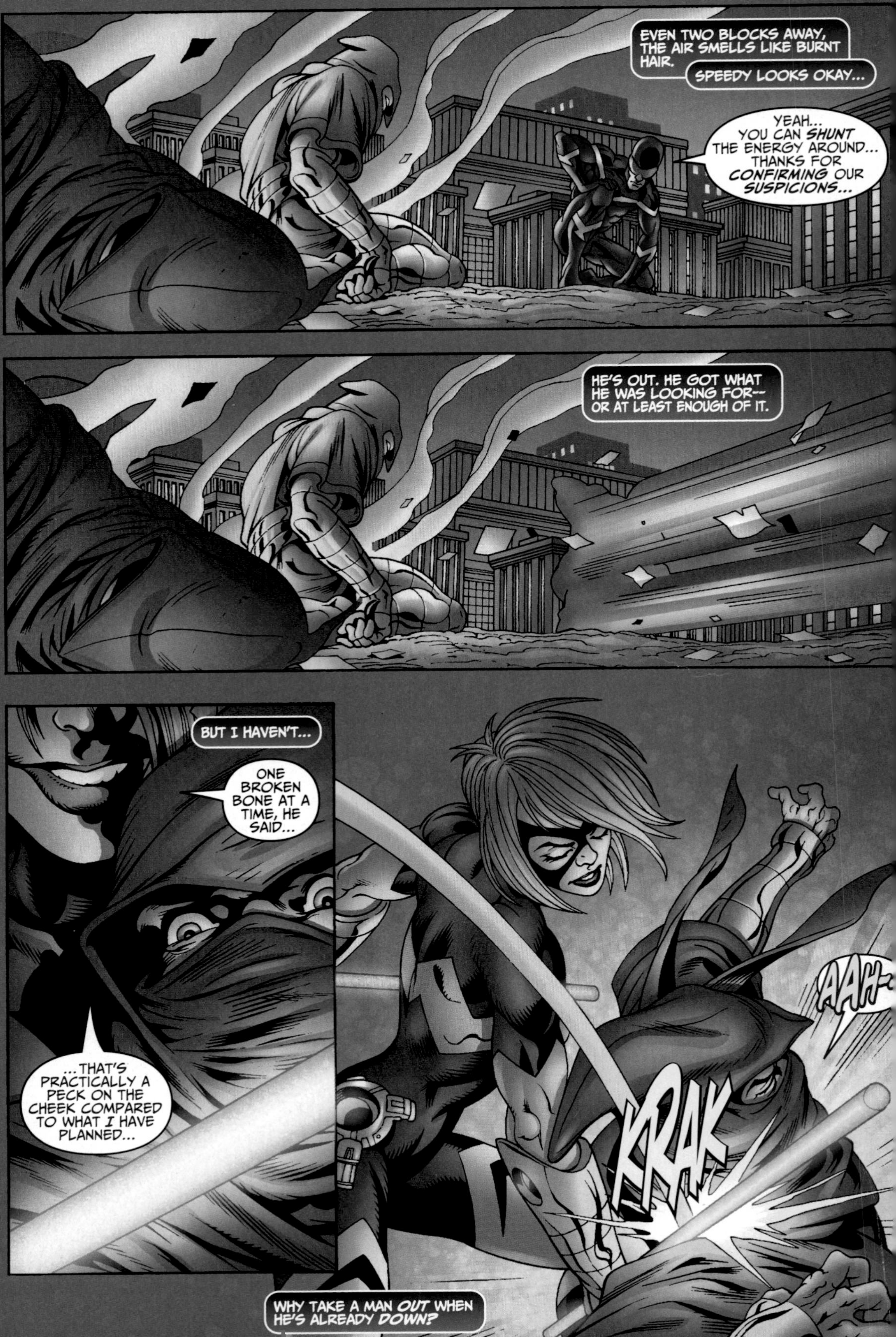

EVEN TWO BLOCKS AWAY, THE AIR SMELLS LIKE BURNT HAIR.
SPEEDY LOOKS OKAY...
YEAH... YOU CAN SHUNT THE ENERGY AROUND... THANKS FOR CONFIRMING OUR SUSPICIONS...
HE'S OUT. HE GOT WHAT HE WAS LOOKING FOR-- OR AT LEAST ENOUGH OF IT.
BUT I HAVEN'T...
ONE BROKEN BONE AT A TIME, HE SAID...
...THAT'S PRACTICALLY A PECK ON THE CHEEK COMPARED TO WHAT I HAVE PLANNED...
AAH--
KRAK
WHY TAKE A MAN OUT WHEN HE'S ALREADY DOWN?

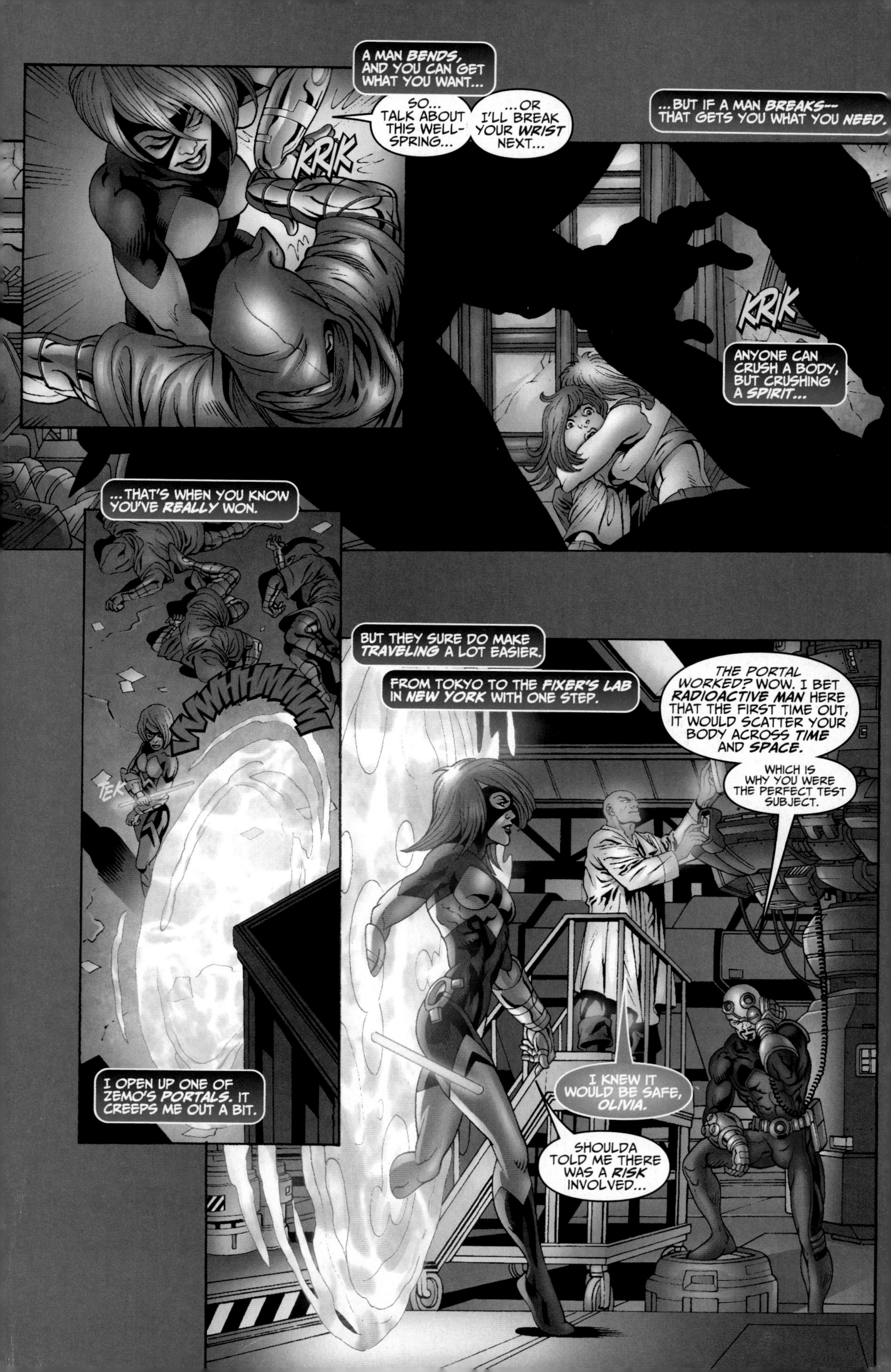
A MAN BENDS, AND YOU CAN GET WHAT YOU WANT...
SO... TALK ABOUT THIS WELL-SPRING...
KRIK
...OR I'LL BREAK YOUR WRIST NEXT...
...BUT IF A MAN BREAKS-- THAT GETS YOU WHAT YOU NEED.
KRIK
ANYONE CAN CRUSH A BODY, BUT CRUSHING A SPIRIT...
...THAT'S WHEN YOU KNOW YOU'VE REALLY WON.
WHHHMMM
TEK
I OPEN UP ONE OF ZEMO'S PORTALS. IT CREEPS ME OUT A BIT.
BUT THEY SURE DO MAKE TRAVELING A LOT EASIER.
FROM TOKYO TO THE FIXER'S LAB IN NEW YORK WITH ONE STEP.
THE PORTAL WORKED? WOW. I BET RADIOACTIVE MAN HERE THAT THE FIRST TIME OUT, IT WOULD SCATTER YOUR BODY ACROSS TIME AND SPACE.
WHICH IS WHY YOU WERE THE PERFECT TEST SUBJECT.
I KNEW IT WOULD BE SAFE, OLIVIA.
SHOULDA TOLD ME THERE WAS A RISK INVOLVED...

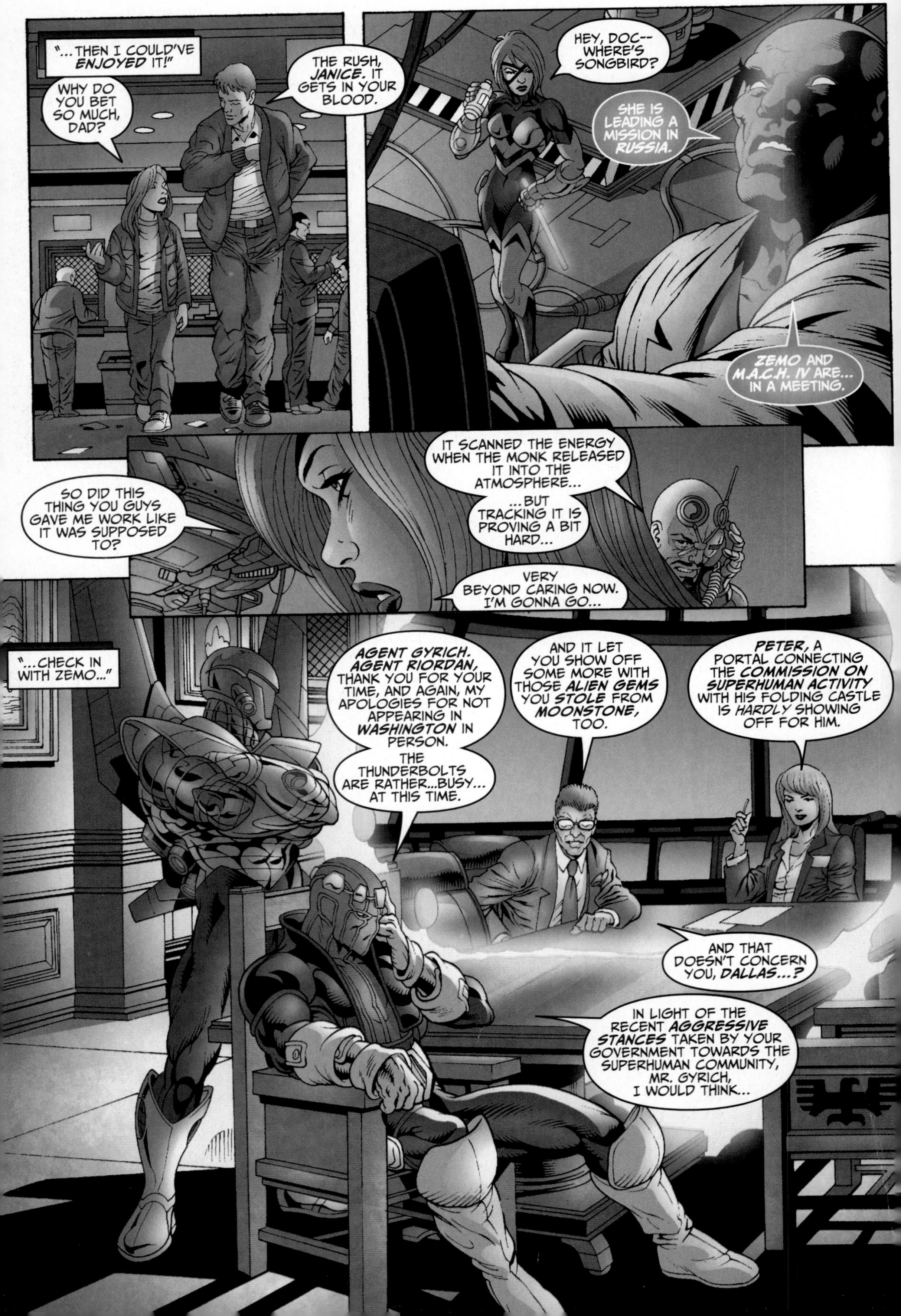

"...THEN I COULD'VE ENJOYED IT!"
WHY DO YOU BET SO MUCH, DAD?
THE RUSH, JANICE. IT GETS IN YOUR BLOOD.
HEY, DOC-- WHERE'S SONGBIRD?
SHE IS LEADING A MISSION IN RUSSIA.
ZEMO AND M.A.C.H. IV ARE... IN A MEETING.
SO DID THIS THING YOU GUYS GAVE ME WORK LIKE IT WAS SUPPOSED TO?
IT SCANNED THE ENERGY WHEN THE MONK RELEASED IT INTO THE ATMOSPHERE...
...BUT TRACKING IT IS PROVING A BIT HARD...
VERY BEYOND CARING NOW. I'M GONNA GO...
"...CHECK IN WITH ZEMO..."
AGENT GYRICH. AGENT RIORDAN, THANK YOU FOR YOUR TIME, AND AGAIN, MY APOLOGIES FOR NOT APPEARING IN WASHINGTON IN PERSON.
THE THUNDERBOLTS ARE RATHER...BUSY... AT THIS TIME.
AND IT LET YOU SHOW OFF SOME MORE WITH THOSE ALIEN GEMS YOU STOLE FROM MOONSTONE, TOO.
PETER, A PORTAL CONNECTING THE COMMISSION ON SUPERHUMAN ACTIVITY WITH HIS FOLDING CASTLE IS HARDLY SHOWING OFF FOR HIM.
AND THAT DOESN'T CONCERN YOU, DALLAS...?
IN LIGHT OF THE RECENT AGGRESSIVE STANCES TAKEN BY YOUR GOVERNMENT TOWARDS THE SUPERHUMAN COMMUNITY, MR. GYRICH, I WOULD THINK...

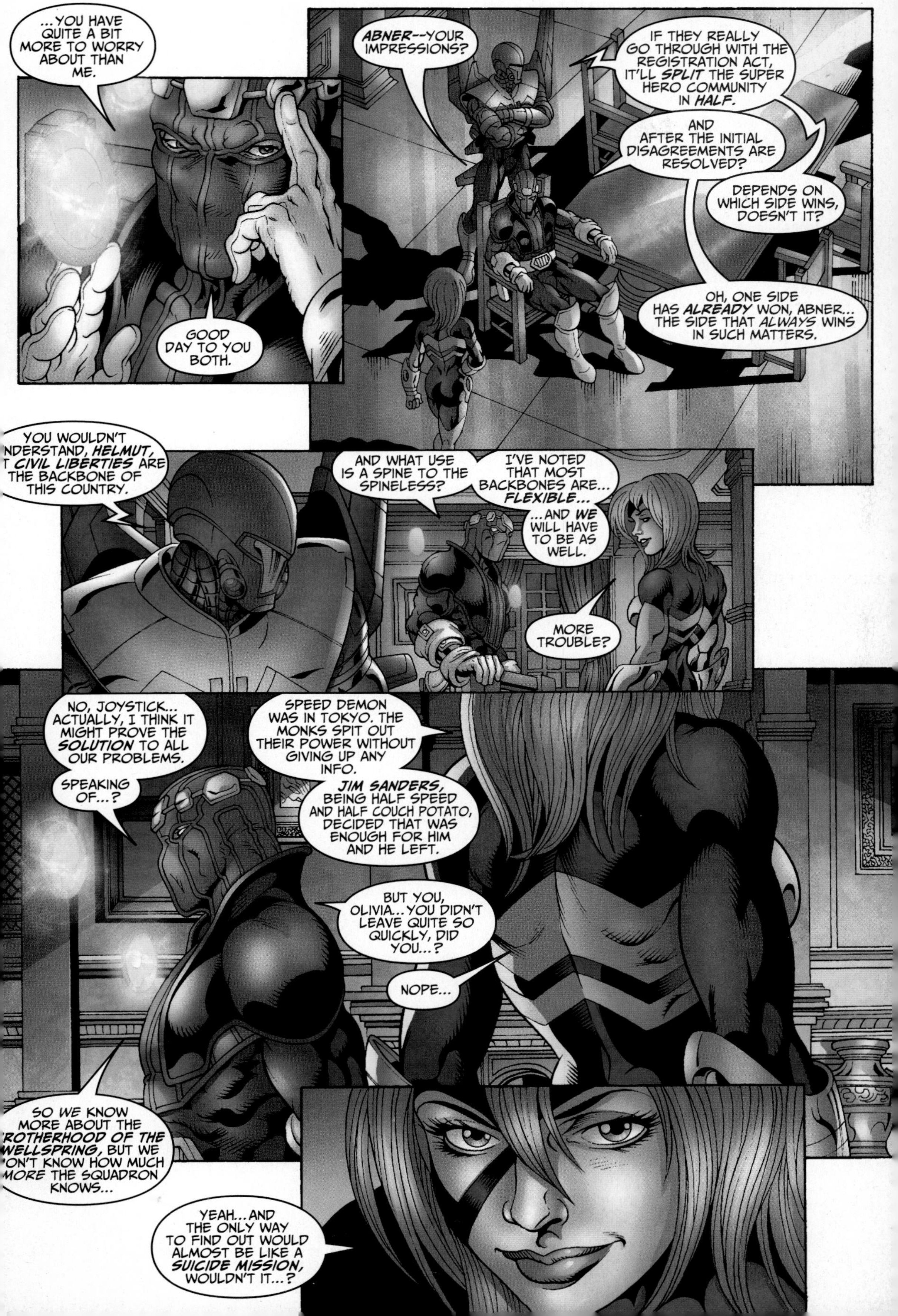
...YOU HAVE QUITE A BIT MORE TO WORRY ABOUT THAN ME.
GOOD DAY TO YOU BOTH.
ABNER--YOUR IMPRESSIONS?
IF THEY REALLY GO THROUGH WITH THE REGISTRATION ACT, IT'LL SPLIT THE SUPER HERO COMMUNITY IN HALF.
AND AFTER THE INITIAL DISAGREEMENTS ARE RESOLVED?
DEPENDS ON WHICH SIDE WINS, DOESN'T IT?
OH, ONE SIDE HAS ALREADY WON, ABNER... THE SIDE THAT ALWAYS WINS IN SUCH MATTERS.
YOU WOULDN'T NDERSTAND, HELMUT, T CIVIL LIBERTIES ARE THE BACKBONE OF THIS COUNTRY.
AND WHAT USE IS A SPINE TO THE SPINELESS?
I'VE NOTED THAT MOST BACKBONES ARE... FLEXIBLE...
...AND WE WILL HAVE TO BE AS WELL.
MORE TROUBLE?
NO, JOYSTICK... ACTUALLY, I THINK IT MIGHT PROVE THE SOLUTION TO ALL OUR PROBLEMS.
SPEAKING OF...?
SPEED DEMON WAS IN TOKYO. THE MONKS SPIT OUT THEIR POWER WITHOUT GIVING UP ANY INFO.
JIM SANDERS, BEING HALF SPEED AND HALF COUCH POTATO, DECIDED THAT WAS ENOUGH FOR HIM AND HE LEFT.
BUT YOU, OLIVIA... YOU DIDN'T LEAVE QUITE SO QUICKLY, DID YOU...?
NOPE...
SO WE KNOW MORE ABOUT THE ROTHERHOOD OF THE WELLSPRING, BUT WE ON'T KNOW HOW MUCH MORE THE SQUADRON KNOWS...
YEAH... AND THE ONLY WAY TO FIND OUT WOULD ALMOST BE LIKE A SUICIDE MISSION, WOULDN'T IT...?

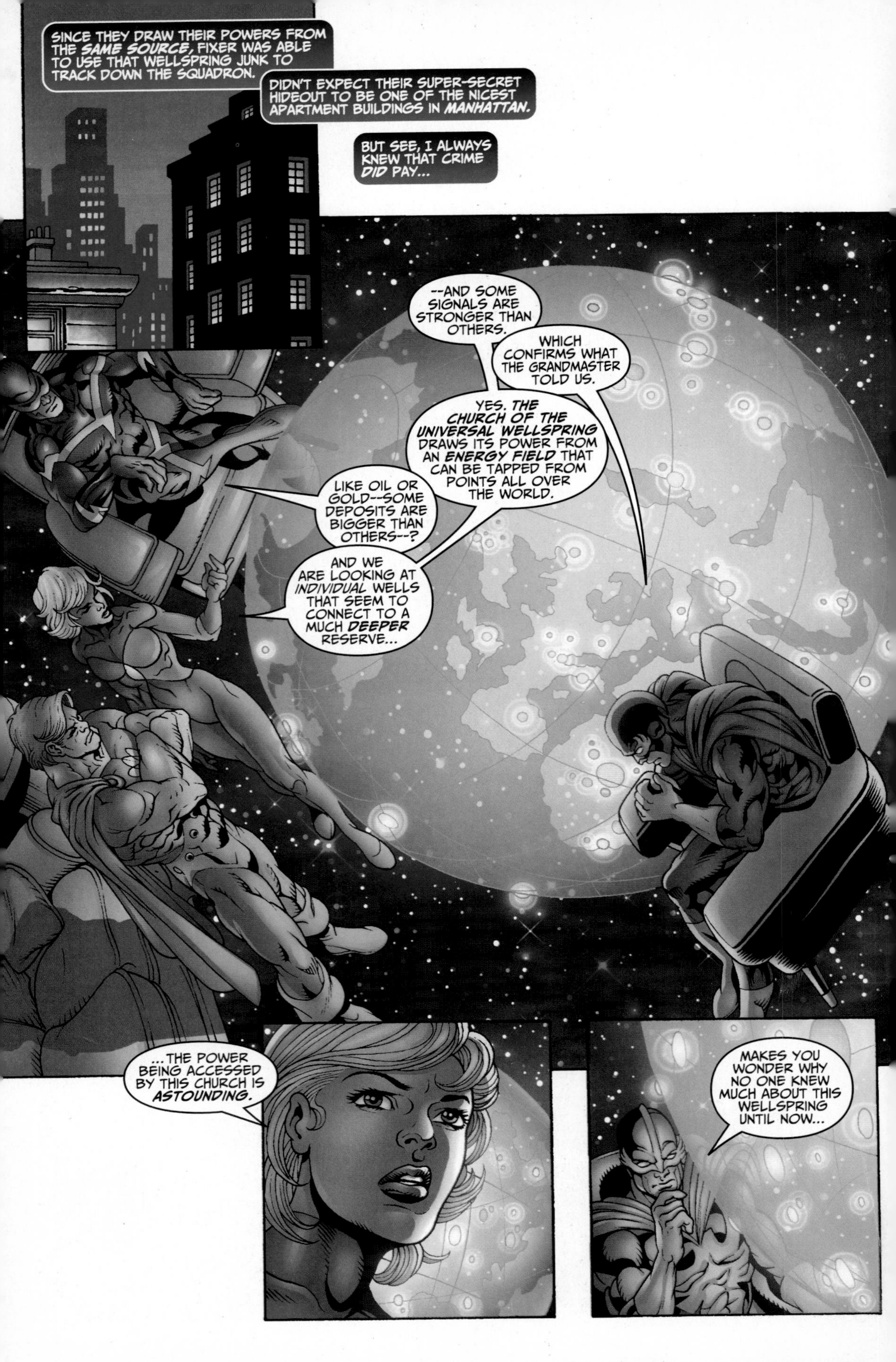
SINCE THEY DRAW THEIR POWERS FROM THE SAME SOURCE, FIXER WAS ABLE TO USE THAT WELLSPRING JUNK TO TRACK DOWN THE SQUADRON.
DIDN'T EXPECT THEIR SUPER-SECRET HIDEOUT TO BE ONE OF THE NICEST APARTMENT BUILDINGS IN MANHATTAN.
BUT SEE, I ALWAYS KNEW THAT CRIME DID PAY...
YES. THE CHURCH OF THE UNIVERSAL WELLSPRING DRAWS ITS POWER FROM AN ENERGY FIELD THAT CAN BE TAPPED FROM POINTS ALL OVER THE WORLD.
LIKE OIL OR GOLD--SOME DEPOSITS ARE BIGGER THAN OTHERS--?
--AND SOME SIGNALS ARE STRONGER THAN OTHERS.
WHICH CONFIRMS WHAT THE GRANDMASTER TOLD US.
AND WE ARE LOOKING AT INDIVIDUAL WELLS THAT SEEM TO CONNECT TO A MUCH DEEPER RESERVE...
...THE POWER BEING ACCESSED BY THIS CHURCH IS ASTOUNDING.
MAKES YOU WONDER WHY NO ONE KNEW MUCH ABOUT THIS WELLSPRING UNTIL NOW...

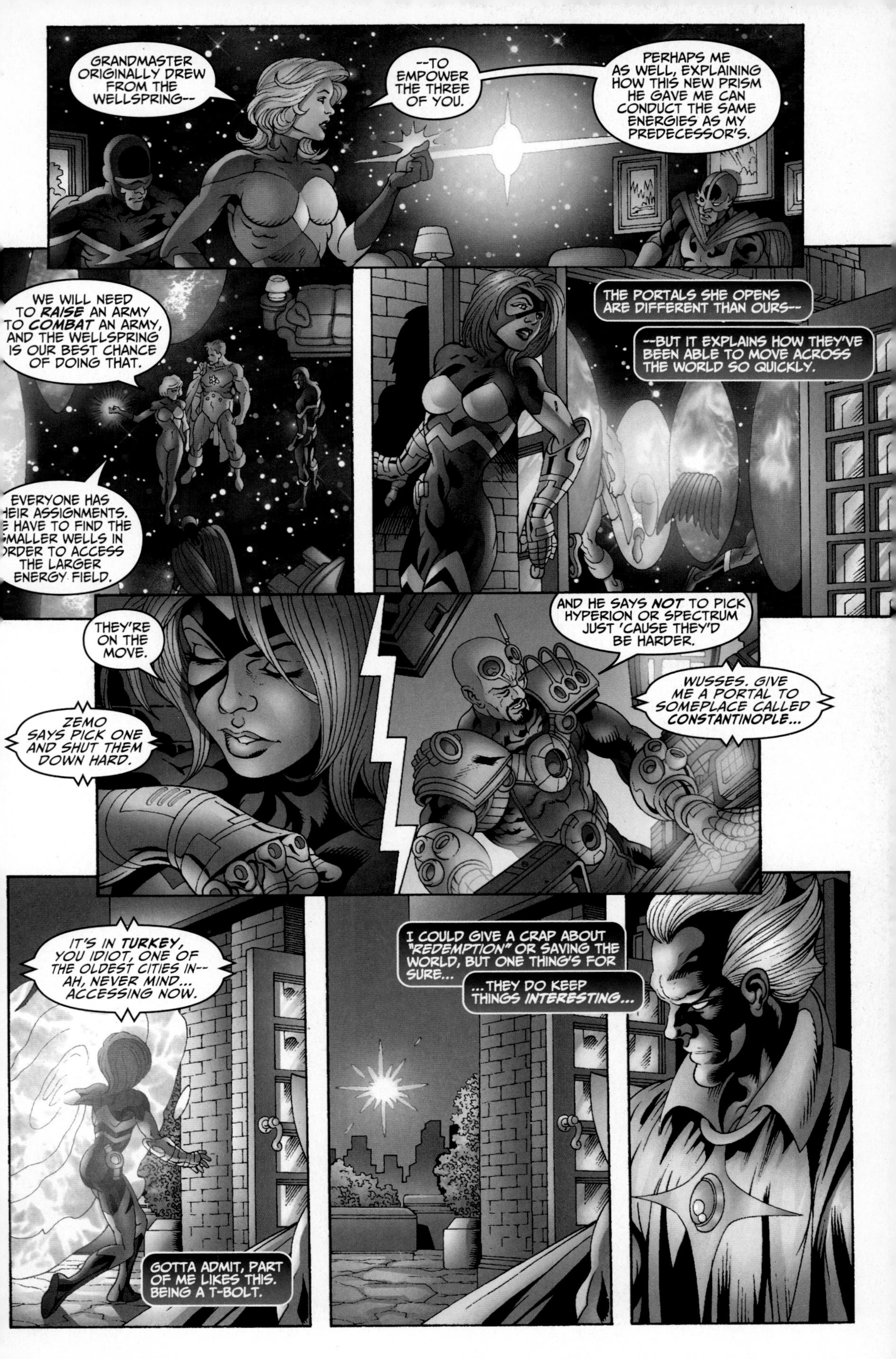
GRANDMASTER ORIGINALLY DREW FROM THE WELLSPRING--
--TO EMPOWER THE THREE OF YOU.
PERHAPS ME AS WELL, EXPLAINING HOW THIS NEW PRISM HE GAVE ME CAN CONDUCT THE SAME ENERGIES AS MY PREDECESSOR'S.
WE WILL NEED TO RAISE AN ARMY TO COMBAT AN ARMY, AND THE WELLSPRING IS OUR BEST CHANCE OF DOING THAT.
EVERYONE HAS HEIR ASSIGNMENTS. E HAVE TO FIND THE SMALLER WELLS IN ORDER TO ACCESS THE LARGER ENERGY FIELD.
THE PORTALS SHE OPENS ARE DIFFERENT THAN OURS--
--BUT IT EXPLAINS HOW THEY'VE BEEN ABLE TO MOVE ACROSS THE WORLD SO QUICKLY.
THEY'RE ON THE MOVE.
ZEMO SAYS PICK ONE AND SHUT THEM DOWN HARD.
AND HE SAYS NOT TO PICK HYPERION OR SPECTRUM JUST 'CAUSE THEY'D BE HARDER.
WUSSES. GIVE ME A PORTAL TO SOMEPLACE CALLED CONSTANTINOPLE...
IT'S IN TURKEY, YOU IDIOT, ONE OF THE OLDEST CITIES IN-- AH, NEVER MIND... ACCESSING NOW.
GOTTA ADMIT, PART OF ME LIKES THIS. BEING A T-BOLT.
I COULD GIVE A CRAP ABOUT "REDEMPTION" OR SAVING THE WORLD, BUT ONE THING'S FOR SURE...
...THEY DO KEEP THINGS INTERESTING...

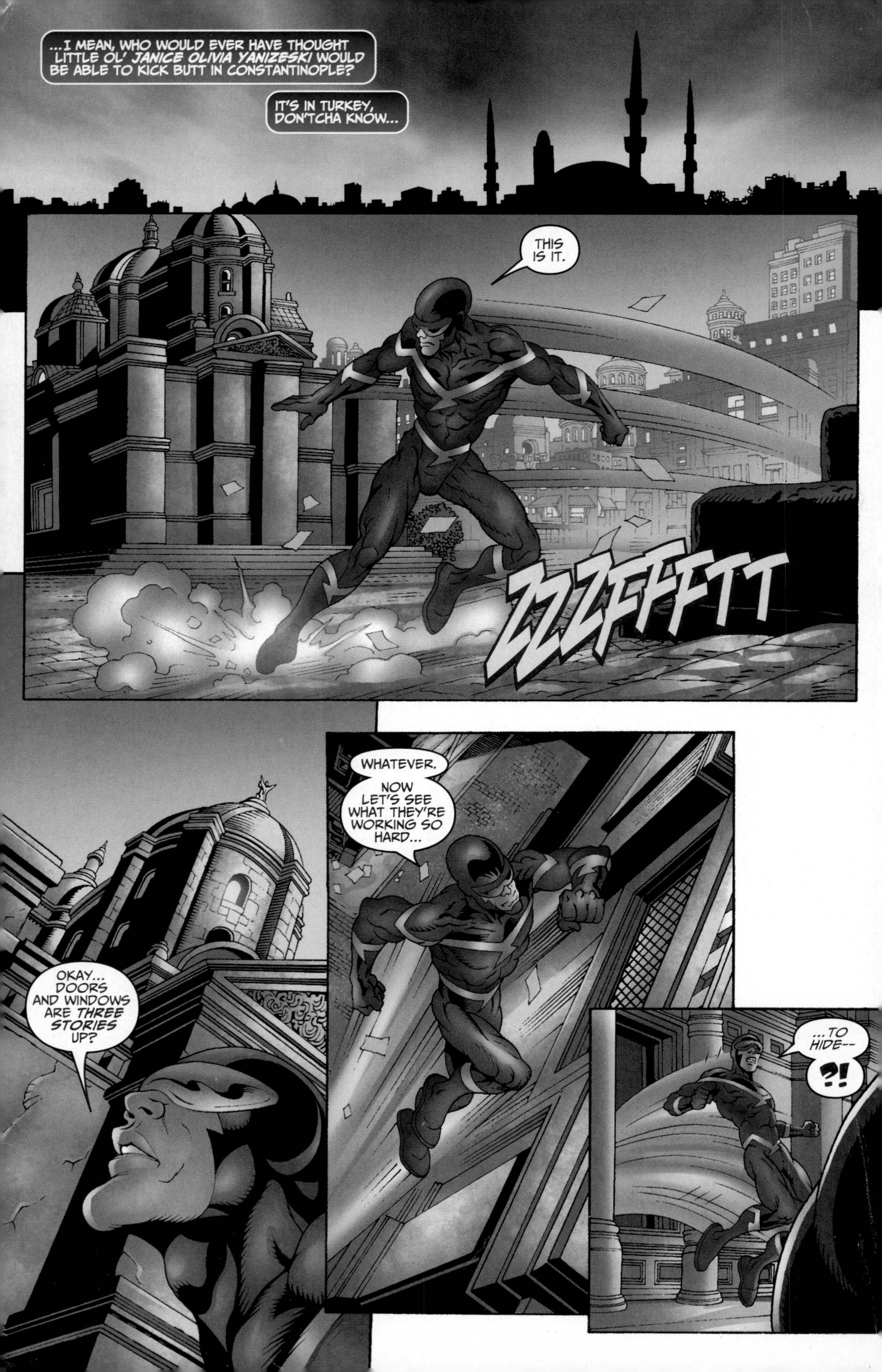
...I MEAN, WHO WOULD EVER HAVE THOUGHT LITTLE OL' JANICE OLIVIA YANIZESKI WOULD BE ABLE TO KICK BUTT IN CONSTANTINOPLE?
IT'S IN TURKEY, DON'TCHA KNOW...
THIS IS IT.
ZZZFFFTT
OKAY... DOORS AND WINDOWS ARE THREE STORIES UP?
WHATEVER.
NOW LET'S SEE WHAT THEY'RE WORKING SO HARD...
...TO HIDE--
?!

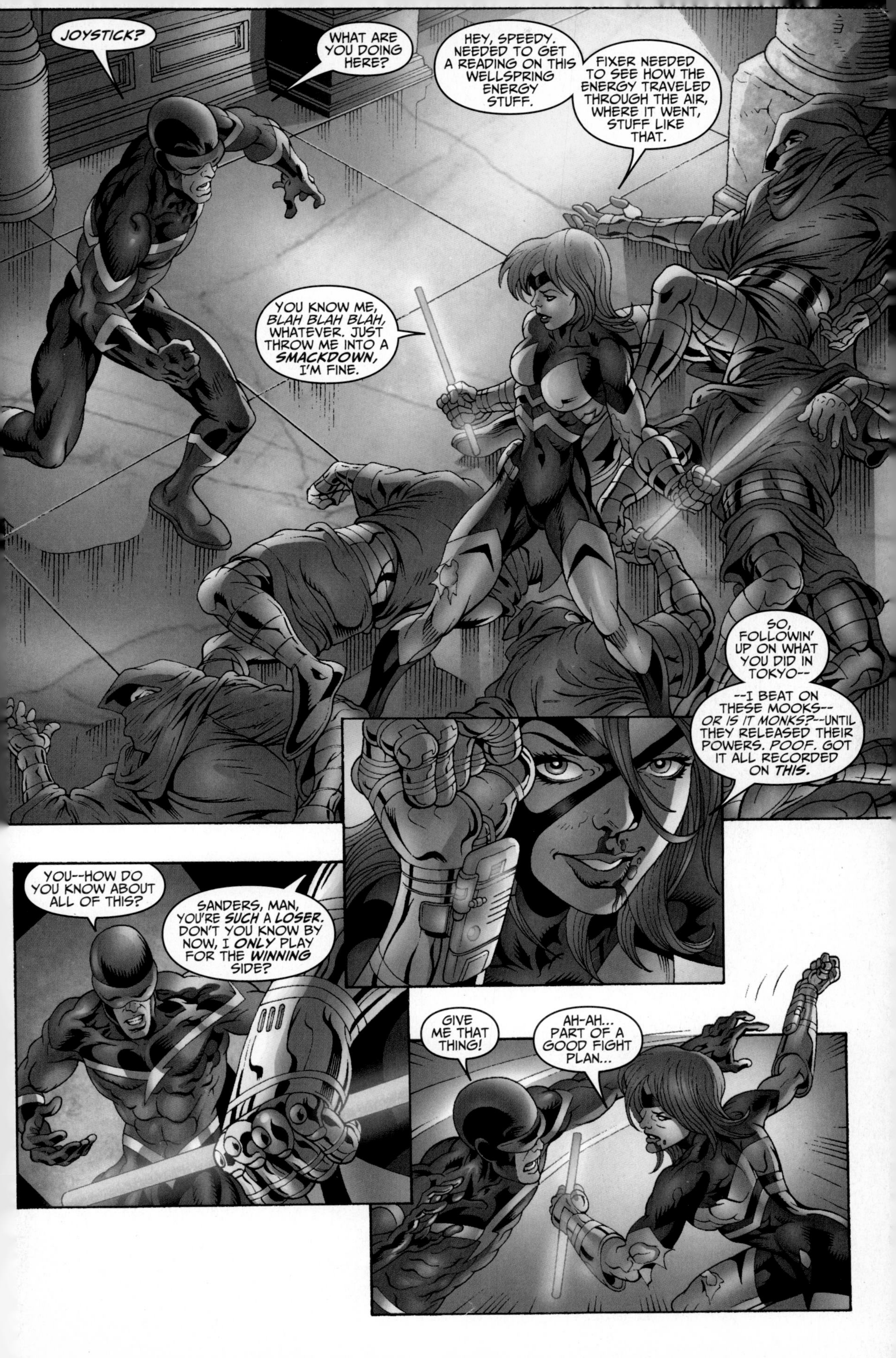
JOYSTICK?
WHAT ARE YOU DOING HERE?
HEY, SPEEDY. NEEDED TO GET A READING ON THIS WELLSPRING ENERGY STUFF.
FIXER NEEDED TO SEE HOW THE ENERGY TRAVELED THROUGH THE AIR, WHERE IT WENT, STUFF LIKE THAT.
YOU KNOW ME, *BLAH BLAH BLAH,* WHATEVER. JUST THROW ME INTO A ***SMACKDOWN,*** I'M FINE.
SO, FOLLOWIN' UP ON WHAT YOU DID IN TOKYO--
--I BEAT ON THESE MOOKS-- *OR IS IT MONKS?*--UNTIL THEY RELEASED THEIR POWERS. *POOF.* GOT IT ALL RECORDED ON ***THIS.***
YOU--HOW DO YOU KNOW ABOUT ALL OF THIS?
SANDERS, MAN, YOU'RE ***SUCH*** A ***LOSER.*** DON'T YOU KNOW BY NOW, I ***ONLY*** PLAY FOR THE ***WINNING*** SIDE?
GIVE ME THAT THING!
AH-AH... PART OF A GOOD FIGHT PLAN...

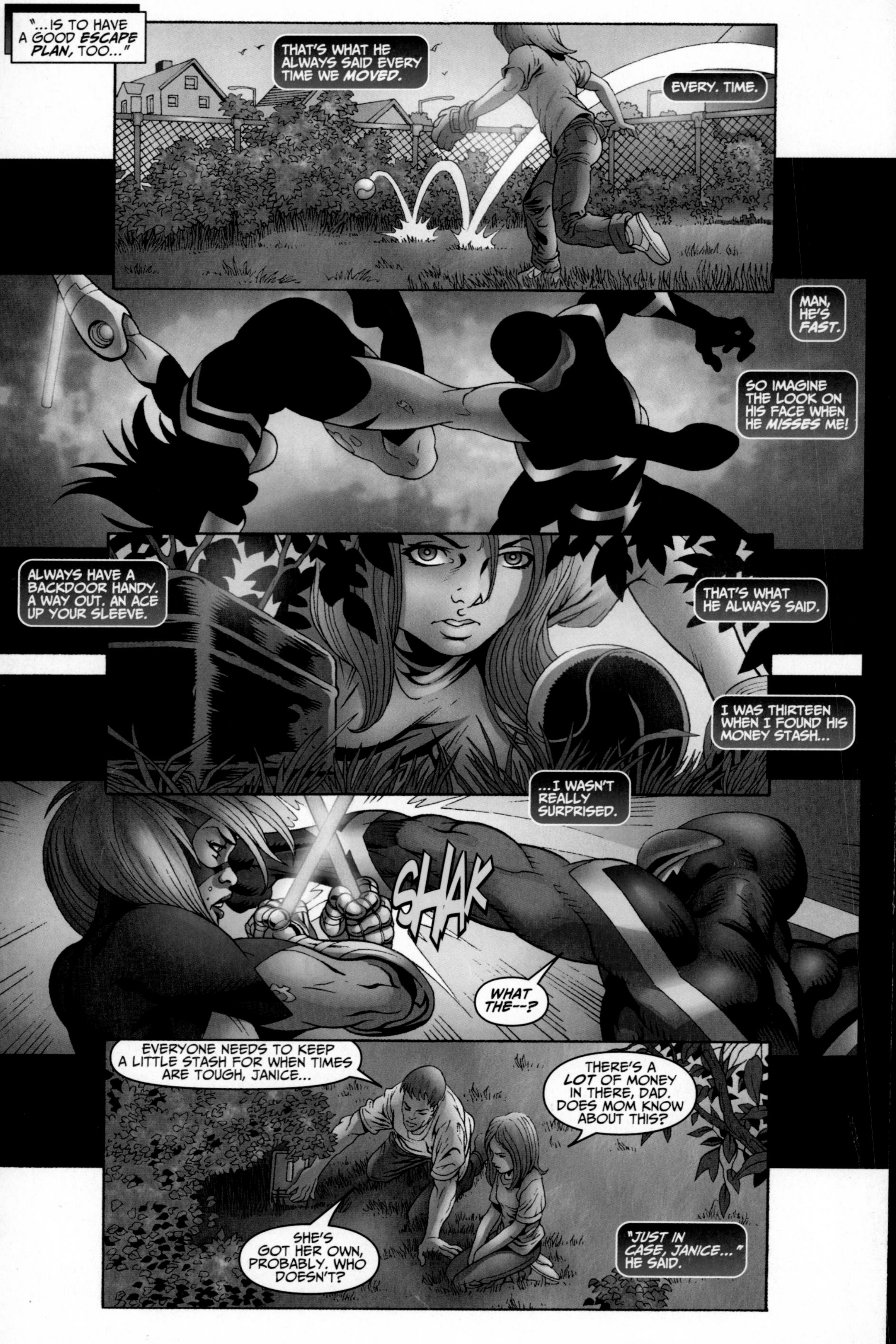
"...IS TO HAVE A GOOD ESCAPE PLAN, TOO..."
THAT'S WHAT HE ALWAYS SAID EVERY TIME WE MOVED.
EVERY. TIME.
MAN, HE'S FAST.
SO IMAGINE THE LOOK ON HIS FACE WHEN HE MISSES ME!
ALWAYS HAVE A BACKDOOR HANDY. A WAY OUT. AN ACE UP YOUR SLEEVE.
THAT'S WHAT HE ALWAYS SAID.
I WAS THIRTEEN WHEN I FOUND HIS MONEY STASH...
...I WASN'T REALLY SURPRISED.
SHAK
WHAT THE--?
EVERYONE NEEDS TO KEEP A LITTLE STASH FOR WHEN TIMES ARE TOUGH, JANICE...
THERE'S A LOT OF MONEY IN THERE, DAD. DOES MOM KNOW ABOUT THIS?
SHE'S GOT HER OWN, PROBABLY. WHO DOESN'T?
"JUST IN CASE, JANICE..." HE SAID.

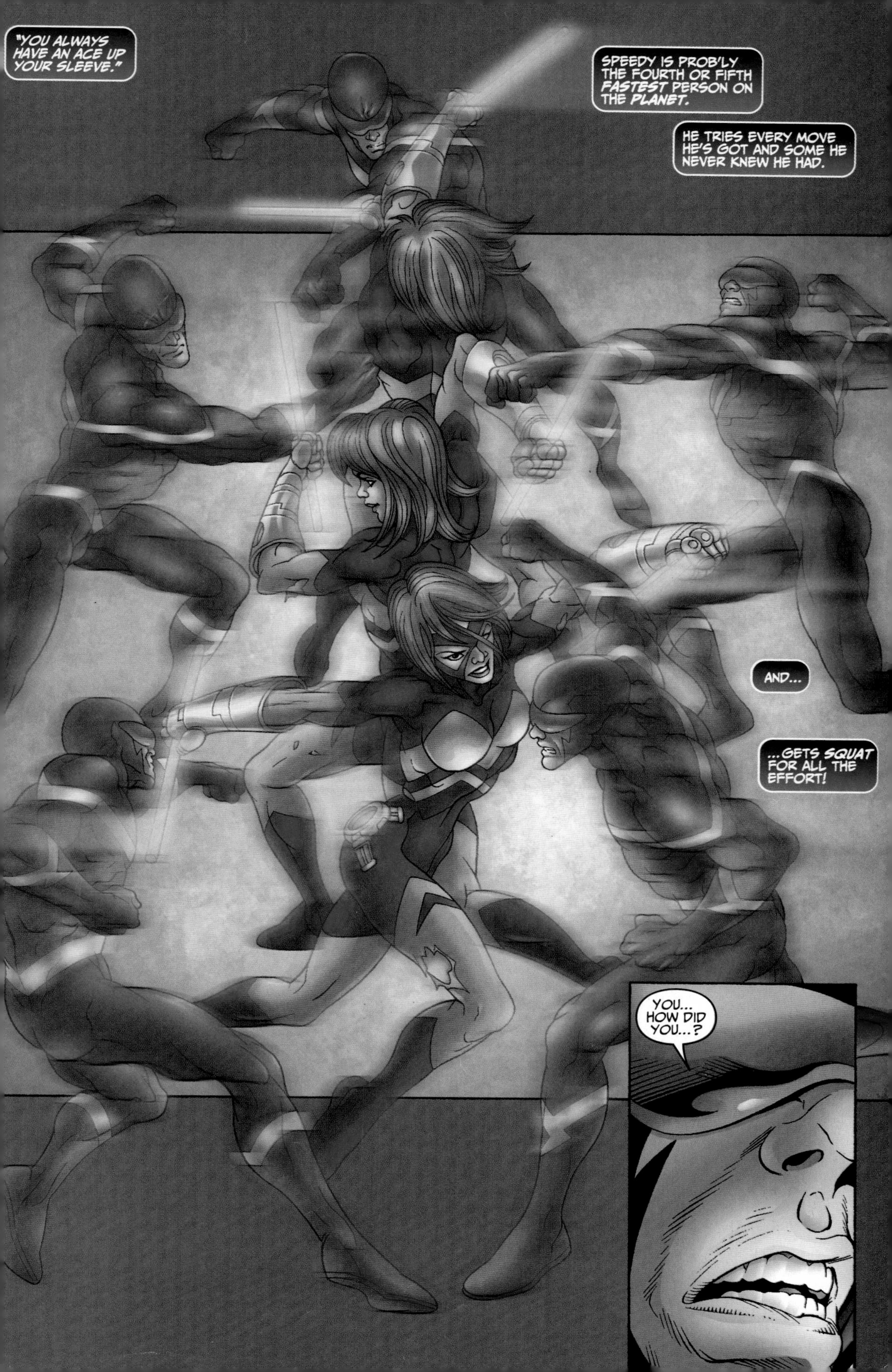
"YOU ALWAYS HAVE AN ACE UP YOUR SLEEVE."
SPEEDY IS PROB'LY THE FOURTH OR FIFTH FASTEST PERSON ON THE PLANET.
HE TRIES EVERY MOVE HE'S GOT AND SOME HE NEVER KNEW HE HAD.
AND...
...GETS SQUAT FOR ALL THE EFFORT!
YOU... HOW DID YOU...?

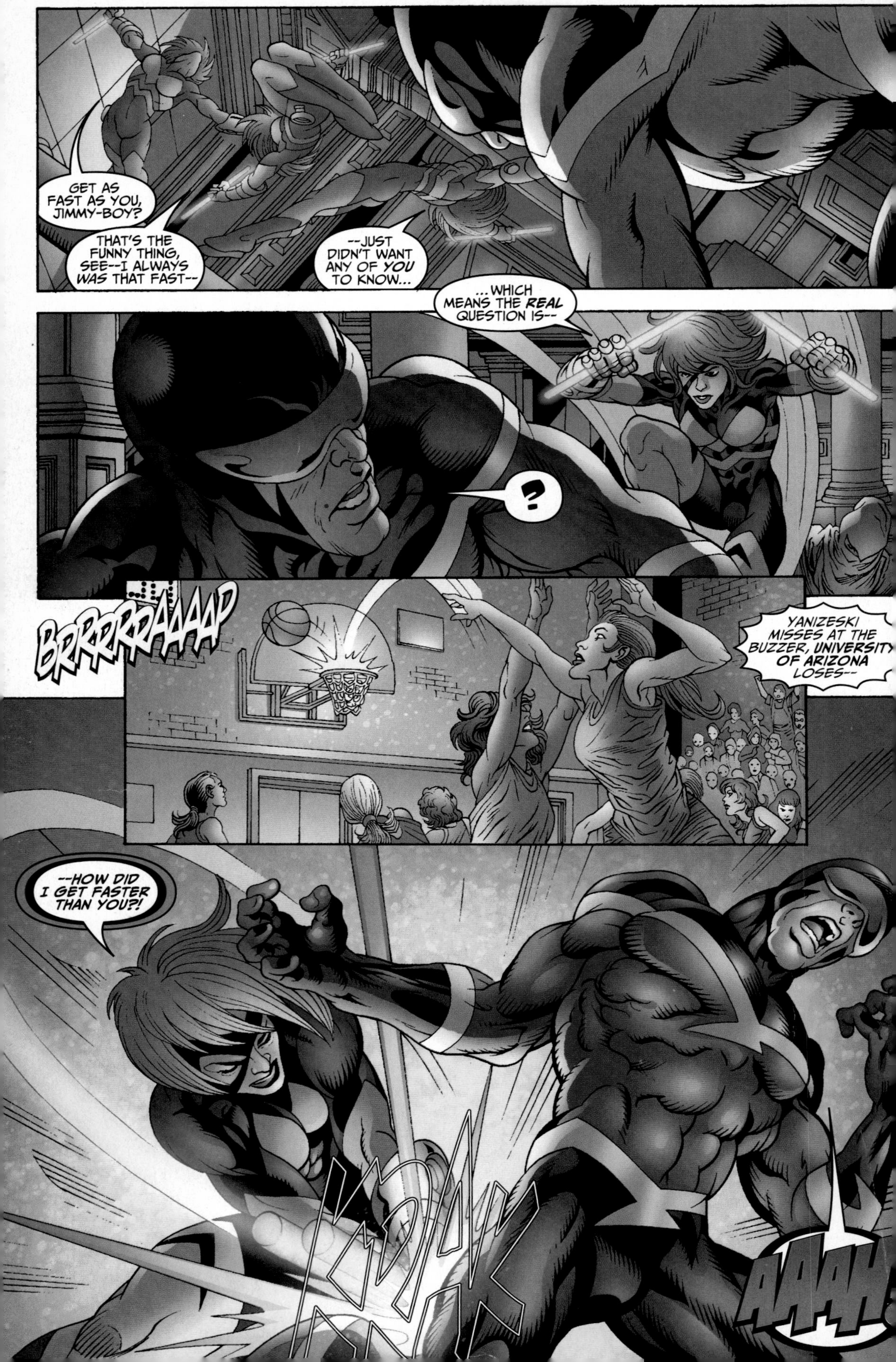
GET AS FAST AS YOU, JIMMY-BOY?
THAT'S THE FUNNY THING, SEE--I ALWAYS *WAS* THAT FAST--
--JUST DIDN'T WANT ANY OF *YOU* TO KNOW...
...WHICH MEANS THE *REAL* QUESTION IS--
?
BRRRRRAAAAP
YANIZESKI MISSES AT THE BUZZER, *UNIVERSITY OF ARIZONA* LOSES--
--HOW DID I GET FASTER THAN YOU?!
AAAH

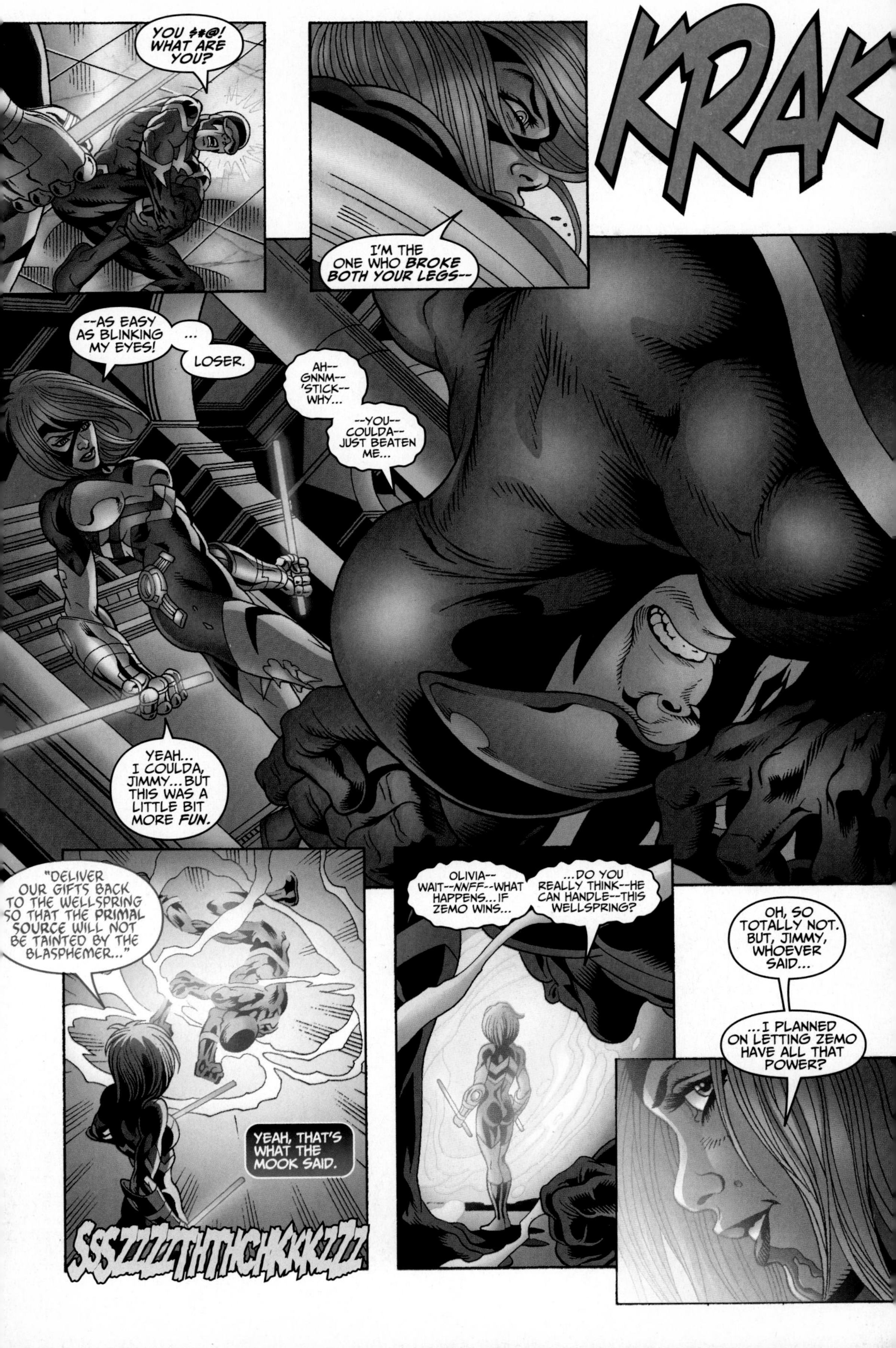
YOU $#@! WHAT ARE YOU?
I'M THE ONE WHO BROKE BOTH YOUR LEGS--
KRAK
--AS EASY AS BLINKING MY EYES!
...
LOSER.
AH-- GNNM-- 'STICK-- WHY...
--YOU-- COULDA-- JUST BEATEN ME...
YEAH... I COULDA, JIMMY... BUT THIS WAS A LITTLE BIT MORE FUN.
"DELIVER OUR GIFTS BACK TO THE WELLSPRING SO THAT THE PRIMAL SOURCE WILL NOT BE TAINTED BY THE BLASPHEMER..."
YEAH, THAT'S WHAT THE MOOK SAID.
SSSZZZZTHTHCHKKKZZZ
OLIVIA-- WAIT--NNFF--WHAT HAPPENS...IF ZEMO WINS...
...DO YOU REALLY THINK--HE CAN HANDLE--THIS WELLSPRING?
OH, SO TOTALLY NOT. BUT, JIMMY, WHOEVER SAID...
...I PLANNED ON LETTING ZEMO HAVE ALL THAT POWER?

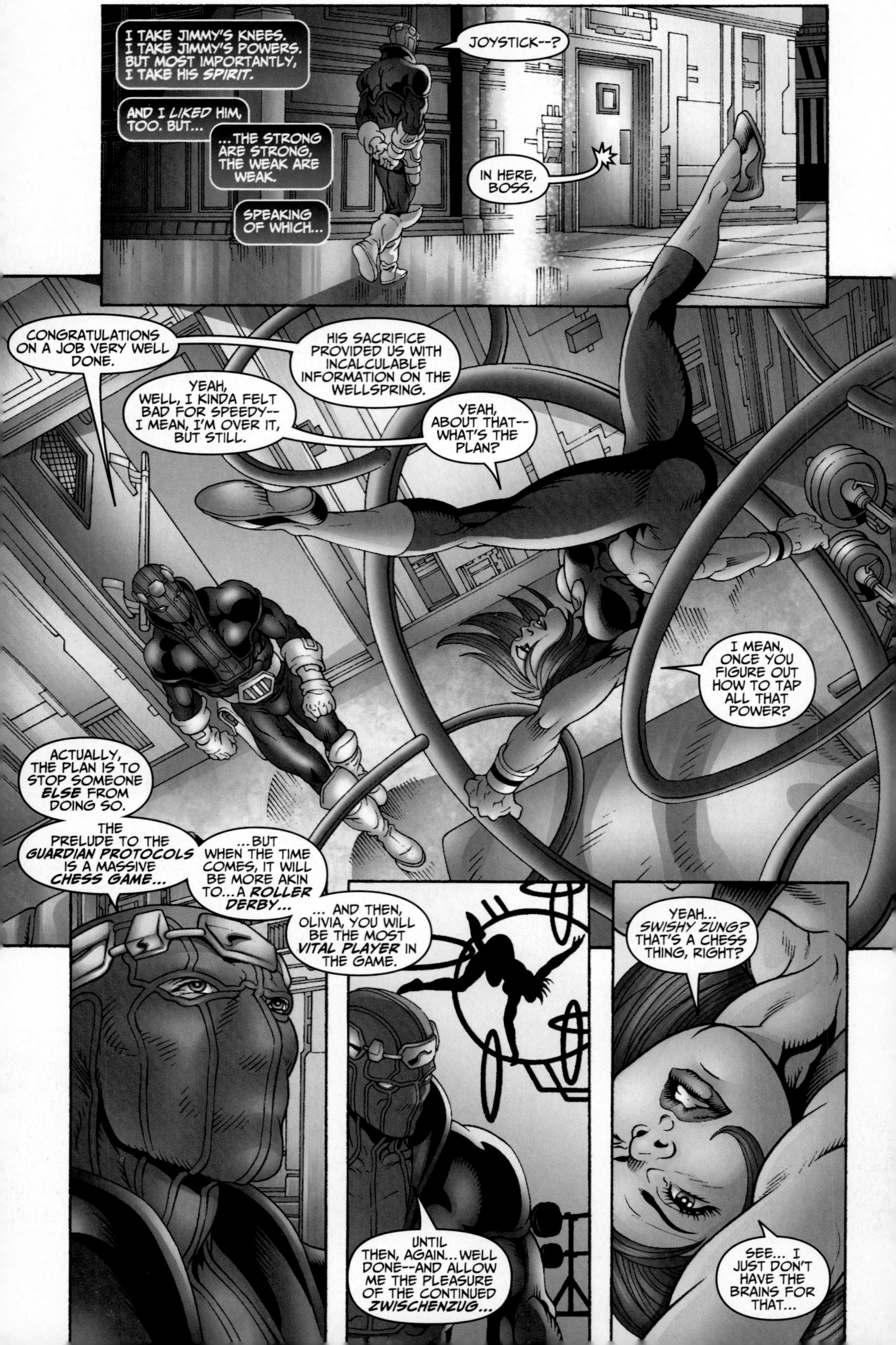
I TAKE JIMMY'S KNEES. I TAKE JIMMY'S POWERS. BUT MOST IMPORTANTLY, I TAKE HIS SPIRIT.
AND I LIKED HIM, TOO. BUT...
...THE STRONG ARE STRONG, THE WEAK ARE WEAK.
SPEAKING OF WHICH...
JOYSTICK--?
IN HERE, BOSS.
CONGRATULATIONS ON A JOB VERY WELL DONE.
HIS SACRIFICE PROVIDED US WITH INCALCULABLE INFORMATION ON THE WELLSPRING.
YEAH, WELL, I KINDA FELT BAD FOR SPEEDY-- I MEAN, I'M OVER IT, BUT STILL.
YEAH, ABOUT THAT-- WHAT'S THE PLAN?
I MEAN, ONCE YOU FIGURE OUT HOW TO TAP ALL THAT POWER?
ACTUALLY, THE PLAN IS TO STOP SOMEONE ELSE FROM DOING SO.
THE PRELUDE TO THE GUARDIAN PROTOCOLS IS A MASSIVE CHESS GAME...
...BUT WHEN THE TIME COMES, IT WILL BE MORE AKIN TO...A ROLLER DERBY...
... AND THEN, OLIVIA, YOU WILL BE THE MOST VITAL PLAYER IN THE GAME.
UNTIL THEN, AGAIN...WELL DONE--AND ALLOW ME THE PLEASURE OF THE CONTINUED ZWISCHENZUG...
YEAH... SWISHY ZUNG? THAT'S A CHESS THING, RIGHT?
SEE... I JUST DON'T HAVE THE BRAINS FOR THAT...

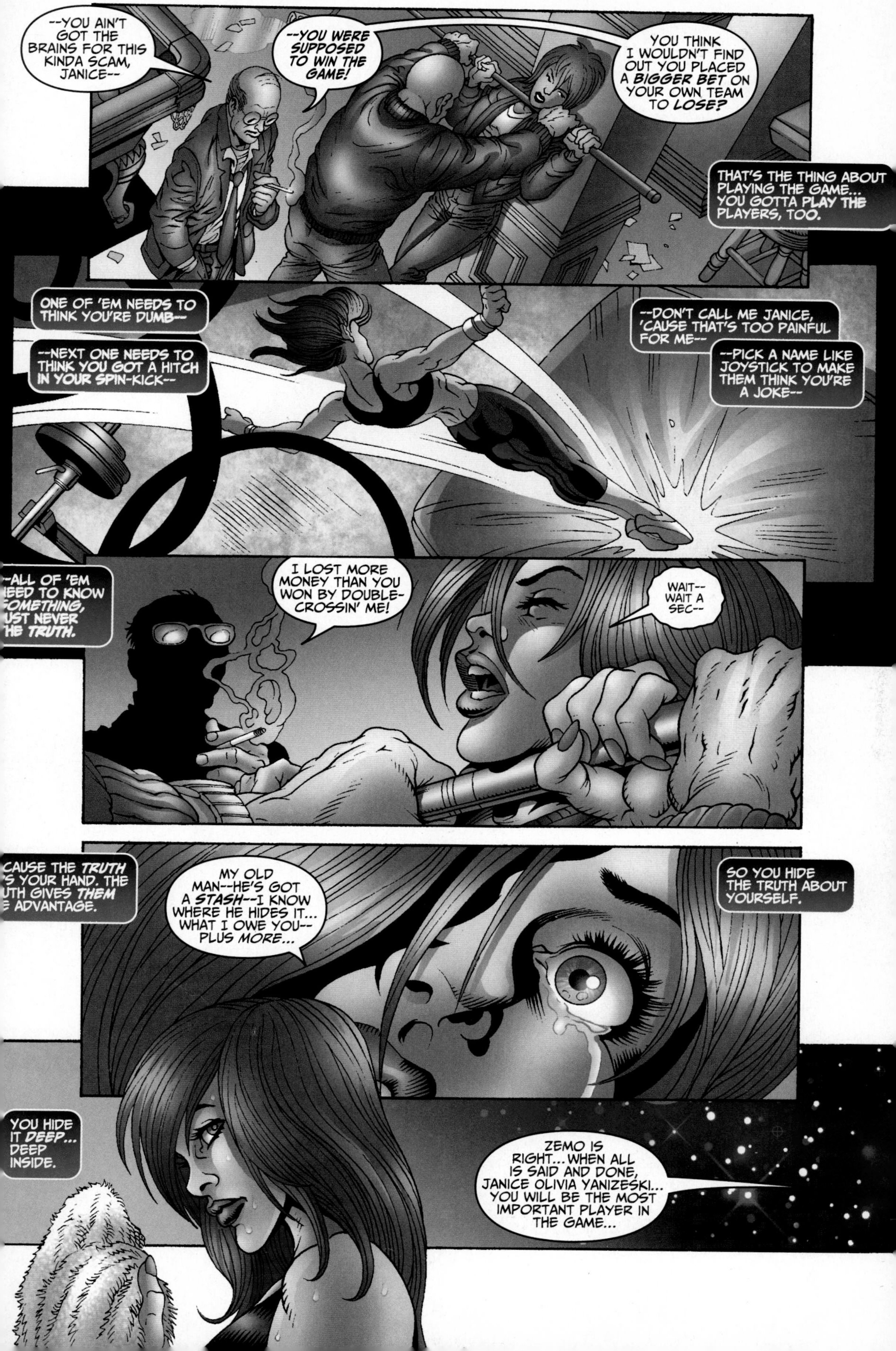
--YOU AIN'T GOT THE BRAINS FOR THIS KINDA SCAM, JANICE--
--YOU WERE SUPPOSED TO WIN THE GAME!
YOU THINK I WOULDN'T FIND OUT YOU PLACED A BIGGER BET ON YOUR OWN TEAM TO LOSE?
THAT'S THE THING ABOUT PLAYING THE GAME... YOU GOTTA PLAY THE PLAYERS, TOO.
ONE OF 'EM NEEDS TO THINK YOU'RE DUMB--
--NEXT ONE NEEDS TO THINK YOU GOT A HITCH IN YOUR SPIN-KICK--
--DON'T CALL ME JANICE, 'CAUSE THAT'S TOO PAINFUL FOR ME--
--PICK A NAME LIKE JOYSTICK TO MAKE THEM THINK YOU'RE A JOKE--
-ALL OF 'EM EED TO KNOW OMETHING, UST NEVER THE TRUTH.
I LOST MORE MONEY THAN YOU WON BY DOUBLE-CROSSIN' ME!
WAIT-- WAIT A SEC--
CAUSE THE TRUTH 'S YOUR HAND. THE UTH GIVES THEM E ADVANTAGE.
MY OLD MAN--HE'S GOT A STASH--I KNOW WHERE HE HIDES IT... WHAT I OWE YOU-- PLUS MORE...
SO YOU HIDE THE TRUTH ABOUT YOURSELF.
YOU HIDE IT DEEP... DEEP INSIDE.
ZEMO IS RIGHT... WHEN ALL IS SAID AND DONE, JANICE OLIVIA YANIZESKI... YOU WILL BE THE MOST IMPORTANT PLAYER IN THE GAME...

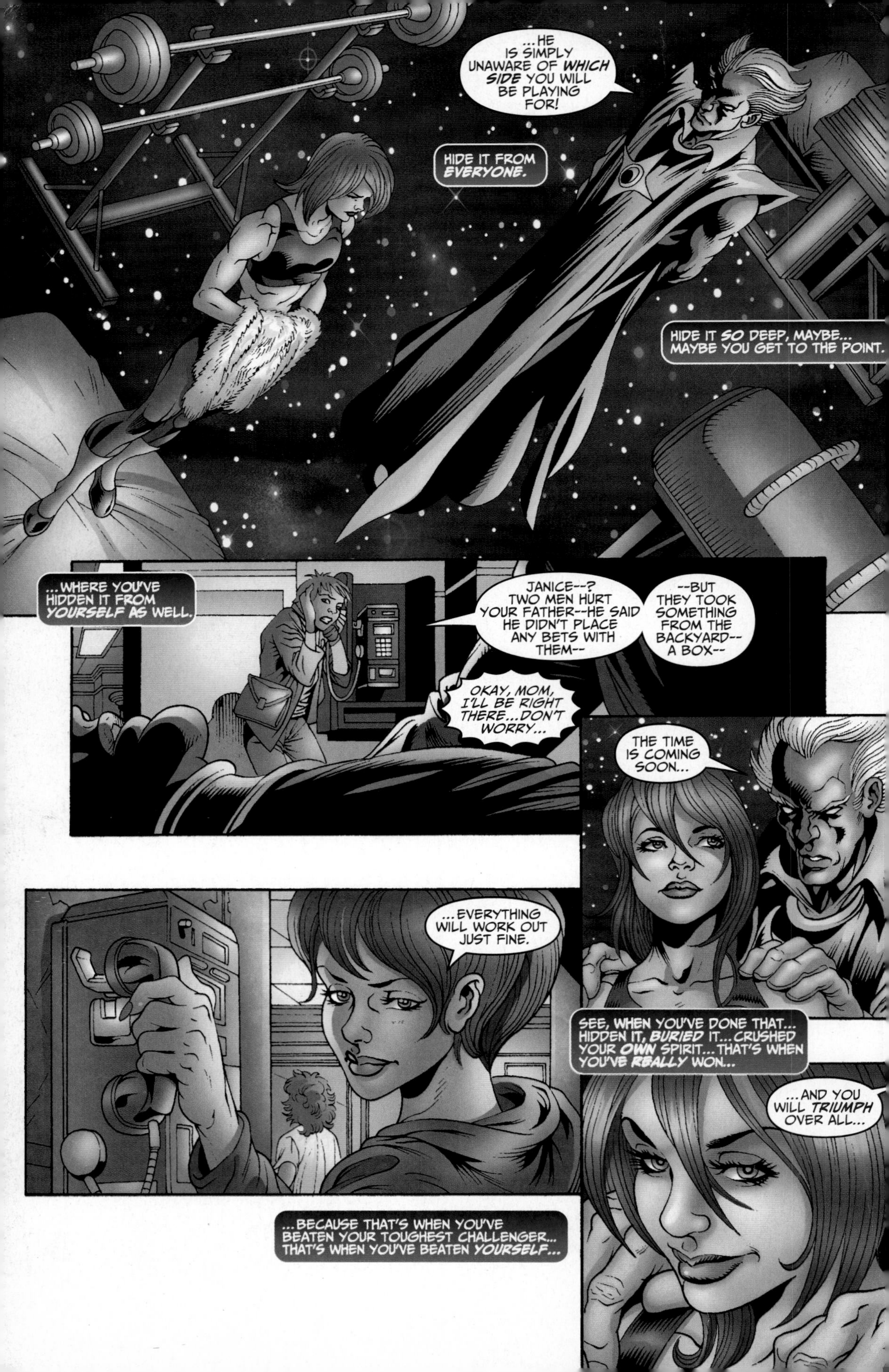
...HE IS SIMPLY UNAWARE OF WHICH SIDE YOU WILL BE PLAYING FOR!
HIDE IT FROM EVERYONE.
HIDE IT SO DEEP, MAYBE... MAYBE YOU GET TO THE POINT.
...WHERE YOU'VE HIDDEN IT FROM YOURSELF AS WELL.
JANICE--? TWO MEN HURT YOUR FATHER--HE SAID HE DIDN'T PLACE ANY BETS WITH THEM--
--BUT THEY TOOK SOMETHING FROM THE BACKYARD-- A BOX--
OKAY, MOM, I'LL BE RIGHT THERE...DON'T WORRY...
THE TIME IS COMING SOON...
...EVERYTHING WILL WORK OUT JUST FINE.
SEE, WHEN YOU'VE DONE THAT... HIDDEN IT, BURIED IT...CRUSHED YOUR OWN SPIRIT...THAT'S WHEN YOU'VE REALLY WON...
...AND YOU WILL TRIUMPH OVER ALL...
...BECAUSE THAT'S WHEN YOU'VE BEATEN YOUR TOUGHEST CHALLENGER... THAT'S WHEN YOU'VE BEATEN YOURSELF...

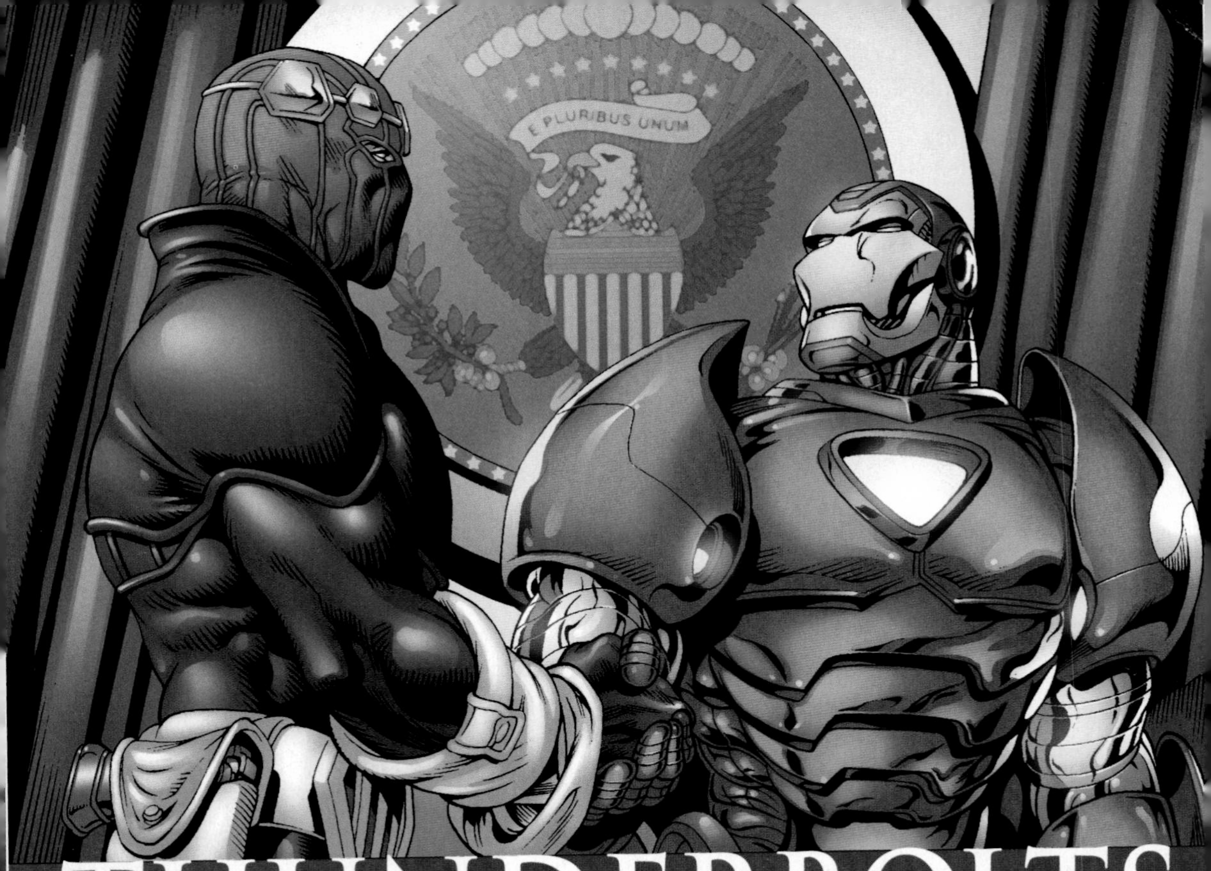
E PLURIBUS UNUM

THUNDERBOLTS

A MARVEL COMICS EVENT

CIVIL WAR

THUNDERBOLTS #103

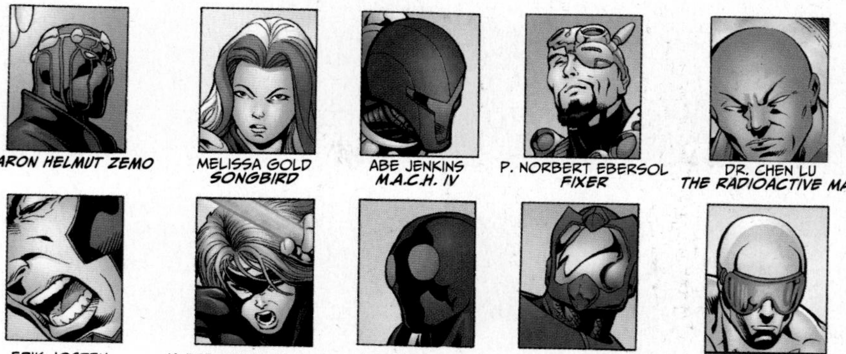

Baron Helmut Zemo | Melissa Gold, Songbird | Abe Jenkins, M.A.C.H. IV | P. Norbert Ebersol, Fixer | Dr. Chen Lu, The Radioactive Man

Erik Josten, Atlas | Janice Olivia Yanizeski, Joystick | Conrad Josten, Smuggler | Andreas Strucker, Swordsman | Donnie Gill, Blizzard

The Avengers foiled a plan by Baron Zemo and the Thunderbolts that could have saved the world. They could not trust Zemo, who repaid their doubt by almost sacrificing his life to save Captain America. After those events, the T-Bolts disbanded. A new team was started by M.A.C.H. IV, who didn't know that Zemo and Songbird had worked behind the scenes to prepare his team for an impending and mysterious global threat.

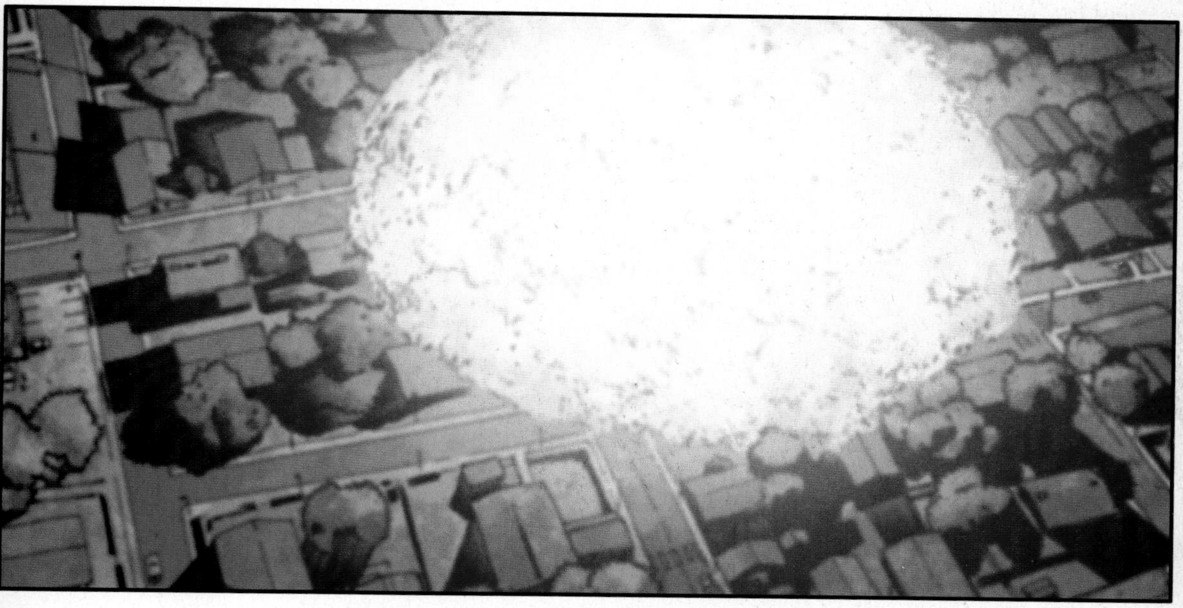

Two Weeks Ago, a horrific explosion at a crowded schoolyard in Stamford, Connecticut killed hundreds of civilians, many of them children. Superhuman irresponsibility was to blame, and the public outcry forced legislators to pass the Superhuman Registration Act. By law, superhumans must now register their identities with the government.

This Act has created a schism in the super hero community. Many have refused to register, including Captain America, who leads a group of renegade heroes against the status quo. Those in favor of using registration to create a nationwide "superhuman police force," have encouraged a startling public unmasking from a hero who has closely guarded his identity...

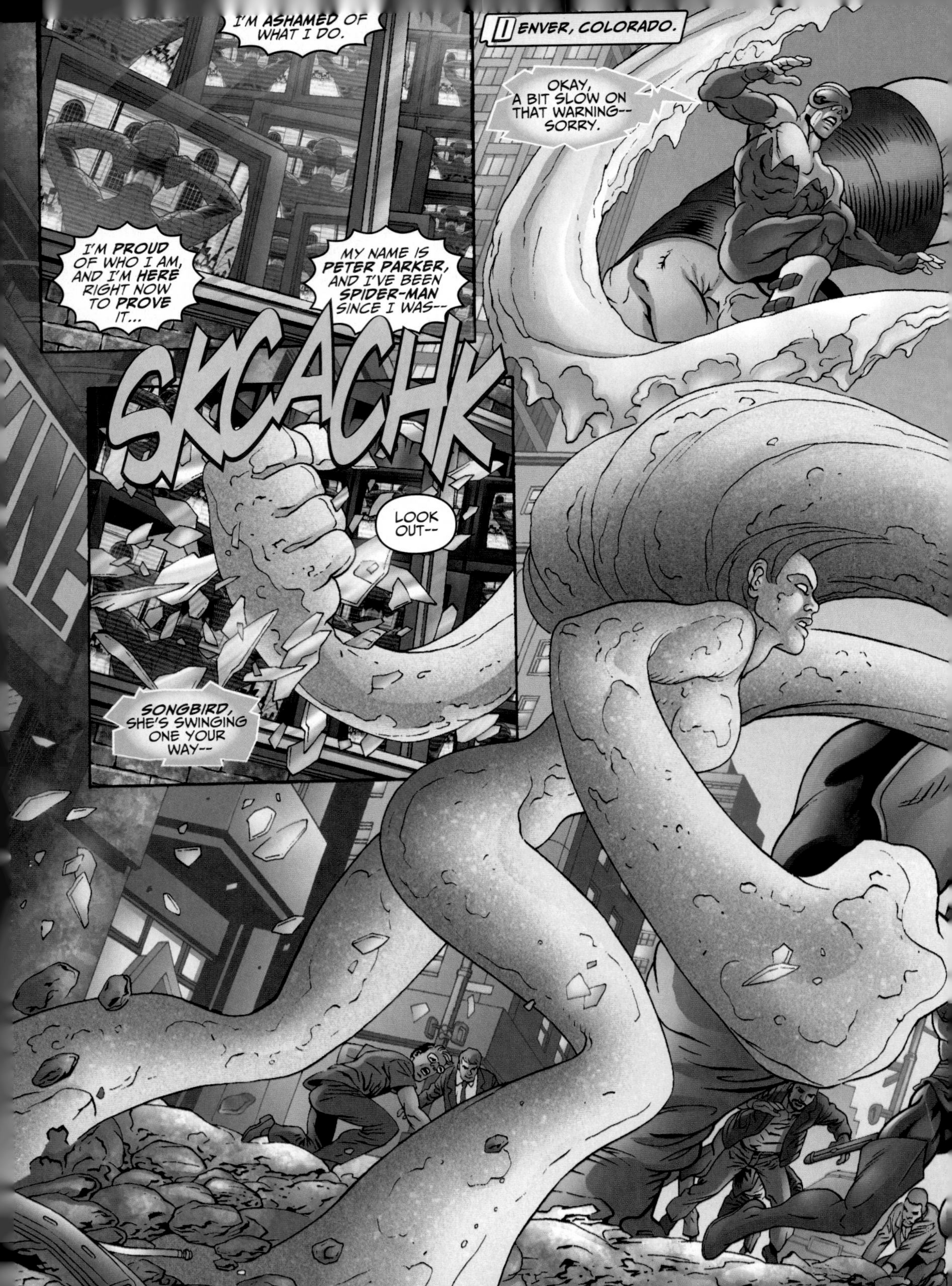
I'M ASHAMED OF WHAT I DO.
I'M PROUD OF WHO I AM, AND I'M HERE RIGHT NOW TO PROVE IT...
MY NAME IS PETER PARKER, AND I'VE BEEN SPIDER-MAN SINCE I WAS--
SKCACHK
LOOK OUT--
SONGBIRD, SHE'S SWINGING ONE YOUR WAY--
DENVER, COLORADO.
OKAY, A BIT SLOW ON THAT WARNING-- SORRY.

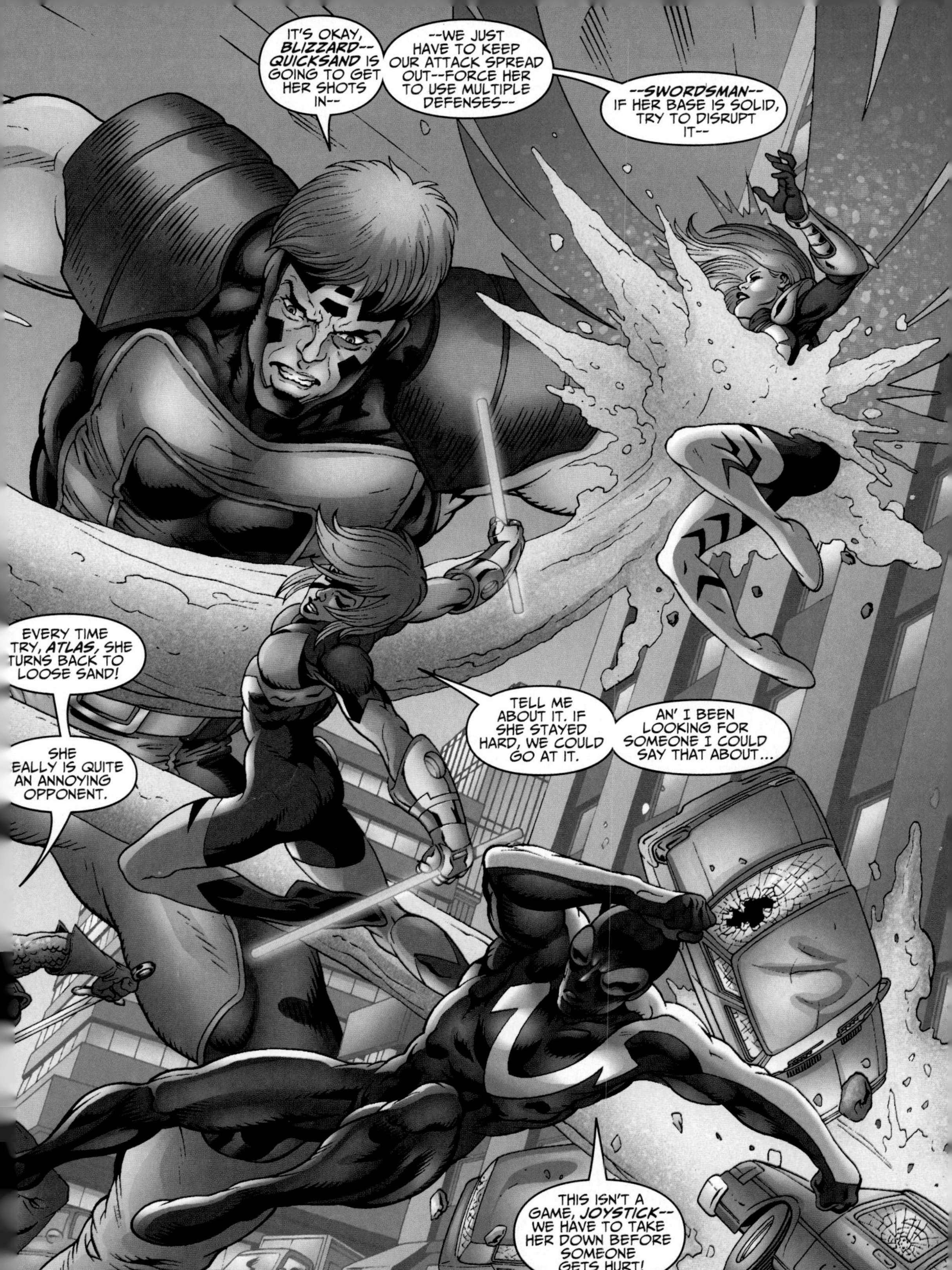

IT'S OKAY, **BLIZZARD--** **QUICKSAND** IS GOING TO GET HER SHOTS IN--
--WE JUST HAVE TO KEEP OUR ATTACK SPREAD OUT--FORCE HER TO USE MULTIPLE DEFENSES--
--SWORDSMAN-- IF HER BASE IS SOLID, TRY TO DISRUPT IT--
EVERY TIME TRY, **ATLAS,** SHE TURNS BACK TO LOOSE SAND!
TELL ME ABOUT IT. IF SHE STAYED HARD, WE COULD GO AT IT.
AN' I BEEN LOOKING FOR SOMEONE I COULD SAY THAT ABOUT...
SHE EALLY IS QUITE AN ANNOYING OPPONENT.
THIS ISN'T A GAME, **JOYSTICK--** WE HAVE TO TAKE HER DOWN BEFORE SOMEONE GETS HURT!

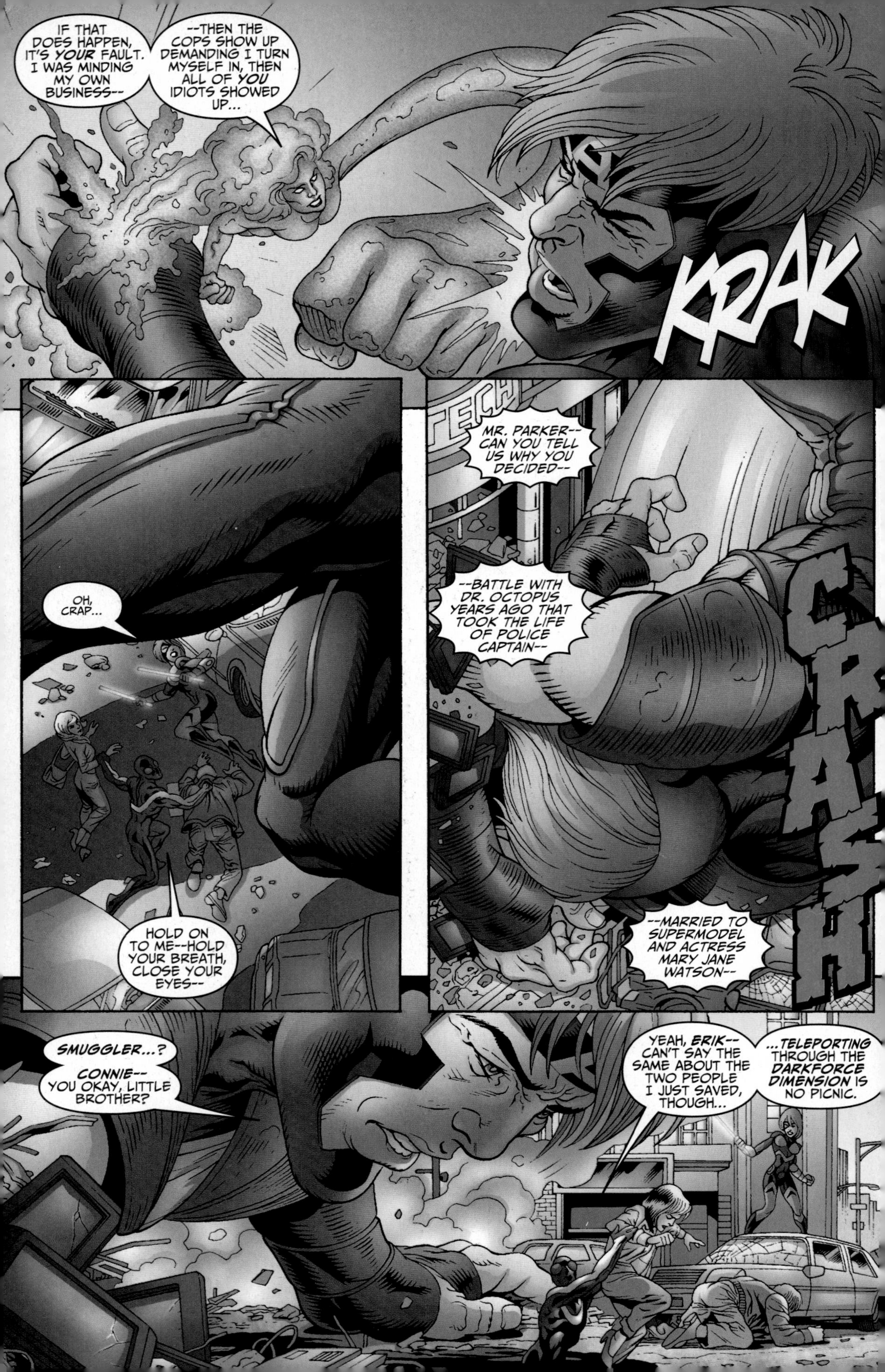
IF THAT DOES HAPPEN, IT'S YOUR FAULT. I WAS MINDING MY OWN BUSINESS--
--THEN THE COPS SHOW UP DEMANDING I TURN MYSELF IN, THEN ALL OF YOU IDIOTS SHOWED UP...
KRAK
OH, CRAP...
HOLD ON TO ME--HOLD YOUR BREATH, CLOSE YOUR EYES--
MR. PARKER--CAN YOU TELL US WHY YOU DECIDED--
--BATTLE WITH DR. OCTOPUS YEARS AGO THAT TOOK THE LIFE OF POLICE CAPTAIN--
--MARRIED TO SUPERMODEL AND ACTRESS MARY JANE WATSON--
CRASH
SMUGGLER...?
CONNIE--YOU OKAY, LITTLE BROTHER?
YEAH, ERIK--CAN'T SAY THE SAME ABOUT THE TWO PEOPLE I JUST SAVED, THOUGH...
...TELEPORTING THROUGH THE DARKFORCE DIMENSION IS NO PICNIC.

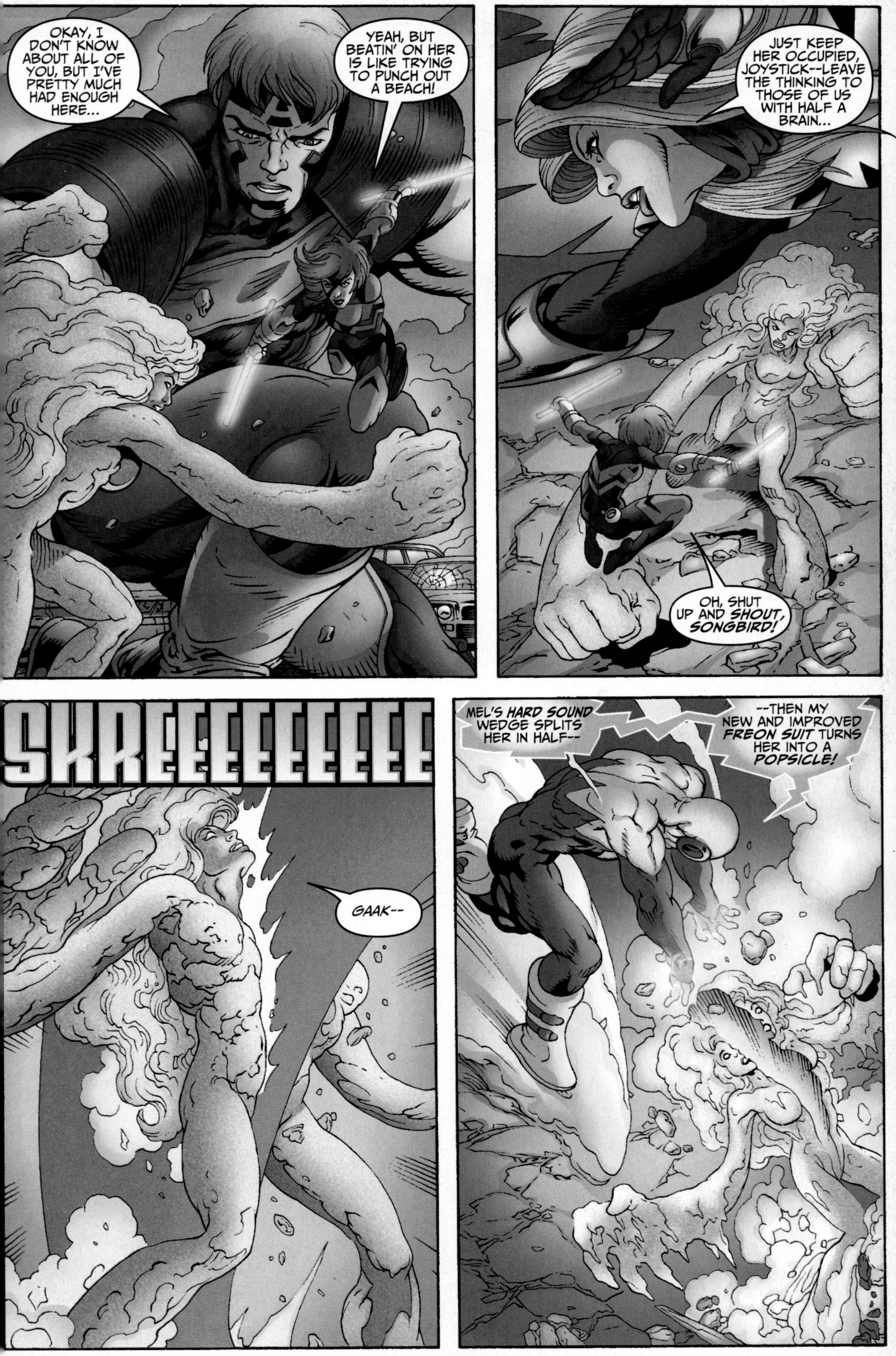
OKAY, I DON'T KNOW ABOUT ALL OF YOU, BUT I'VE PRETTY MUCH HAD ENOUGH HERE...
YEAH, BUT BEATIN' ON HER IS LIKE TRYING TO PUNCH OUT A BEACH!
JUST KEEP HER OCCUPIED, JOYSTICK--LEAVE THE THINKING TO THOSE OF US WITH HALF A BRAIN...
OH, SHUT UP AND SHOUT, SONGBIRD!
SKREEEEEEEEEE
GAAK--
MEL'S HARD SOUND WEDGE SPLITS HER IN HALF--
--THEN MY NEW AND IMPROVED FREON SUIT TURNS HER INTO A POPSICLE!

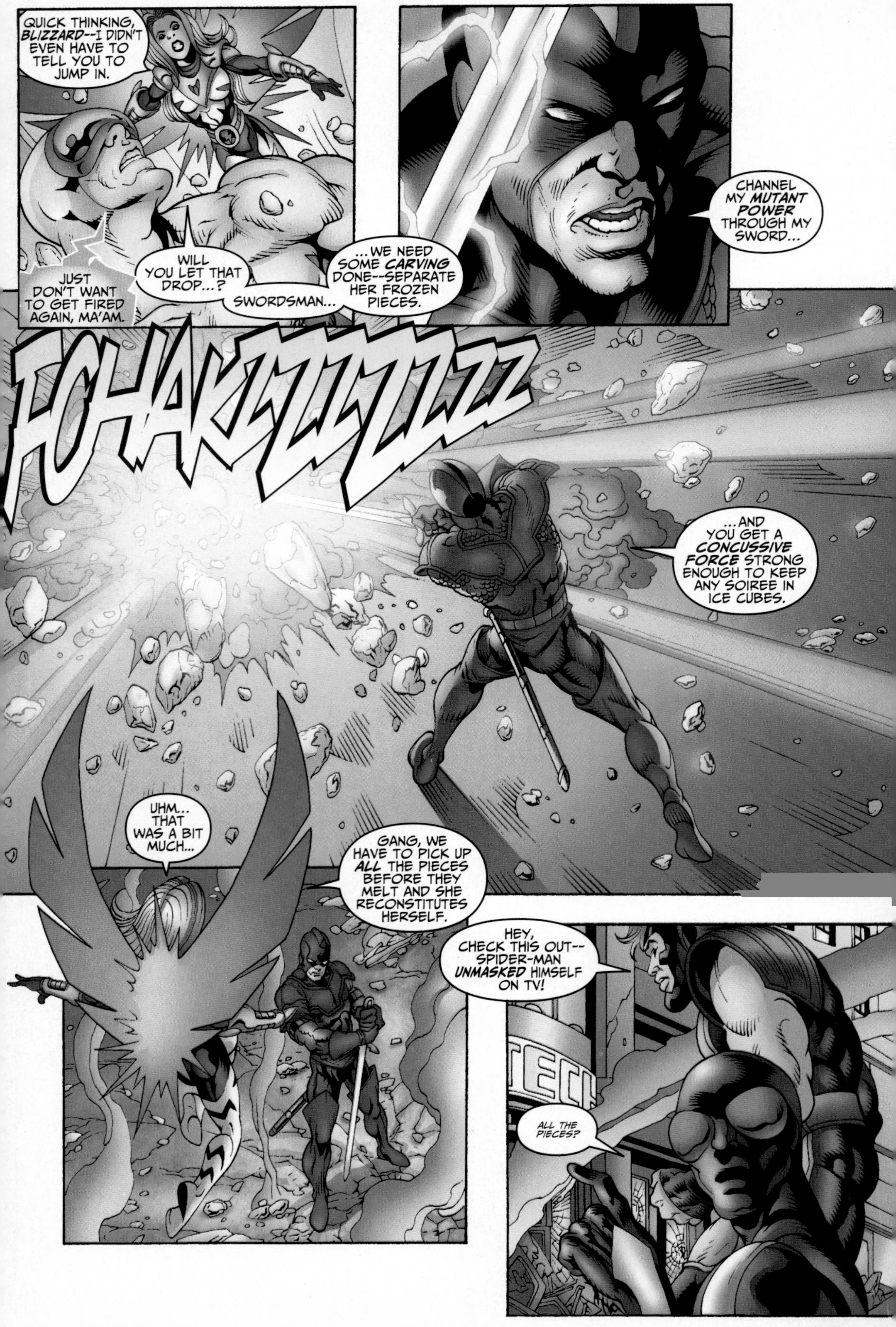
QUICK THINKING, BLIZZARD--I DIDN'T EVEN HAVE TO TELL YOU TO JUMP IN.
JUST DON'T WANT TO GET FIRED AGAIN, MA'AM.
WILL YOU LET THAT DROP...?
SWORDSMAN...
...WE NEED SOME CARVING DONE--SEPARATE HER FROZEN PIECES.
CHANNEL MY MUTANT POWER THROUGH MY SWORD...
FCHAKZZZZZZZZ
...AND YOU GET A CONCUSSIVE FORCE STRONG ENOUGH TO KEEP ANY SOIREE IN ICE CUBES.
UHM... THAT WAS A BIT MUCH...
GANG, WE HAVE TO PICK UP ALL THE PIECES BEFORE THEY MELT AND SHE RECONSTITUTES HERSELF.
HEY, CHECK THIS OUT-- SPIDER-MAN UNMASKED HIMSELF ON TV!
ALL THE PIECES?

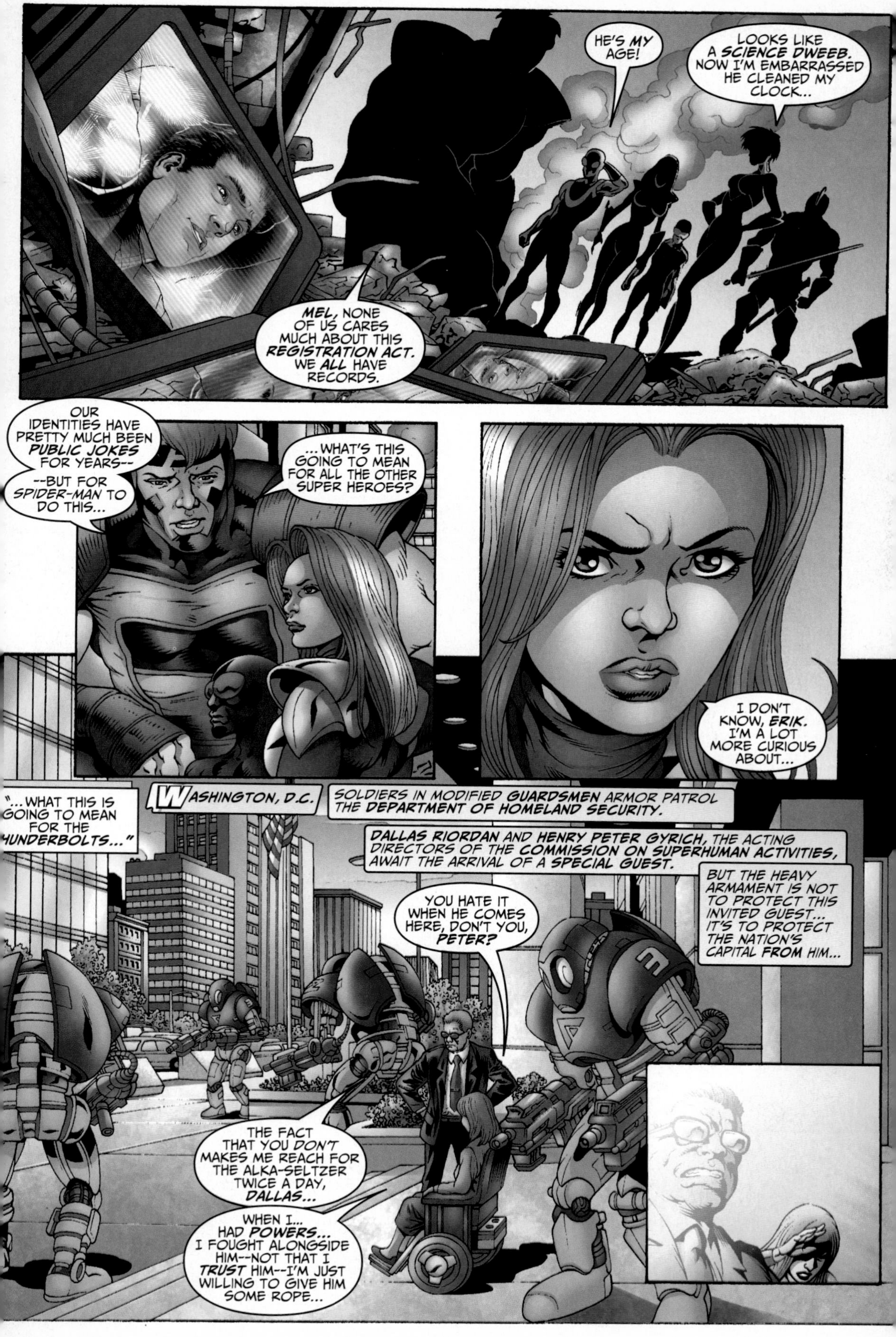
HE'S MY AGE!
LOOKS LIKE A SCIENCE DWEEB. NOW I'M EMBARRASSED HE CLEANED MY CLOCK...
MEL, NONE OF US CARES MUCH ABOUT THIS REGISTRATION ACT. WE ALL HAVE RECORDS.
OUR IDENTITIES HAVE PRETTY MUCH BEEN PUBLIC JOKES FOR YEARS--
--BUT FOR SPIDER-MAN TO DO THIS...
...WHAT'S THIS GOING TO MEAN FOR ALL THE OTHER SUPER HEROES?
I DON'T KNOW, ERIK. I'M A LOT MORE CURIOUS ABOUT...
"...WHAT THIS IS GOING TO MEAN FOR THE HUNDERBOLTS..."
WASHINGTON, D.C.
SOLDIERS IN MODIFIED GUARDSMEN ARMOR PATROL THE DEPARTMENT OF HOMELAND SECURITY.
DALLAS RIORDAN AND HENRY PETER GYRICH, THE ACTING DIRECTORS OF THE COMMISSION ON SUPERHUMAN ACTIVITIES, AWAIT THE ARRIVAL OF A SPECIAL GUEST.
BUT THE HEAVY ARMAMENT IS NOT TO PROTECT THIS INVITED GUEST... IT'S TO PROTECT THE NATION'S CAPITAL FROM HIM...
YOU HATE IT WHEN HE COMES HERE, DON'T YOU, PETER?
THE FACT THAT YOU DON'T MAKES ME REACH FOR THE ALKA-SELTZER TWICE A DAY, DALLAS...
WHEN I... HAD POWERS... I FOUGHT ALONGSIDE HIM--NOT THAT I TRUST HIM--I'M JUST WILLING TO GIVE HIM SOME ROPE...

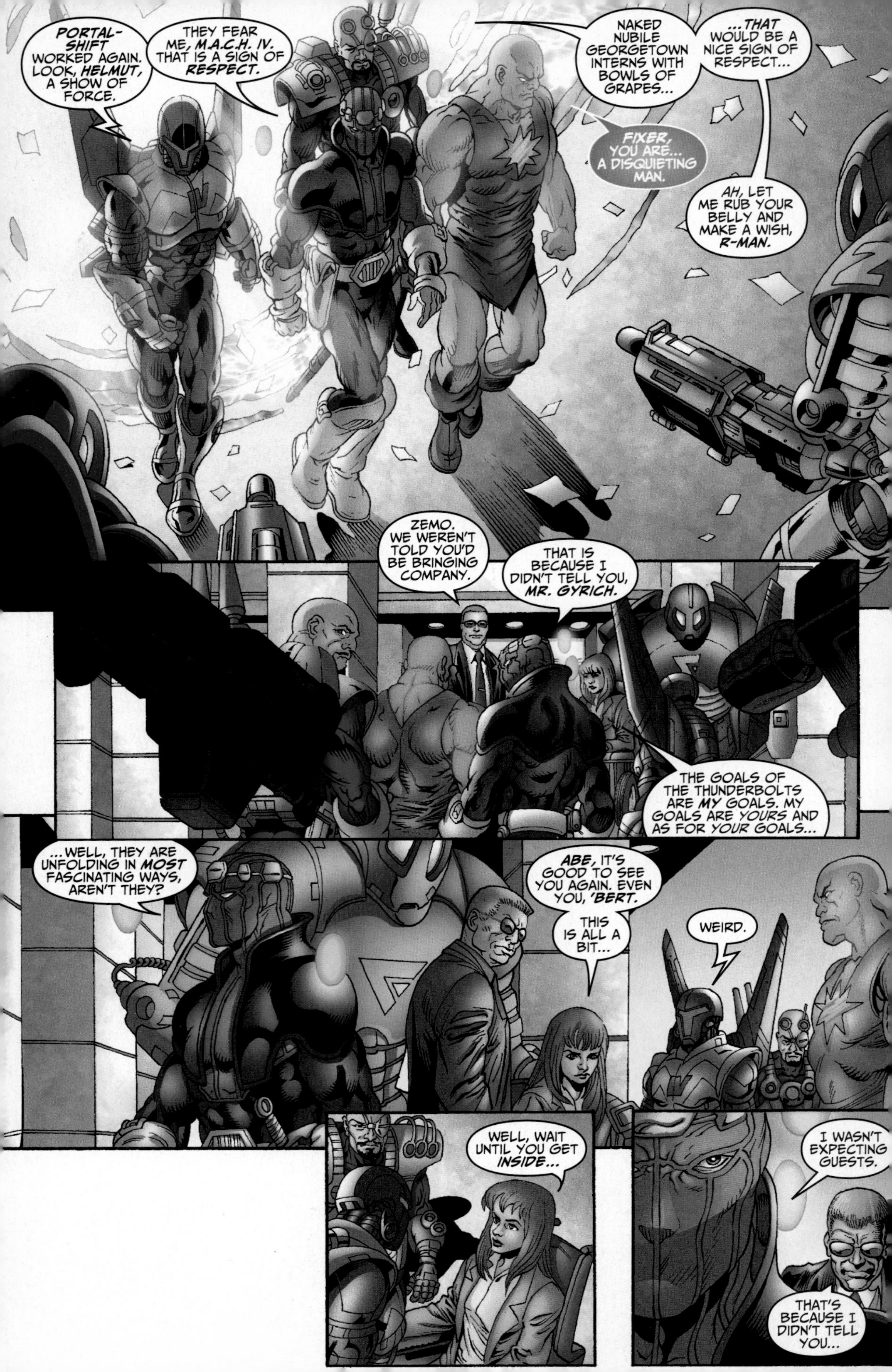
PORTAL-SHIFT WORKED AGAIN. LOOK, HELMUT, A SHOW OF FORCE.
THEY FEAR ME, M.A.C.H. IV. THAT IS A SIGN OF RESPECT.
NAKED NUBILE GEORGETOWN INTERNS WITH BOWLS OF GRAPES...
...THAT WOULD BE A NICE SIGN OF RESPECT...
FIXER, YOU ARE... A DISQUIETING MAN.
AH, LET ME RUB YOUR BELLY AND MAKE A WISH, R-MAN.
ZEMO. WE WEREN'T TOLD YOU'D BE BRINGING COMPANY.
THAT IS BECAUSE I DIDN'T TELL YOU, MR. GYRICH.
THE GOALS OF THE THUNDERBOLTS ARE MY GOALS. MY GOALS ARE YOURS AND AS FOR YOUR GOALS...
...WELL, THEY ARE UNFOLDING IN MOST FASCINATING WAYS, AREN'T THEY?
ABE, IT'S GOOD TO SEE YOU AGAIN. EVEN YOU, 'BERT.
THIS IS ALL A BIT...
WEIRD.
WELL, WAIT UNTIL YOU GET INSIDE...
I WASN'T EXPECTING GUESTS.
THAT'S BECAUSE I DIDN'T TELL YOU...

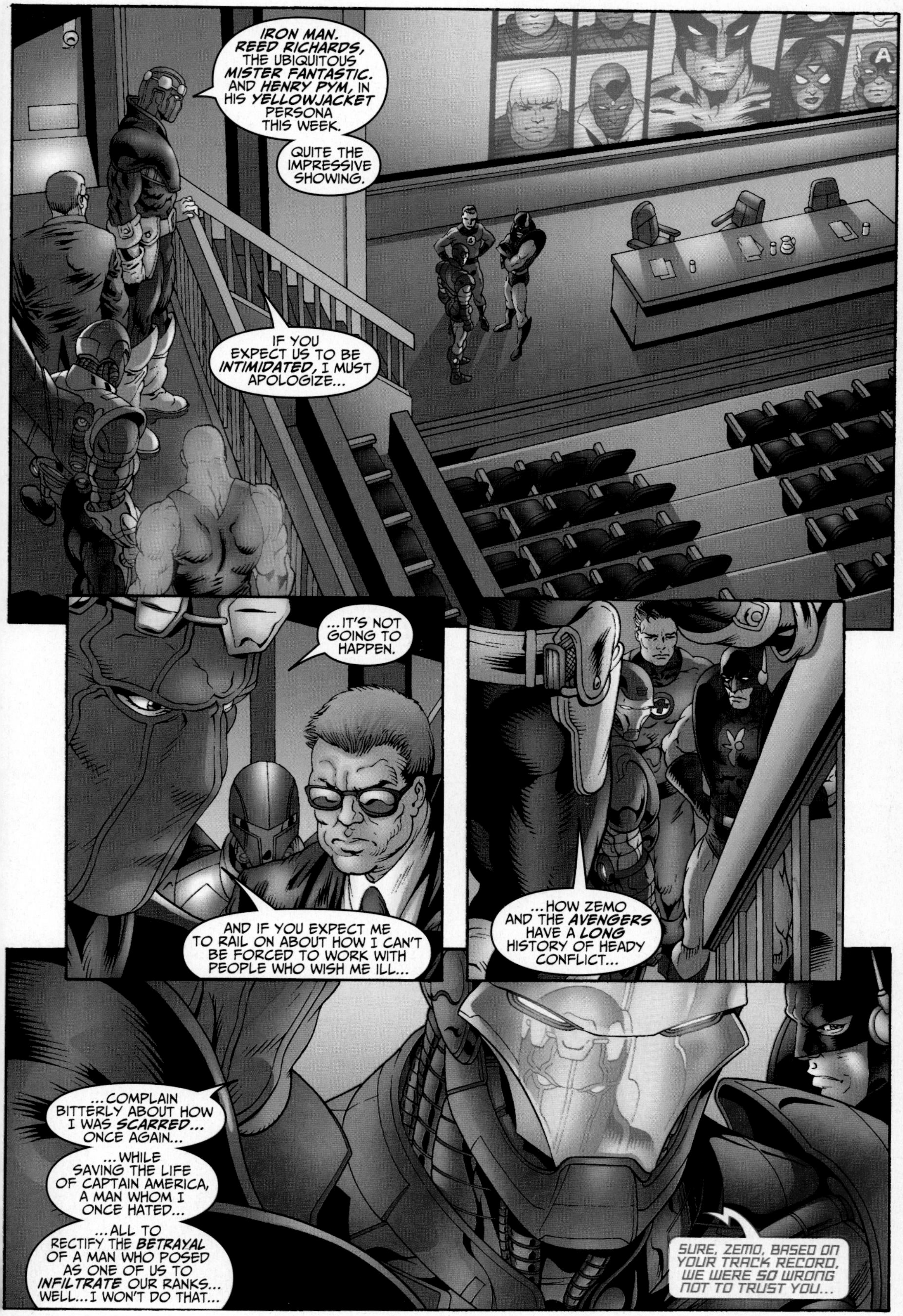
IRON MAN. REED RICHARDS, THE UBIQUITOUS MISTER FANTASTIC. AND HENRY PYM, IN HIS YELLOWJACKET PERSONA THIS WEEK.
QUITE THE IMPRESSIVE SHOWING.
IF YOU EXPECT US TO BE INTIMIDATED, I MUST APOLOGIZE...
...IT'S NOT GOING TO HAPPEN.
AND IF YOU EXPECT ME TO RAIL ON ABOUT HOW I CAN'T BE FORCED TO WORK WITH PEOPLE WHO WISH ME ILL...
...HOW ZEMO AND THE AVENGERS HAVE A LONG HISTORY OF HEADY CONFLICT...
...COMPLAIN BITTERLY ABOUT HOW I WAS SCARRED... ONCE AGAIN...
...WHILE SAVING THE LIFE OF CAPTAIN AMERICA, A MAN WHOM I ONCE HATED...
...ALL TO RECTIFY THE BETRAYAL OF A MAN WHO POSED AS ONE OF US TO INFILTRATE OUR RANKS... WELL...I WON'T DO THAT...
SURE, ZEMO, BASED ON YOUR TRACK RECORD, WE WERE SO WRONG NOT TO TRUST YOU...

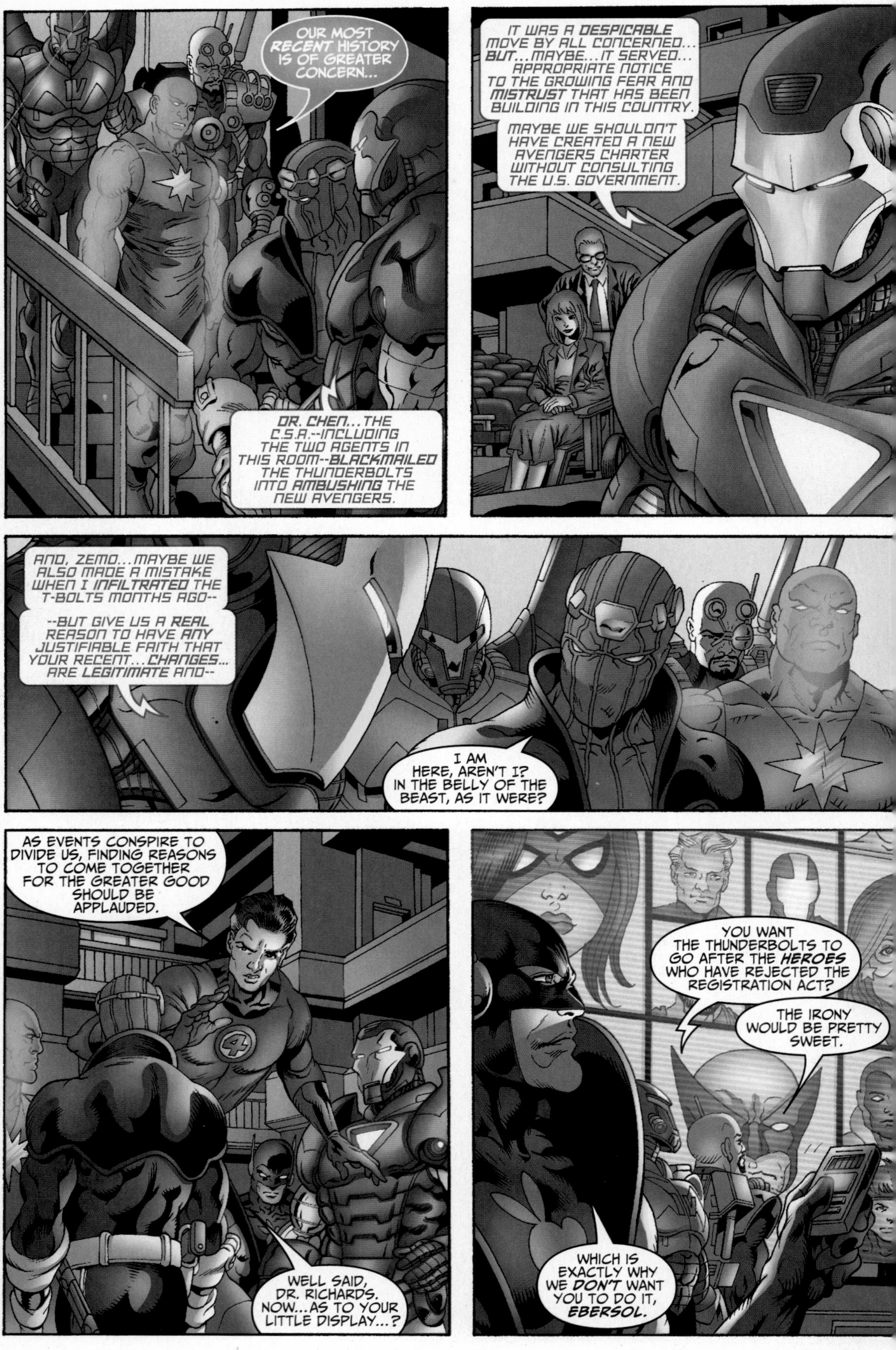
OUR MOST RECENT HISTORY IS OF GREATER CONCERN...
DR. CHEN... THE C.S.A.--INCLUDING THE TWO AGENTS IN THIS ROOM--BLACKMAILED THE THUNDERBOLTS INTO AMBUSHING THE NEW AVENGERS.
IT WAS A DESPICABLE MOVE BY ALL CONCERNED... BUT... MAYBE... IT SERVED... APPROPRIATE NOTICE TO THE GROWING FEAR AND MISTRUST THAT HAS BEEN BUILDING IN THIS COUNTRY.
MAYBE WE SHOULDN'T HAVE CREATED A NEW AVENGERS CHARTER WITHOUT CONSULTING THE U.S. GOVERNMENT.
AND, ZEMO... MAYBE WE ALSO MADE A MISTAKE WHEN I INFILTRATED THE T-BOLTS MONTHS AGO--
--BUT GIVE US A REAL REASON TO HAVE ANY JUSTIFIABLE FAITH THAT YOUR RECENT... CHANGES... ARE LEGITIMATE AND--
I AM HERE, AREN'T I? IN THE BELLY OF THE BEAST, AS IT WERE?
AS EVENTS CONSPIRE TO DIVIDE US, FINDING REASONS TO COME TOGETHER FOR THE GREATER GOOD SHOULD BE APPLAUDED.
WELL SAID, DR. RICHARDS. NOW... AS TO YOUR LITTLE DISPLAY...?
YOU WANT THE THUNDERBOLTS TO GO AFTER THE HEROES WHO HAVE REJECTED THE REGISTRATION ACT?
THE IRONY WOULD BE PRETTY SWEET.
WHICH IS EXACTLY WHY WE DON'T WANT YOU TO DO IT, EBERSOL.

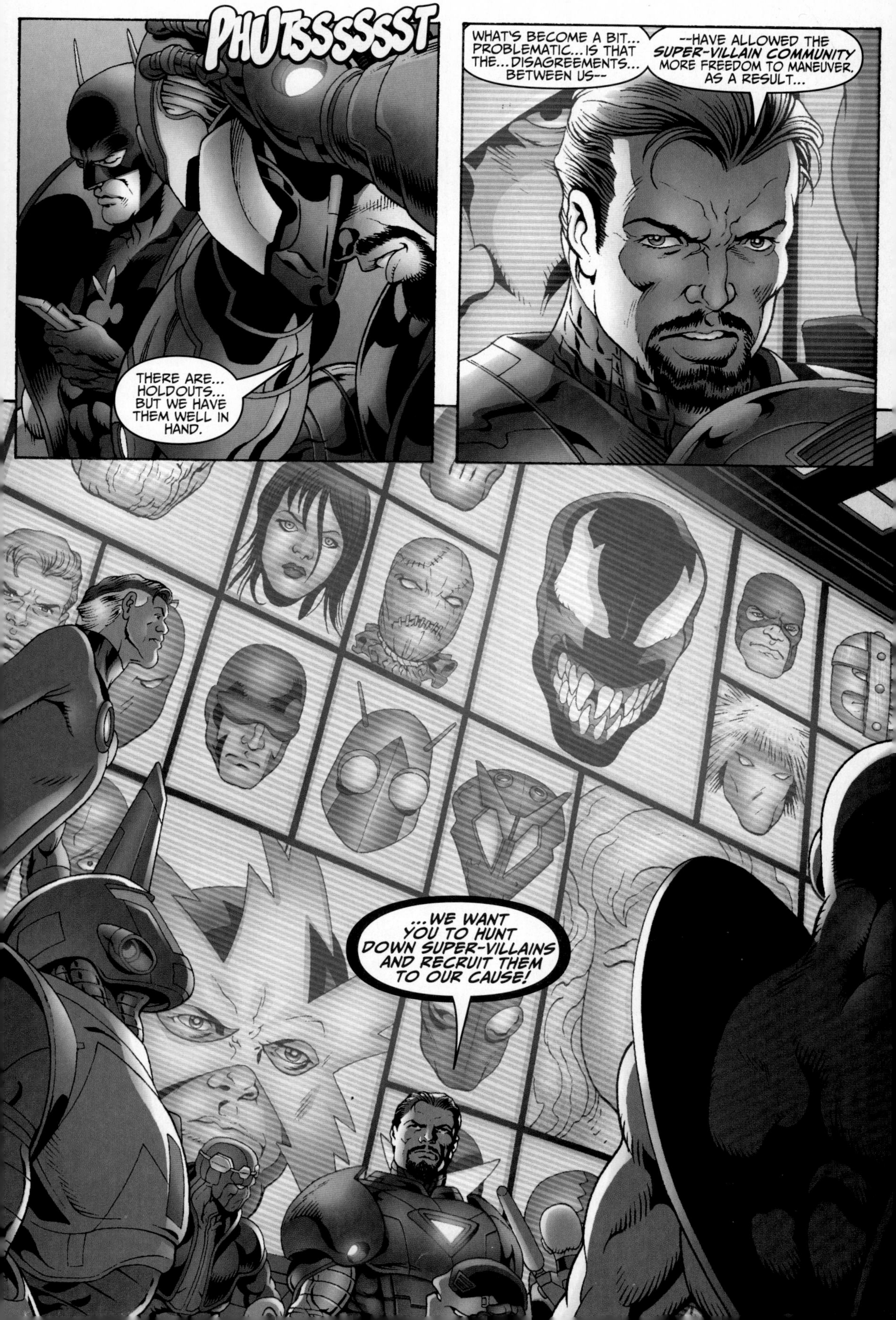
PHUTSSSSSST
THERE ARE... HOLDOUTS... BUT WE HAVE THEM WELL IN HAND.
WHAT'S BECOME A BIT... PROBLEMATIC...IS THAT THE...DISAGREEMENTS... BETWEEN US--
--HAVE ALLOWED THE SUPER-VILLAIN COMMUNITY MORE FREEDOM TO MANEUVER. AS A RESULT...
...WE WANT YOU TO HUNT DOWN SUPER-VILLAINS AND RECRUIT THEM TO OUR CAUSE!

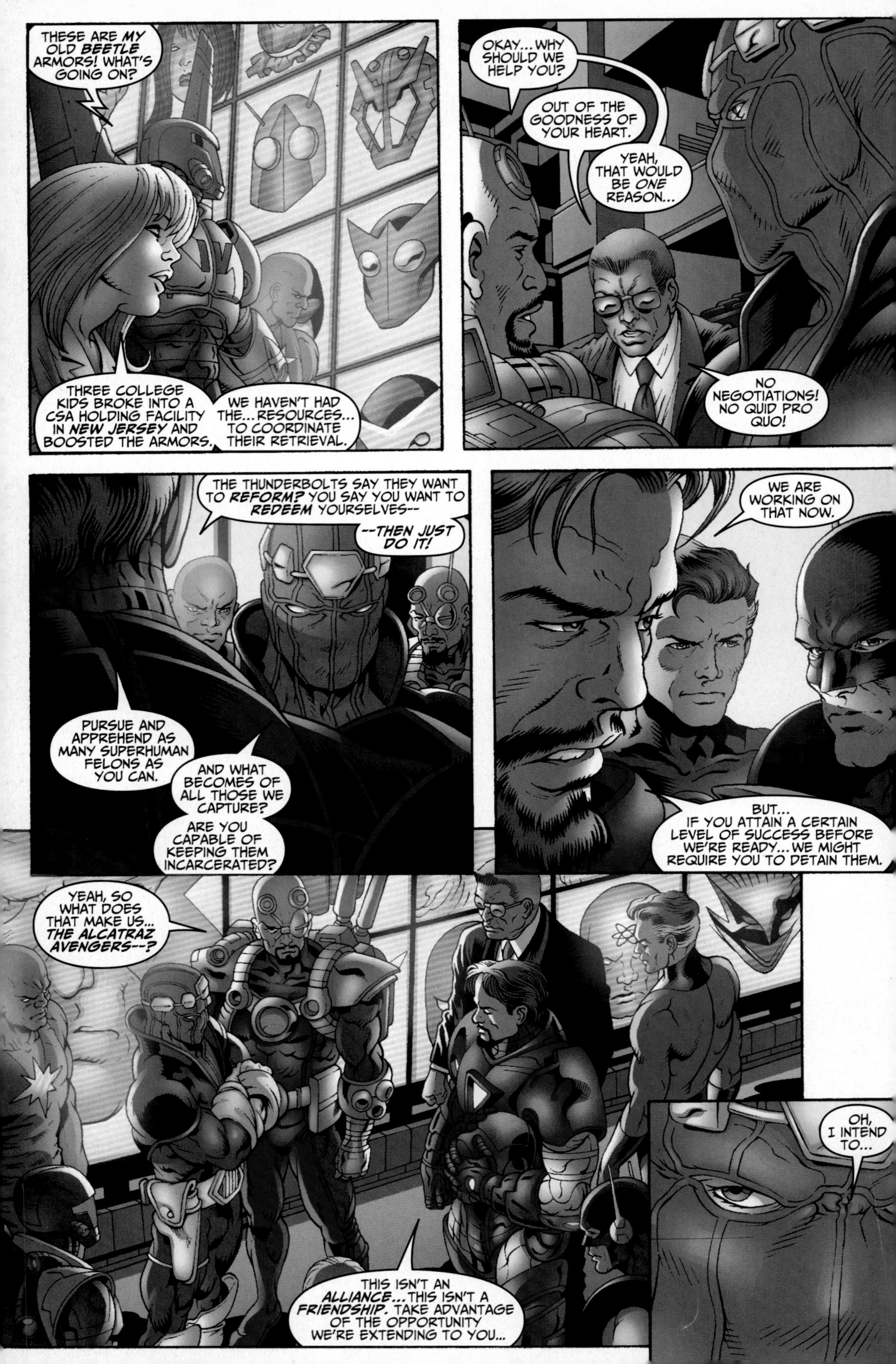

THESE ARE MY OLD BEETLE ARMORS! WHAT'S GOING ON?
THREE COLLEGE KIDS BROKE INTO A CSA HOLDING FACILITY IN NEW JERSEY AND BOOSTED THE ARMORS.
WE HAVEN'T HAD THE... RESOURCES... TO COORDINATE THEIR RETRIEVAL.
OKAY... WHY SHOULD WE HELP YOU?
OUT OF THE GOODNESS OF YOUR HEART.
YEAH, THAT WOULD BE ONE REASON...
NO NEGOTIATIONS! NO QUID PRO QUO!
THE THUNDERBOLTS SAY THEY WANT TO REFORM? YOU SAY YOU WANT TO REDEEM YOURSELVES--
--THEN JUST DO IT!
PURSUE AND APPREHEND AS MANY SUPERHUMAN FELONS AS YOU CAN.
AND WHAT BECOMES OF ALL THOSE WE CAPTURE?
ARE YOU CAPABLE OF KEEPING THEM INCARCERATED?
WE ARE WORKING ON THAT NOW.
BUT... IF YOU ATTAIN A CERTAIN LEVEL OF SUCCESS BEFORE WE'RE READY... WE MIGHT REQUIRE YOU TO DETAIN THEM.
YEAH, SO WHAT DOES THAT MAKE US... THE ALCATRAZ AVENGERS--?
THIS ISN'T AN ALLIANCE... THIS ISN'T A FRIENDSHIP. TAKE ADVANTAGE OF THE OPPORTUNITY WE'RE EXTENDING TO YOU...
OH, I INTEND TO...

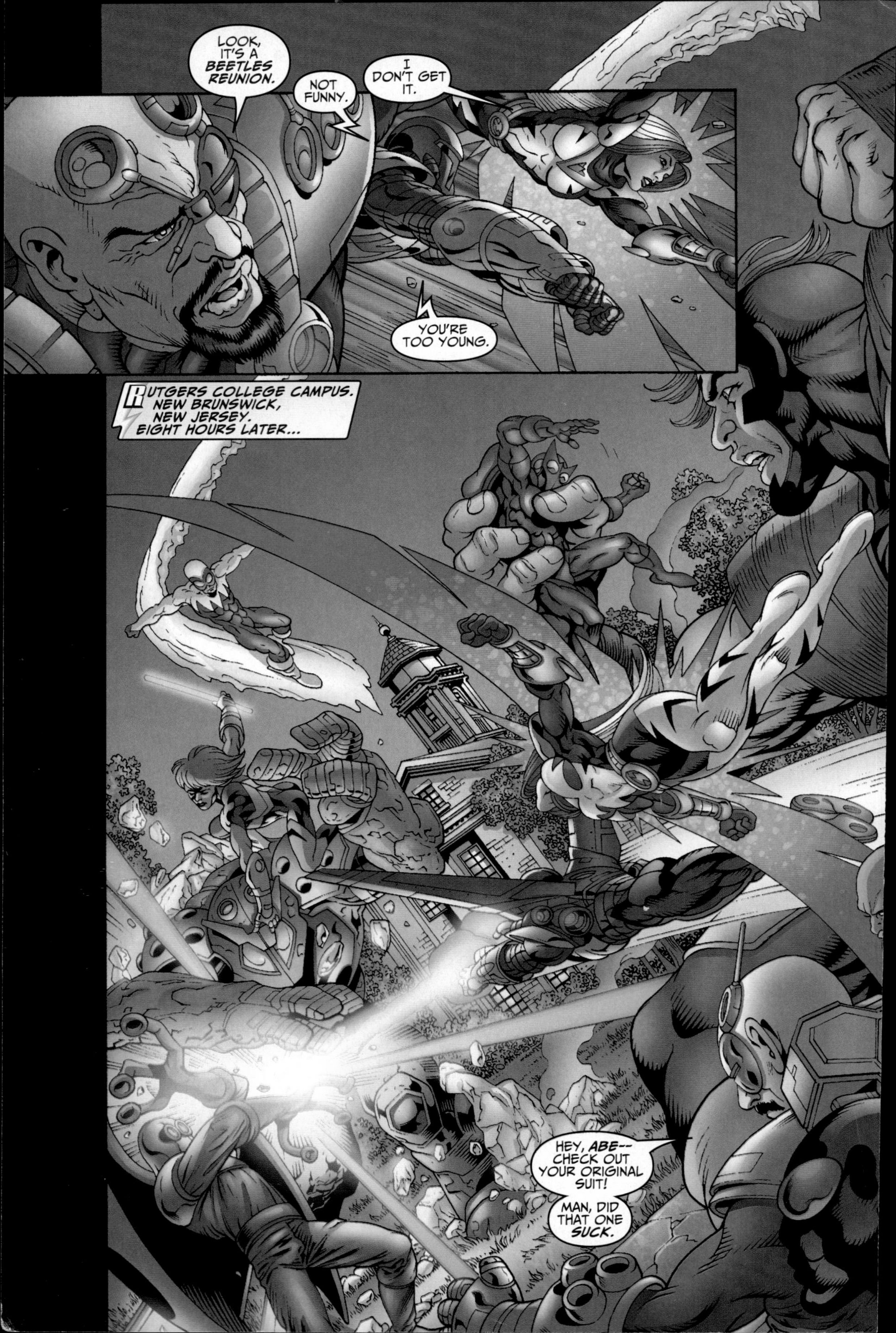
LOOK, IT'S A BEETLES REUNION.
NOT FUNNY.
I DON'T GET IT.
YOU'RE TOO YOUNG.
RUTGERS COLLEGE CAMPUS. NEW BRUNSWICK, NEW JERSEY. EIGHT HOURS LATER...
HEY, ABE-- CHECK OUT YOUR ORIGINAL SUIT!
MAN, DID THAT ONE SUCK.

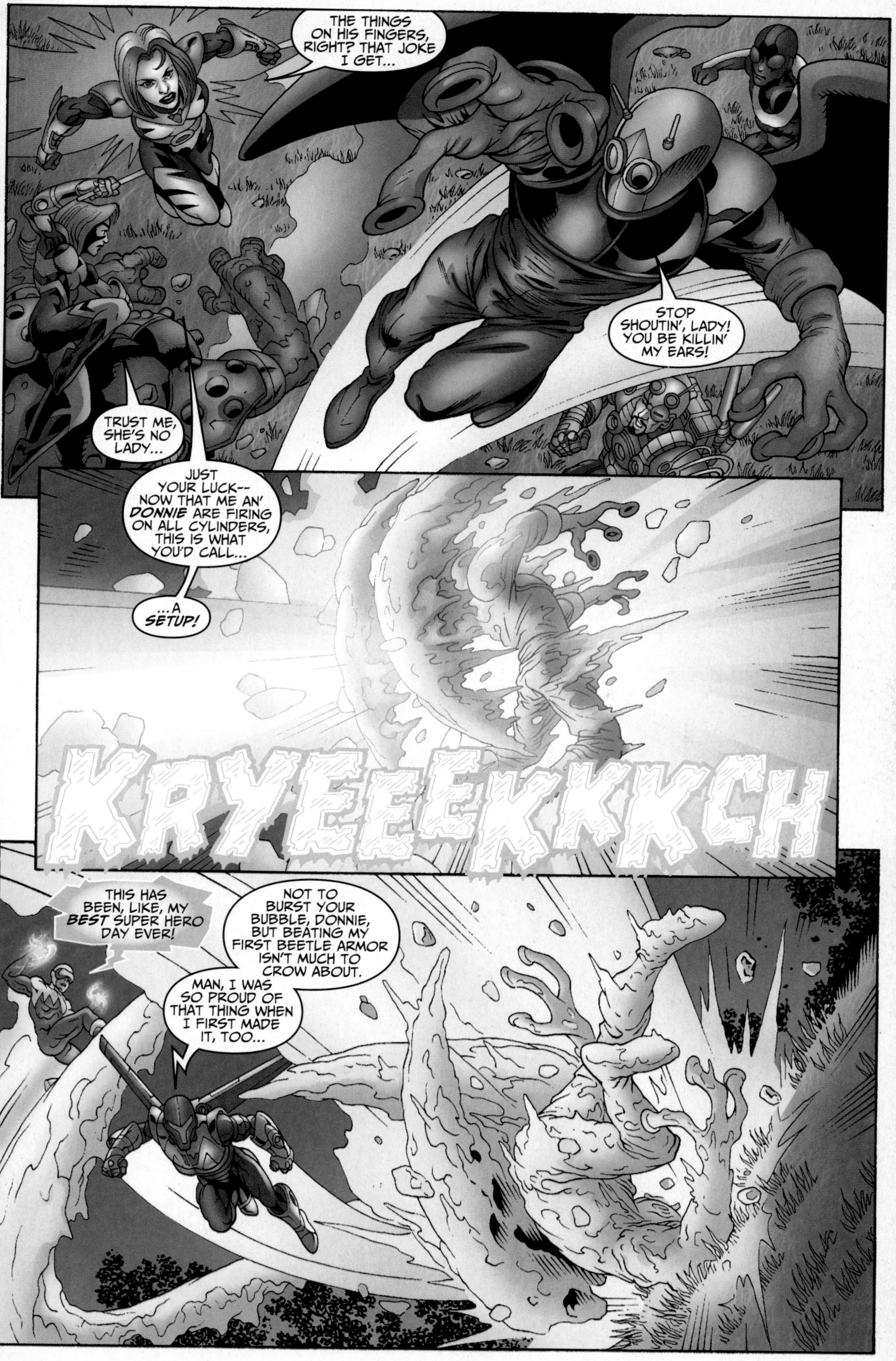

THE THINGS ON HIS FINGERS, RIGHT? THAT JOKE I GET...
STOP SHOUTIN', LADY! YOU BE KILLIN' MY EARS!
TRUST ME, SHE'S NO LADY...
JUST YOUR LUCK-- NOW THAT ME AN' DONNIE ARE FIRING ON ALL CYLINDERS, THIS IS WHAT YOU'D CALL...
...A SETUP!
KRYEEEKKKCH
THIS HAS BEEN, LIKE, MY BEST SUPER HERO DAY EVER!
NOT TO BURST YOUR BUBBLE, DONNIE, BUT BEATING MY FIRST BEETLE ARMOR ISN'T MUCH TO CROW ABOUT.
MAN, I WAS SO PROUD OF THAT THING WHEN I FIRST MADE IT, TOO...

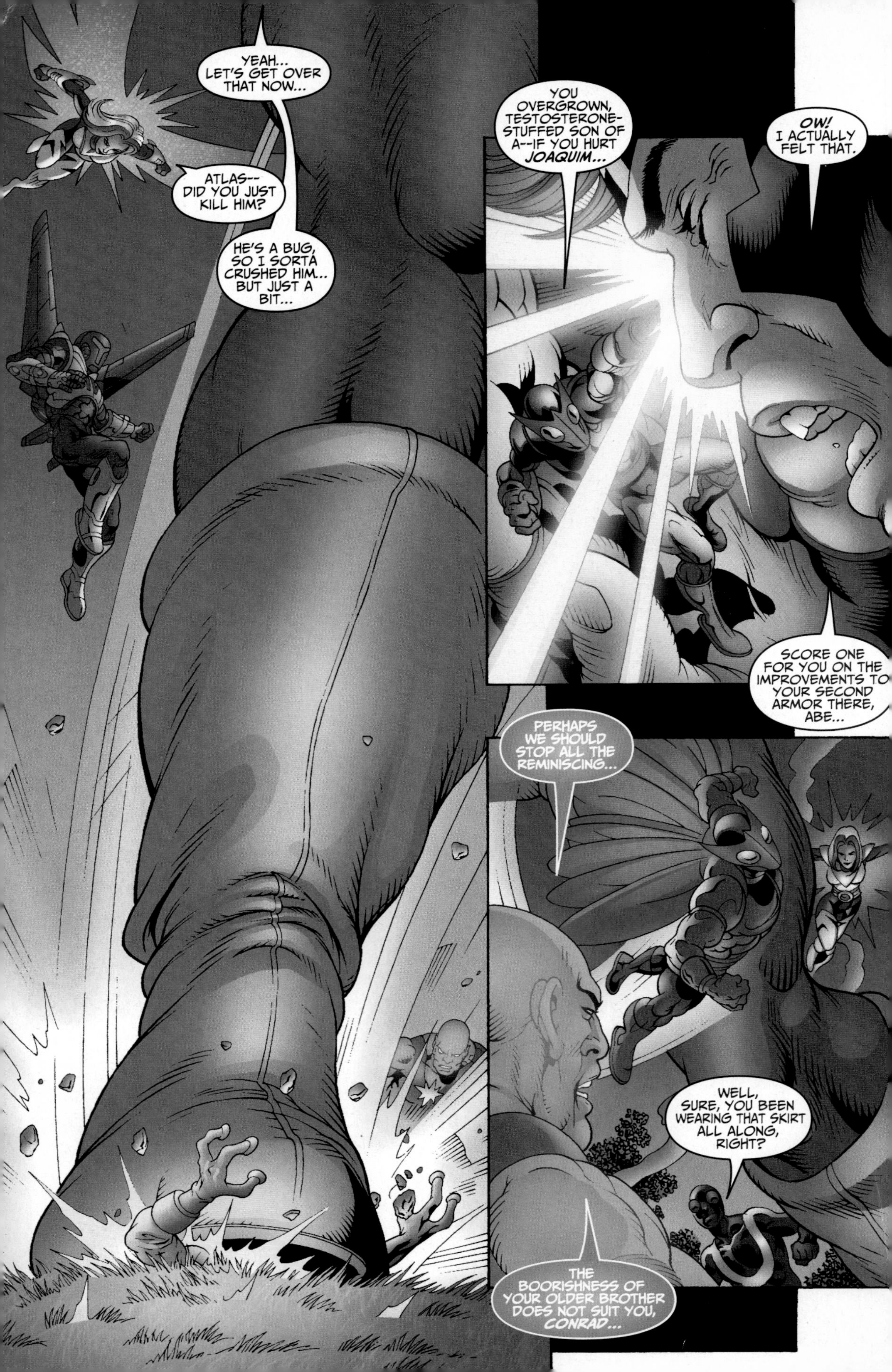
ATLAS-- DID YOU JUST KILL HIM?
HE'S A BUG, SO I SORTA CRUSHED HIM... BUT JUST A BIT...
YEAH... LET'S GET OVER THAT NOW...
YOU OVERGROWN, TESTOSTERONE-STUFFED SON OF A--IF YOU HURT JOAQUIM...
OW! I ACTUALLY FELT THAT.
SCORE ONE FOR YOU ON THE IMPROVEMENTS TO YOUR SECOND ARMOR THERE, ABE...
PERHAPS WE SHOULD STOP ALL THE REMINISCING...
WELL, SURE, YOU BEEN WEARING THAT SKIRT ALL ALONG, RIGHT?
THE BOORISHNESS OF YOUR OLDER BROTHER DOES NOT SUIT YOU, CONRAD...

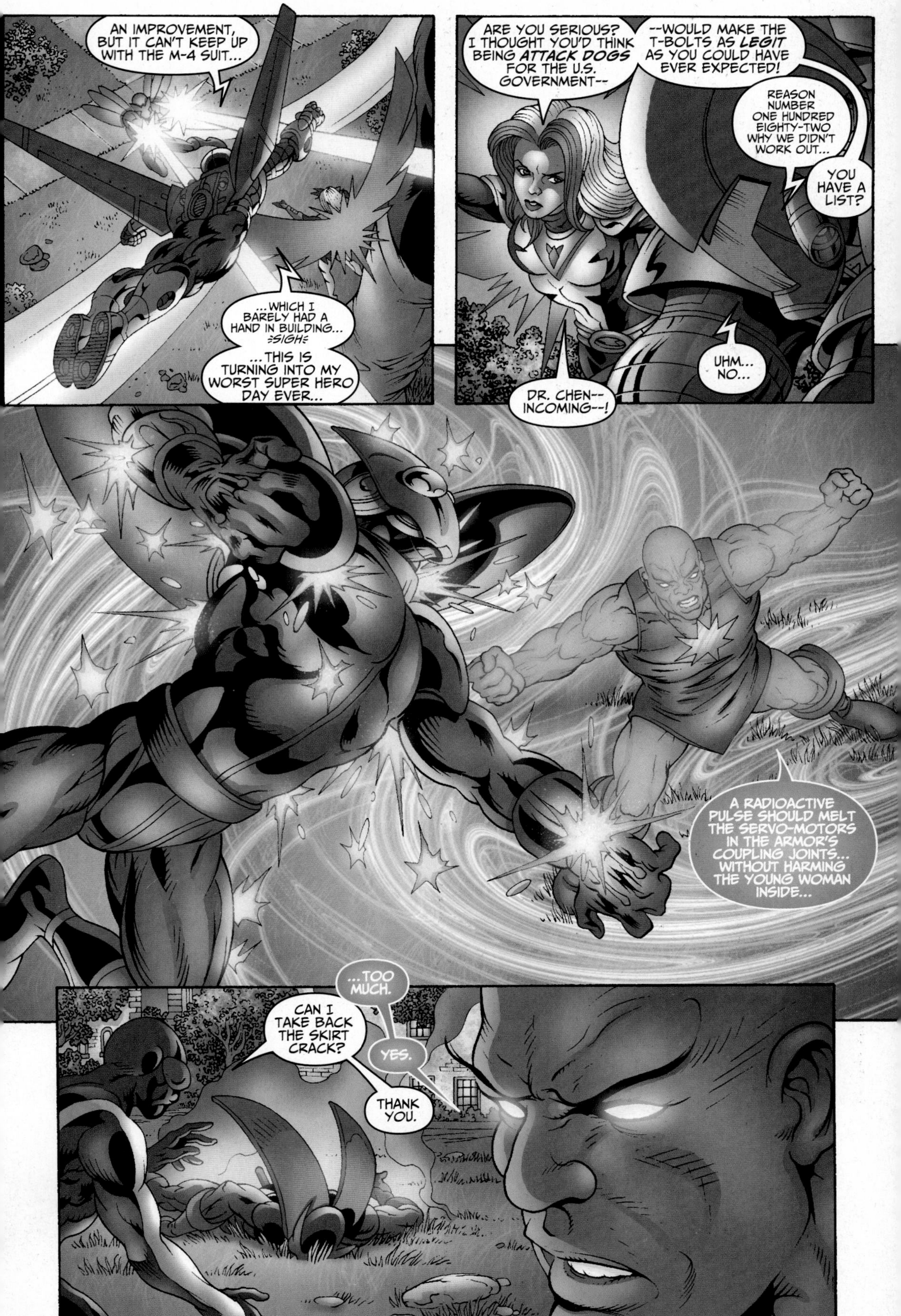
AN IMPROVEMENT, BUT IT CAN'T KEEP UP WITH THE M-4 SUIT...
...WHICH I BARELY HAD A HAND IN BUILDING... =SIGH=
...THIS IS TURNING INTO MY WORST SUPER HERO DAY EVER...
ARE YOU SERIOUS? I THOUGHT YOU'D THINK BEING ATTACK DOGS FOR THE U.S. GOVERNMENT--
--WOULD MAKE THE T-BOLTS AS LEGIT AS YOU COULD HAVE EVER EXPECTED!
REASON NUMBER ONE HUNDRED EIGHTY-TWO WHY WE DIDN'T WORK OUT...
YOU HAVE A LIST?
UHM... NO...
DR. CHEN-- INCOMING--!
A RADIOACTIVE PULSE SHOULD MELT THE SERVO-MOTORS IN THE ARMOR'S COUPLING JOINTS... WITHOUT HARMING THE YOUNG WOMAN INSIDE...
CAN I TAKE BACK THE SKIRT CRACK?
...TOO MUCH.
YES.
THANK YOU.

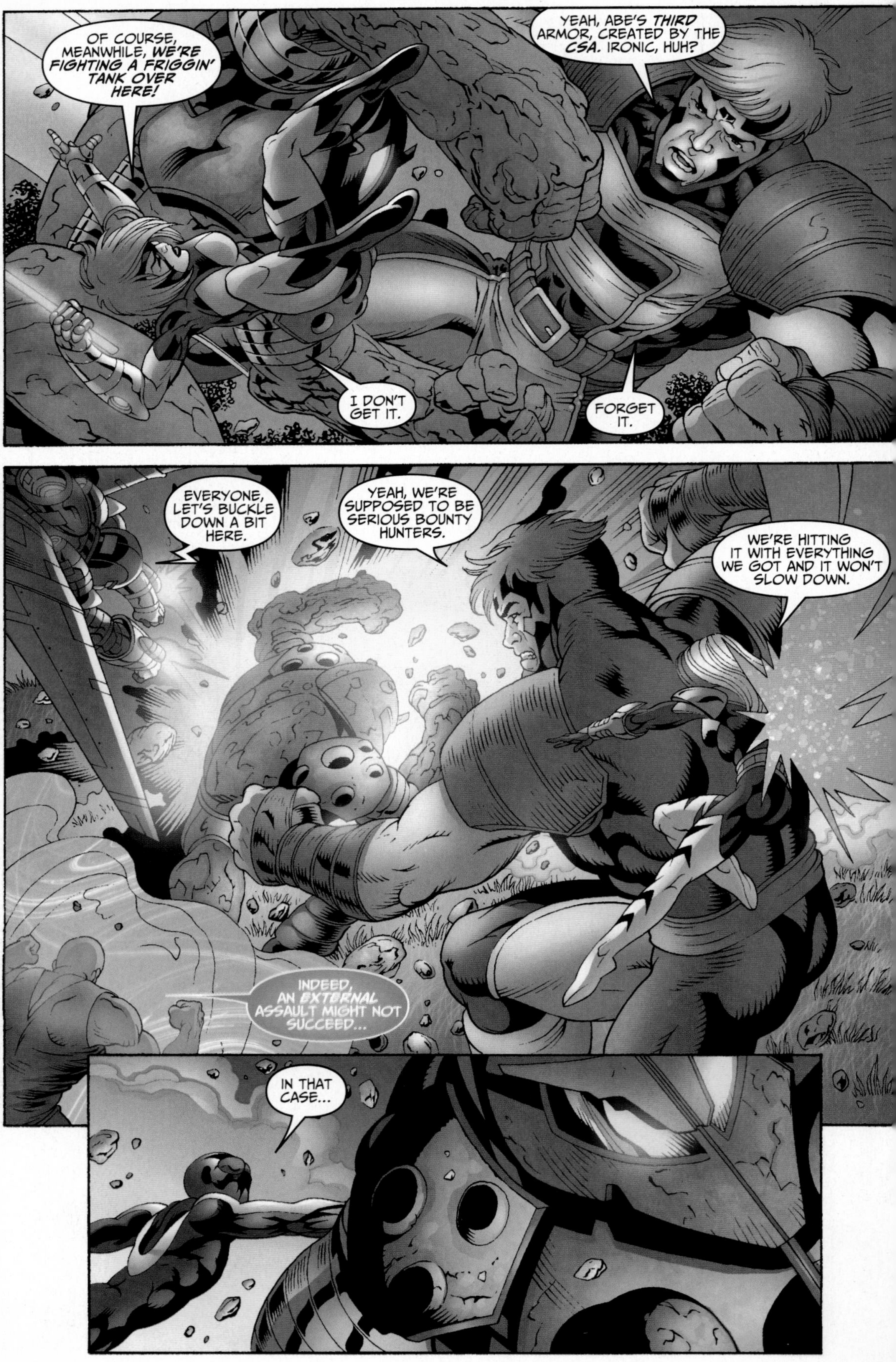
OF COURSE, MEANWHILE, WE'RE FIGHTING A FRIGGIN' TANK OVER HERE!
YEAH, ABE'S THIRD ARMOR, CREATED BY THE CSA. IRONIC, HUH?
I DON'T GET IT.
FORGET IT.
EVERYONE, LET'S BUCKLE DOWN A BIT HERE.
YEAH, WE'RE SUPPOSED TO BE SERIOUS BOUNTY HUNTERS.
WE'RE HITTING IT WITH EVERYTHING WE GOT AND IT WON'T SLOW DOWN.
INDEED, AN EXTERNAL ASSAULT MIGHT NOT SUCCEED...
IN THAT CASE...

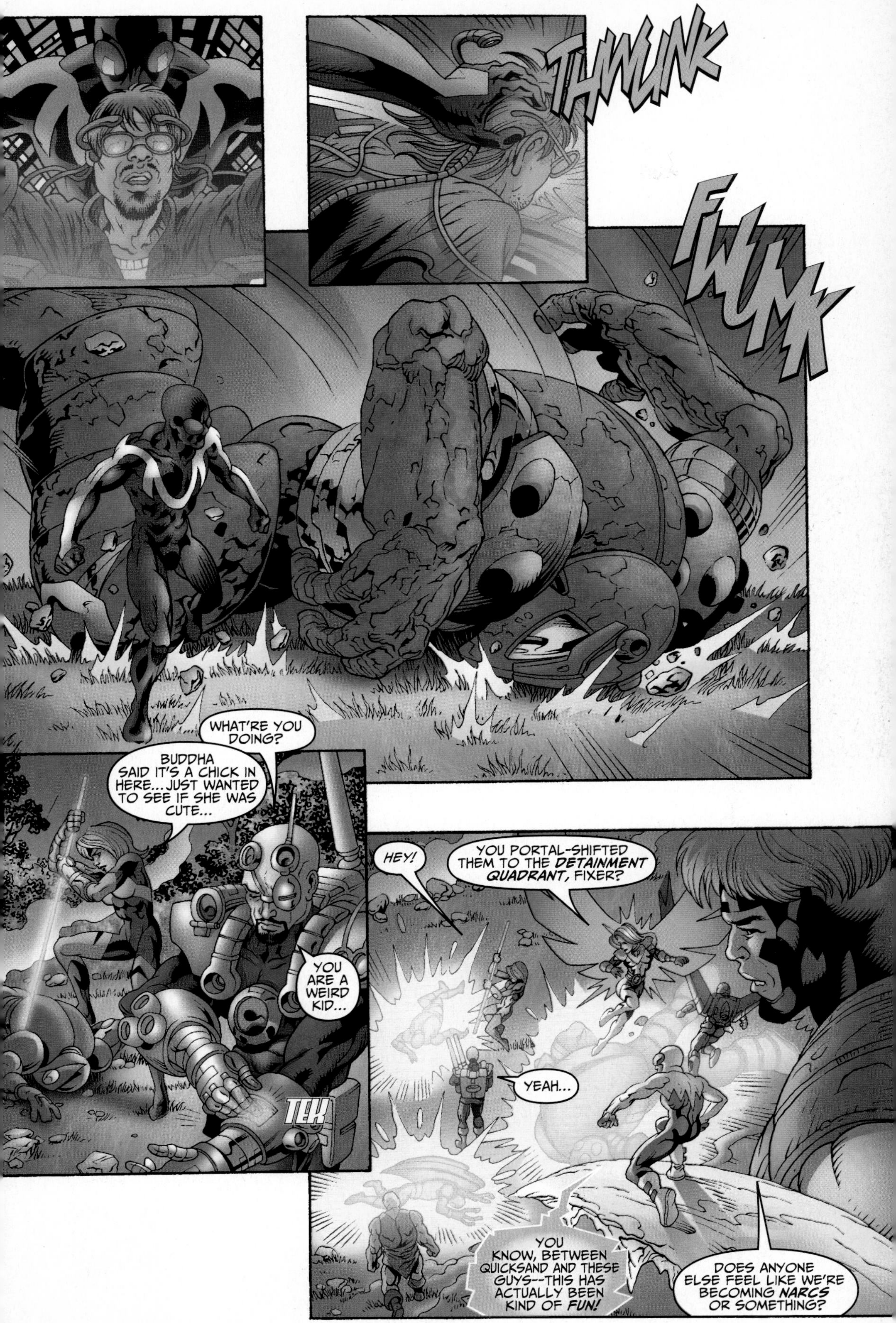
THWUNK
FWUNK
WHAT'RE YOU DOING?
BUDDHA SAID IT'S A CHICK IN HERE...JUST WANTED TO SEE IF SHE WAS CUTE...
YOU ARE A WEIRD KID...
TEK
HEY!
YOU PORTAL-SHIFTED THEM TO THE DETAINMENT QUADRANT, FIXER?
YEAH...
YOU KNOW, BETWEEN QUICKSAND AND THESE GUYS--THIS HAS ACTUALLY BEEN KIND OF FUN!
DOES ANYONE ELSE FEEL LIKE WE'RE BECOMING NARCS OR SOMETHING?

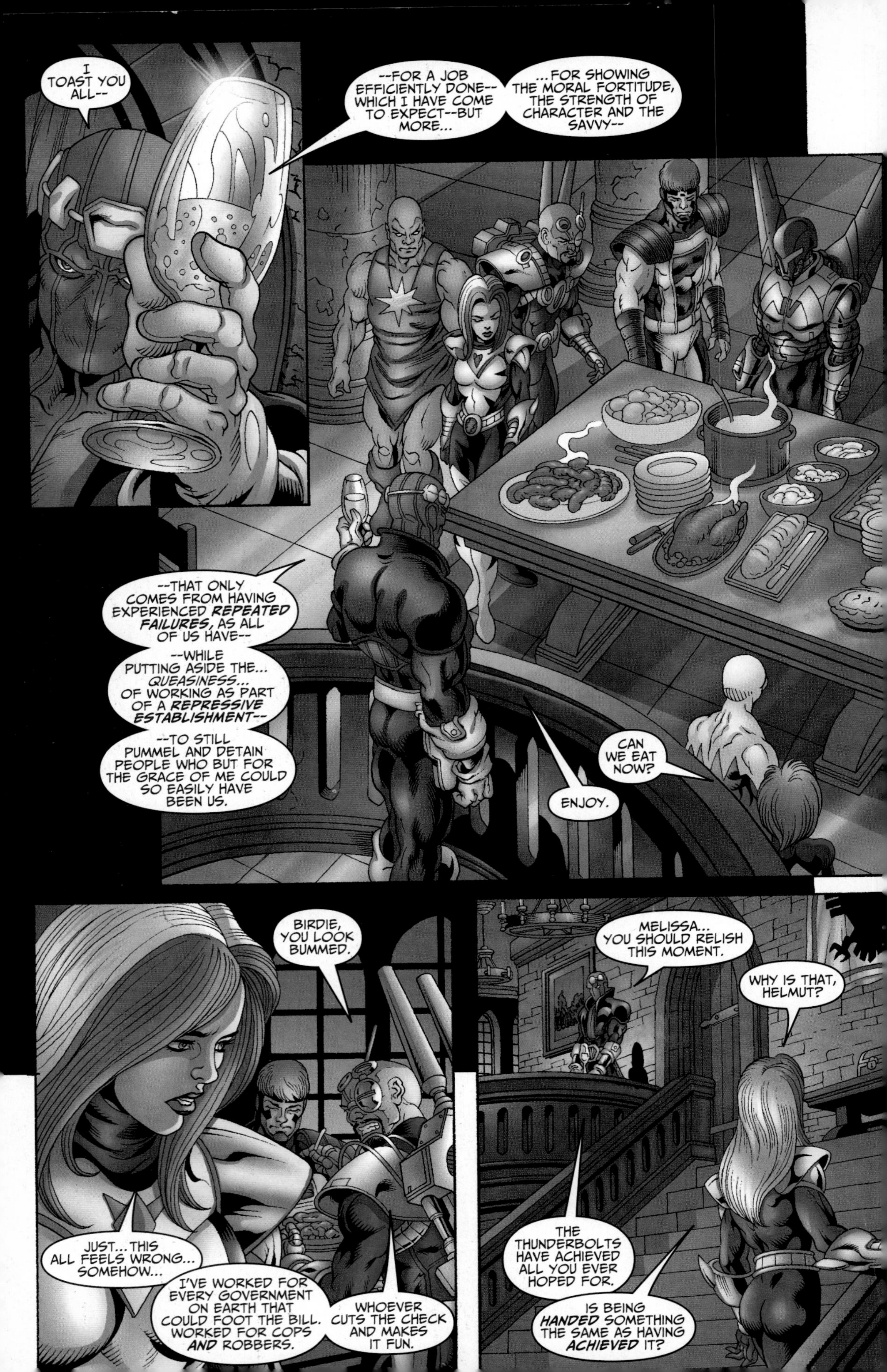
I TOAST YOU ALL--
--FOR A JOB EFFICIENTLY DONE--WHICH I HAVE COME TO EXPECT--BUT MORE...
...FOR SHOWING THE MORAL FORTITUDE, THE STRENGTH OF CHARACTER AND THE SAVVY--
--THAT ONLY COMES FROM HAVING EXPERIENCED *REPEATED FAILURES*, AS ALL OF US HAVE--
--WHILE PUTTING ASIDE THE... *QUEASINESS*... OF WORKING AS PART OF A *REPRESSIVE ESTABLISHMENT*--
--TO STILL PUMMEL AND DETAIN PEOPLE WHO BUT FOR THE GRACE OF ME COULD SO EASILY HAVE BEEN US.
CAN WE EAT NOW?
ENJOY.
BIRDIE, YOU LOOK BUMMED.
JUST... THIS ALL FEELS WRONG... SOMEHOW...
I'VE WORKED FOR EVERY GOVERNMENT ON EARTH THAT COULD FOOT THE BILL. WORKED FOR COPS *AND* ROBBERS.
WHOEVER CUTS THE CHECK AND MAKES IT FUN.
MELISSA... YOU SHOULD RELISH THIS MOMENT.
WHY IS THAT, HELMUT?
THE THUNDERBOLTS HAVE ACHIEVED ALL YOU EVER HOPED FOR.
IS BEING *HANDED* SOMETHING THE SAME AS HAVING *ACHIEVED* IT?

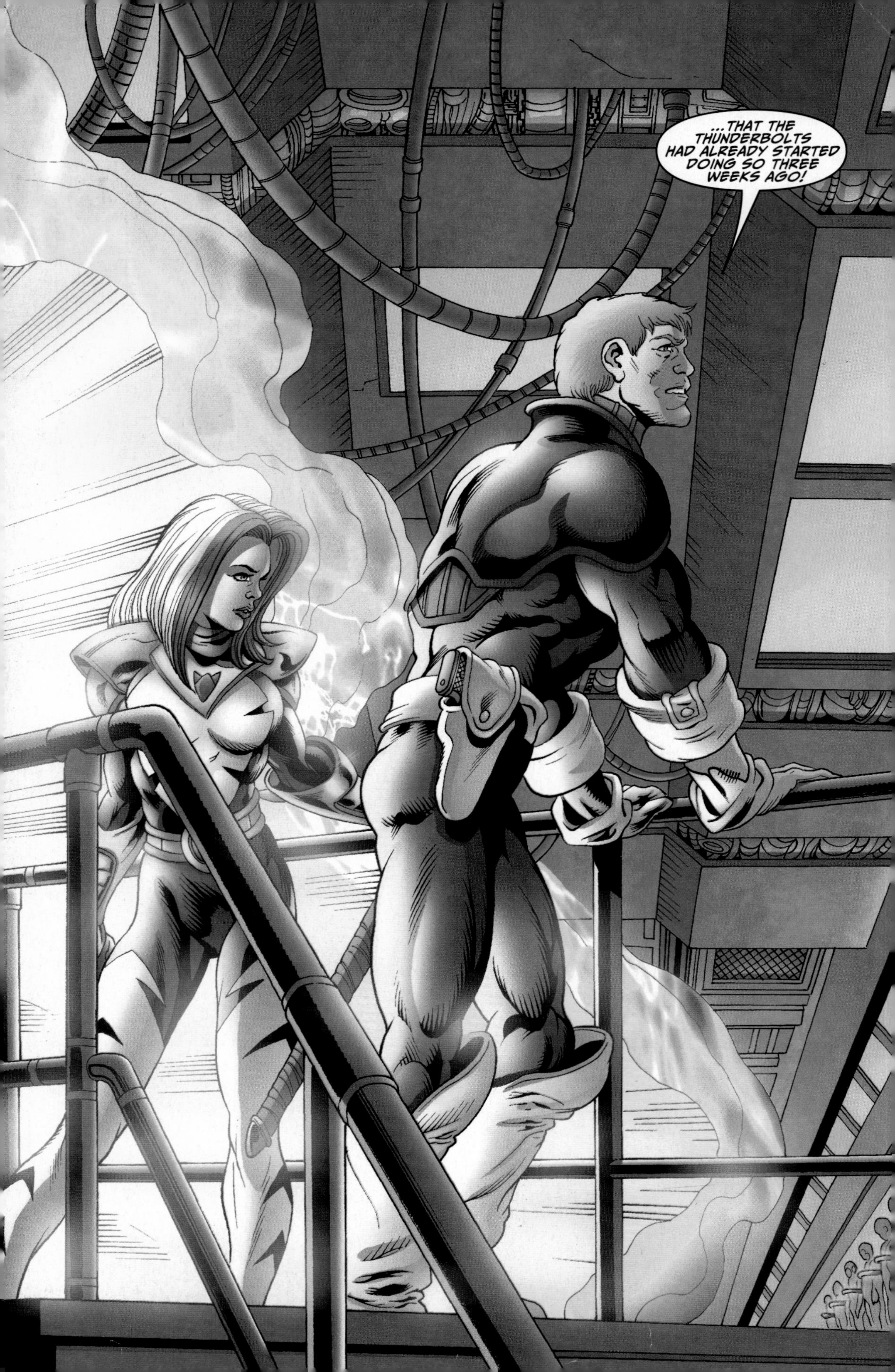
...THAT THE THÜNDERBOLTS HAD ALREADY STARTED DOING SO THREE WEEKS AGO!

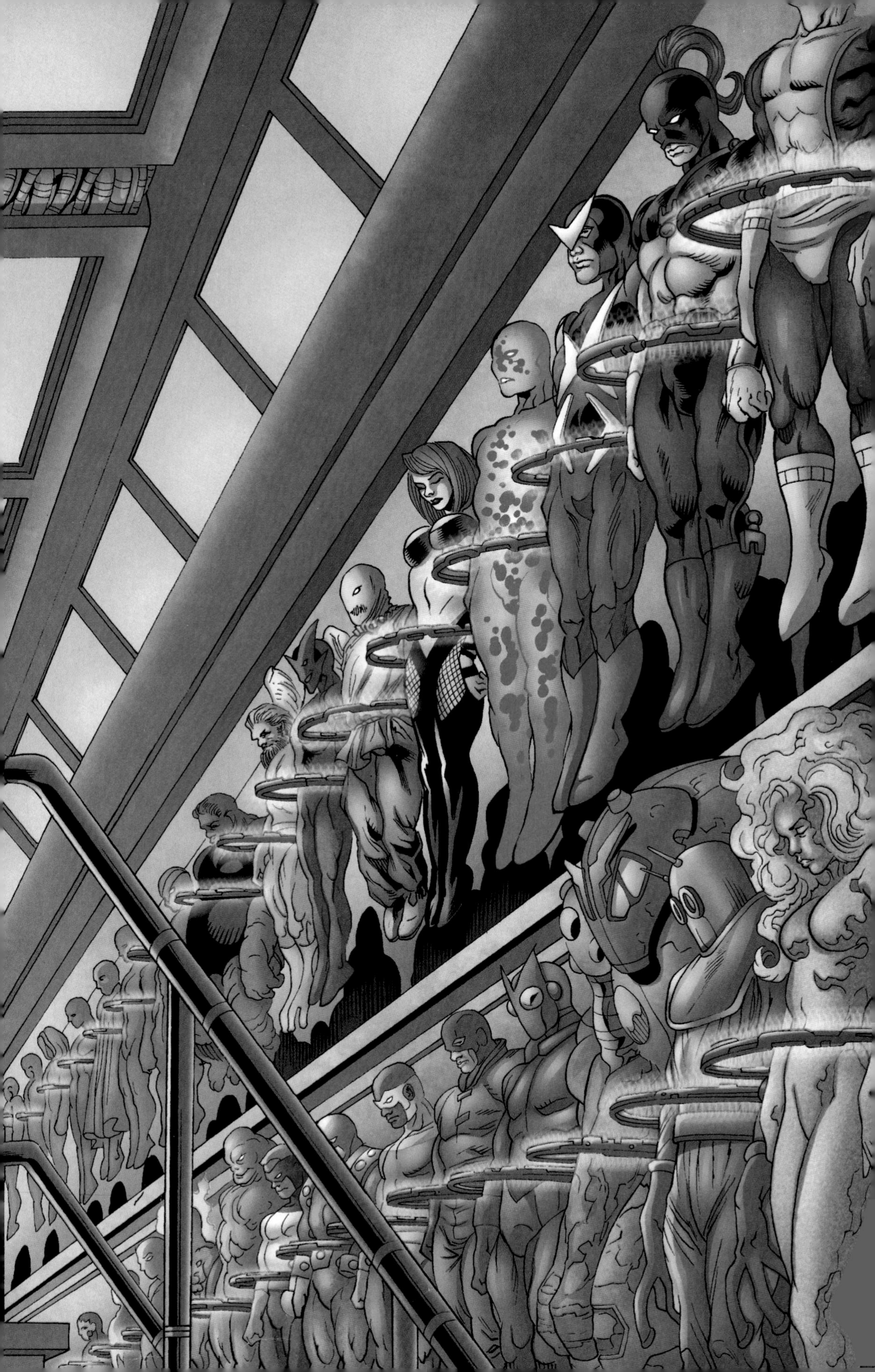

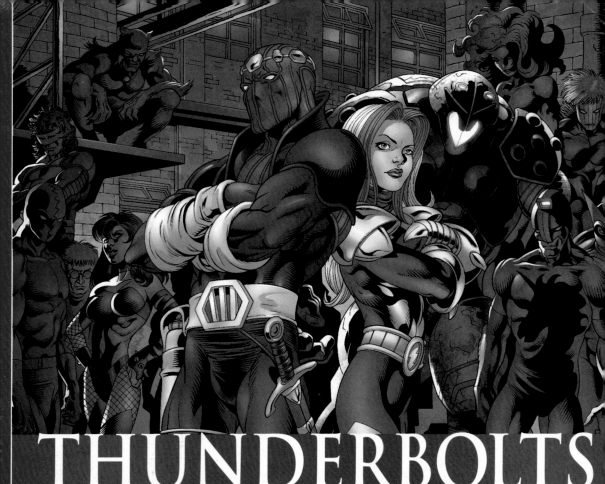

THUNDERBOLTS

A MARVEL COMICS EVENT

CIVIL
WAR

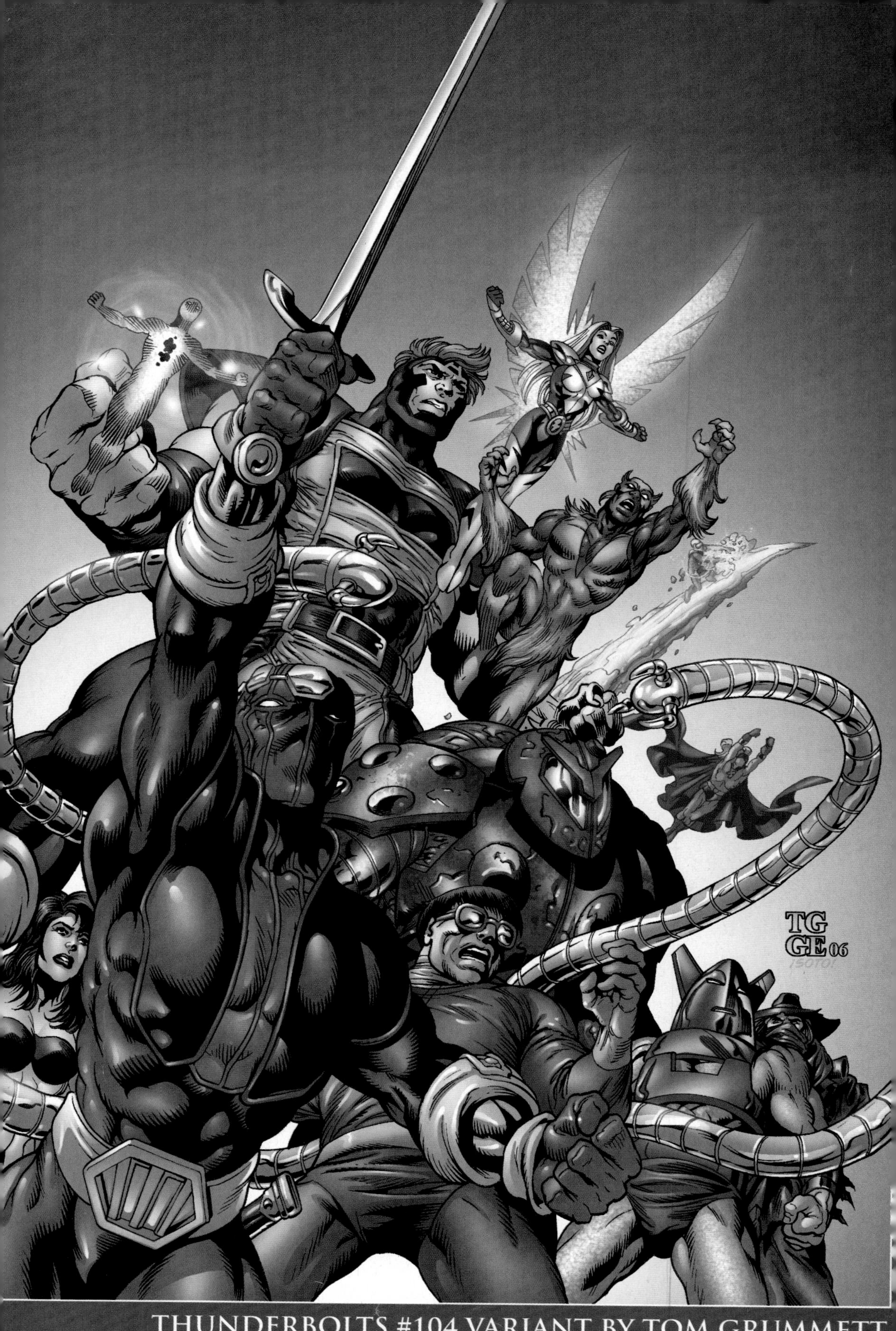
TG
GE 06
¡SOTO!
THUNDERBOLTS #104 VARIANT BY TOM GRUMMETT

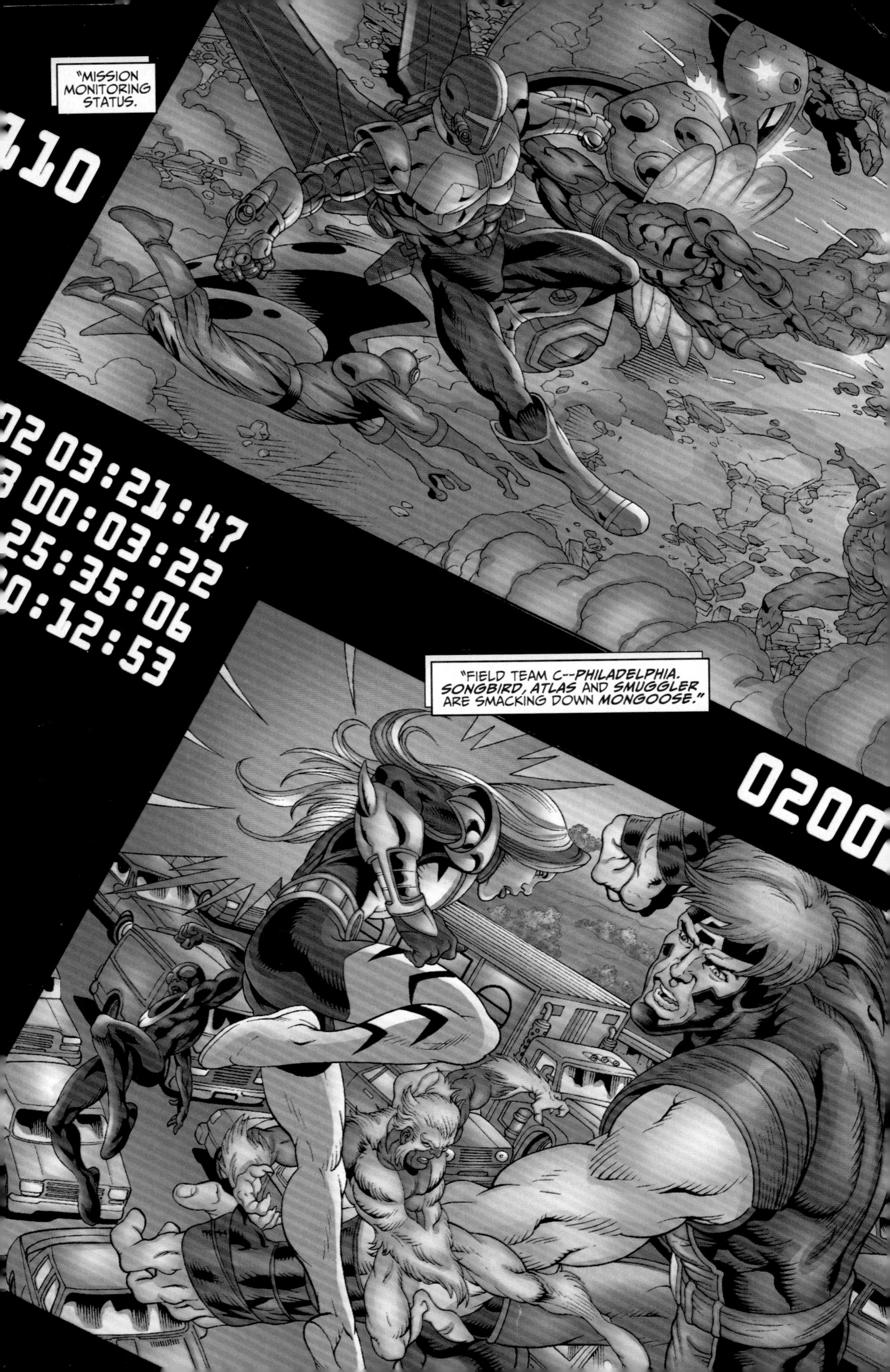

"MISSION MONITORING STATUS.
110
02 03:21:47
3 00:03:22
25:35:06
0:12:53
"FIELD TEAM C--*PHILADELPHIA*. *SONGBIRD*, *ATLAS* AND *SMUGGLER* ARE SMACKING DOWN *MONGOOSE*."
0200

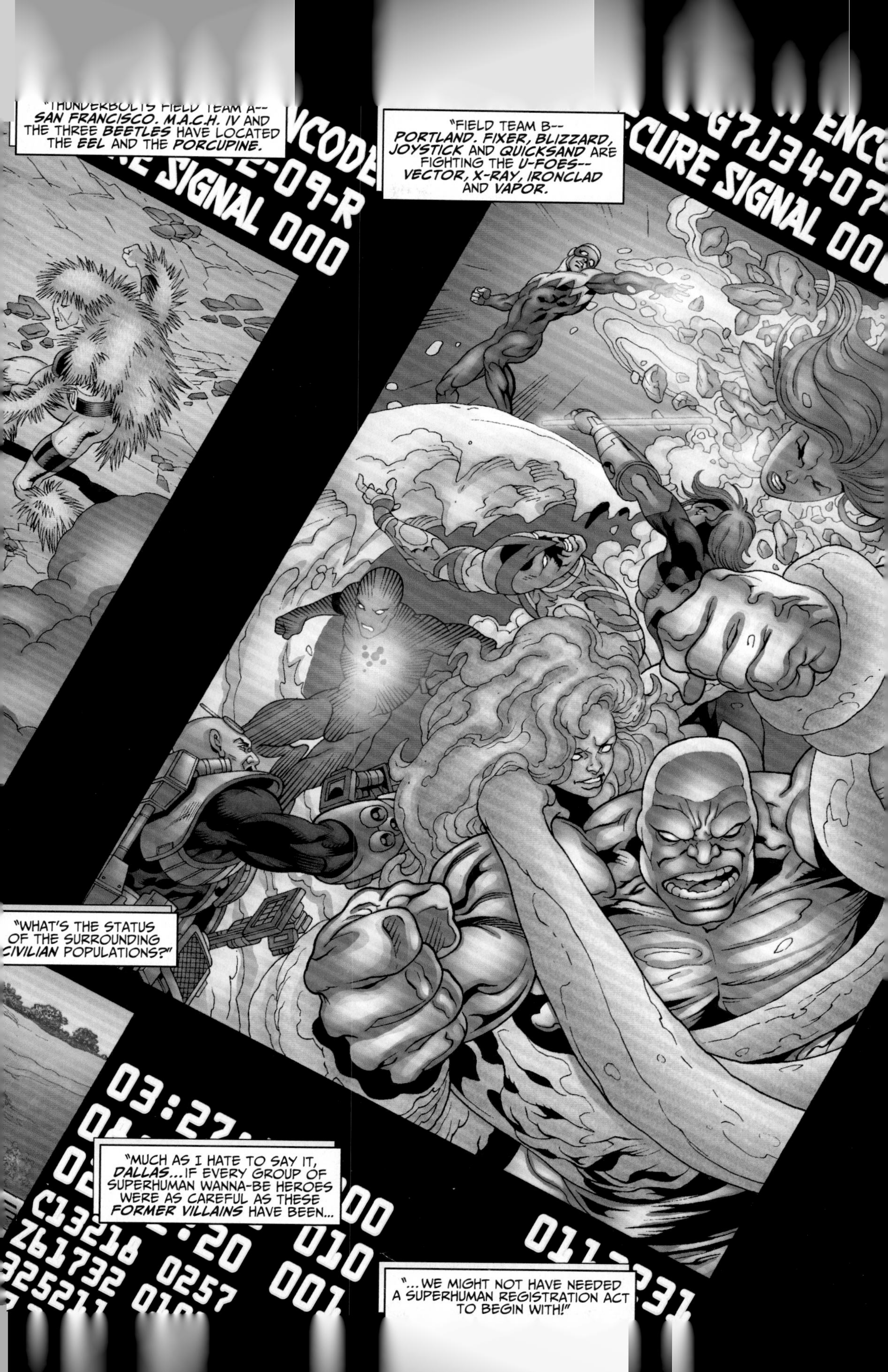
"THUNDERBOLTS FIELD TEAM A-- SAN FRANCISCO. M.A.C.H. IV AND THE THREE BEETLES HAVE LOCATED THE EEL AND THE PORCUPINE.
"FIELD TEAM B-- PORTLAND. FIXER, BLIZZARD, JOYSTICK AND QUICKSAND ARE FIGHTING THE U-FOES-- VECTOR, X-RAY, IRONCLAD AND VAPOR.
"WHAT'S THE STATUS OF THE SURROUNDING CIVILIAN POPULATIONS?"
"MUCH AS I HATE TO SAY IT, DALLAS... IF EVERY GROUP OF SUPERHUMAN WANNA-BE HEROES WERE AS CAREFUL AS THESE FORMER VILLAINS HAVE BEEN...
"...WE MIGHT NOT HAVE NEEDED A SUPERHUMAN REGISTRATION ACT TO BEGIN WITH!"

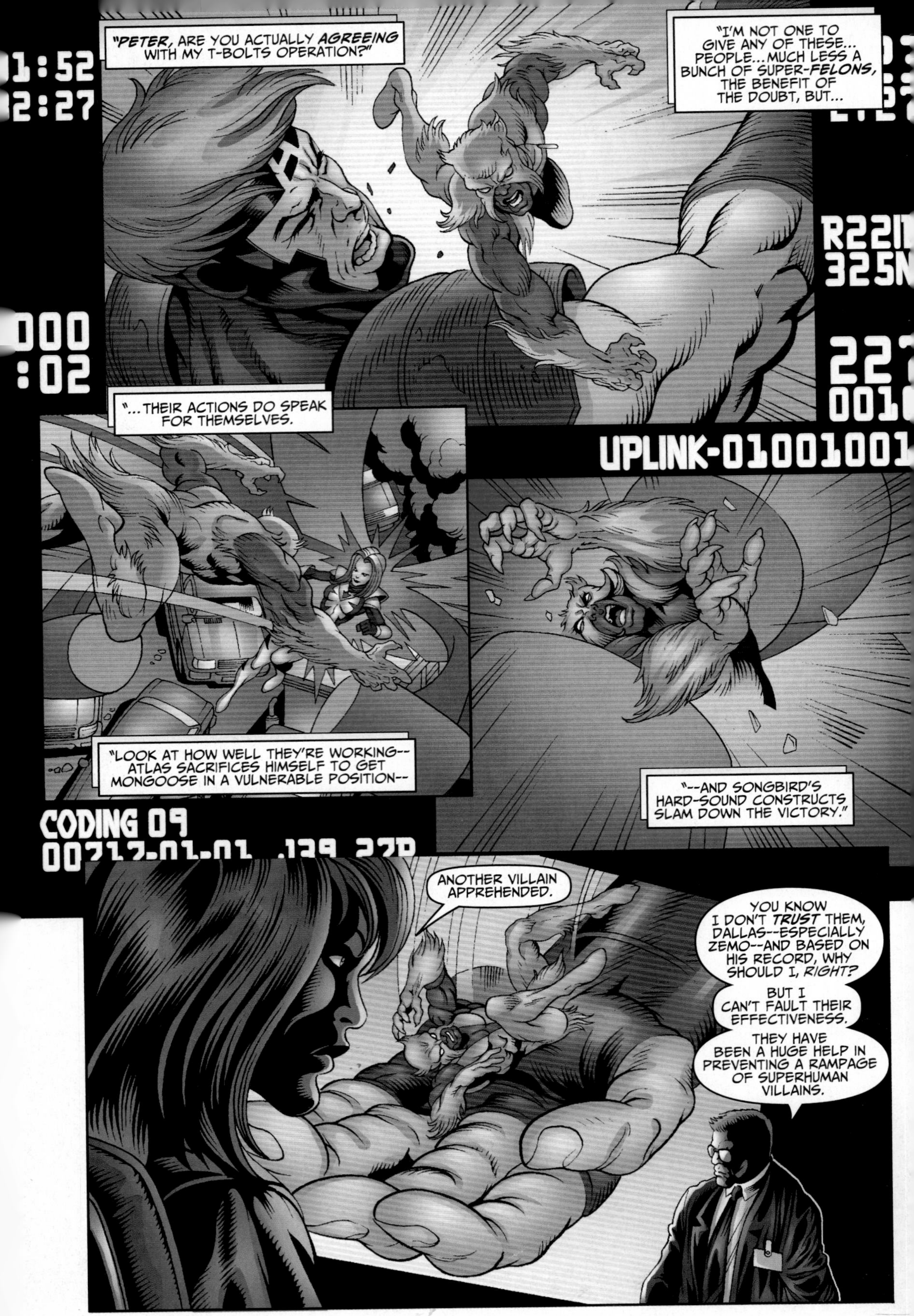
"PETER, ARE YOU ACTUALLY AGREEING WITH MY T-BOLTS OPERATION?"
1:52
2:27
"I'M NOT ONE TO GIVE ANY OF THESE... PEOPLE...MUCH LESS A BUNCH OF SUPER-FELONS, THE BENEFIT OF THE DOUBT, BUT...
000
:02
"...THEIR ACTIONS DO SPEAK FOR THEMSELVES.
UPLINK-0100100
"LOOK AT HOW WELL THEY'RE WORKING--ATLAS SACRIFICES HIMSELF TO GET MONGOOSE IN A VULNERABLE POSITION--
"--AND SONGBIRD'S HARD-SOUND CONSTRUCTS SLAM DOWN THE VICTORY."
CODING 09
ANOTHER VILLAIN APPREHENDED.
YOU KNOW I DON'T TRUST THEM, DALLAS--ESPECIALLY ZEMO--AND BASED ON HIS RECORD, WHY SHOULD I, RIGHT?
BUT I CAN'T FAULT THEIR EFFECTIVENESS.
THEY HAVE BEEN A HUGE HELP IN PREVENTING A RAMPAGE OF SUPERHUMAN VILLAINS.

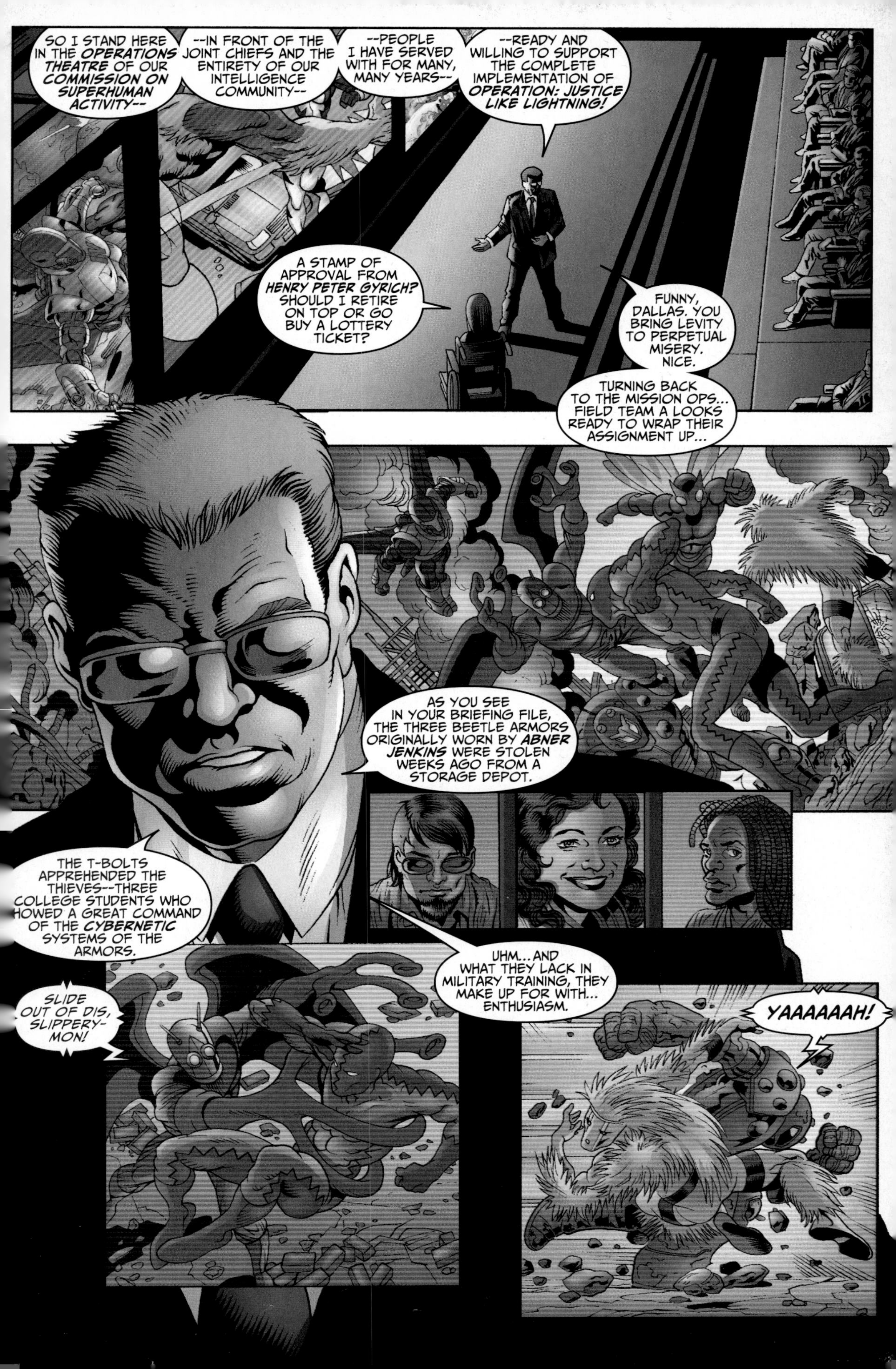
SO I STAND HERE IN THE OPERATIONS THEATRE OF OUR COMMISSION ON SUPERHUMAN ACTIVITY--
--IN FRONT OF THE JOINT CHIEFS AND THE ENTIRETY OF OUR INTELLIGENCE COMMUNITY--
--PEOPLE I HAVE SERVED WITH FOR MANY, MANY YEARS--
--READY AND WILLING TO SUPPORT THE COMPLETE IMPLEMENTATION OF OPERATION: JUSTICE LIKE LIGHTNING!
A STAMP OF APPROVAL FROM HENRY PETER GYRICH? SHOULD I RETIRE ON TOP OR GO BUY A LOTTERY TICKET?
FUNNY, DALLAS. YOU BRING LEVITY TO PERPETUAL MISERY. NICE.
TURNING BACK TO THE MISSION OPS... FIELD TEAM A LOOKS READY TO WRAP THEIR ASSIGNMENT UP...
AS YOU SEE IN YOUR BRIEFING FILE, THE THREE BEETLE ARMORS ORIGINALLY WORN BY ABNER JENKINS WERE STOLEN WEEKS AGO FROM A STORAGE DEPOT.
THE T-BOLTS APPREHENDED THE THIEVES--THREE COLLEGE STUDENTS WHO SHOWED A GREAT COMMAND OF THE CYBERNETIC SYSTEMS OF THE ARMORS.
UHM...AND WHAT THEY LACK IN MILITARY TRAINING, THEY MAKE UP FOR WITH... ENTHUSIASM.
SLIDE OUT OF DIS, SLIPPERY-MON!
YAAAAAAH!

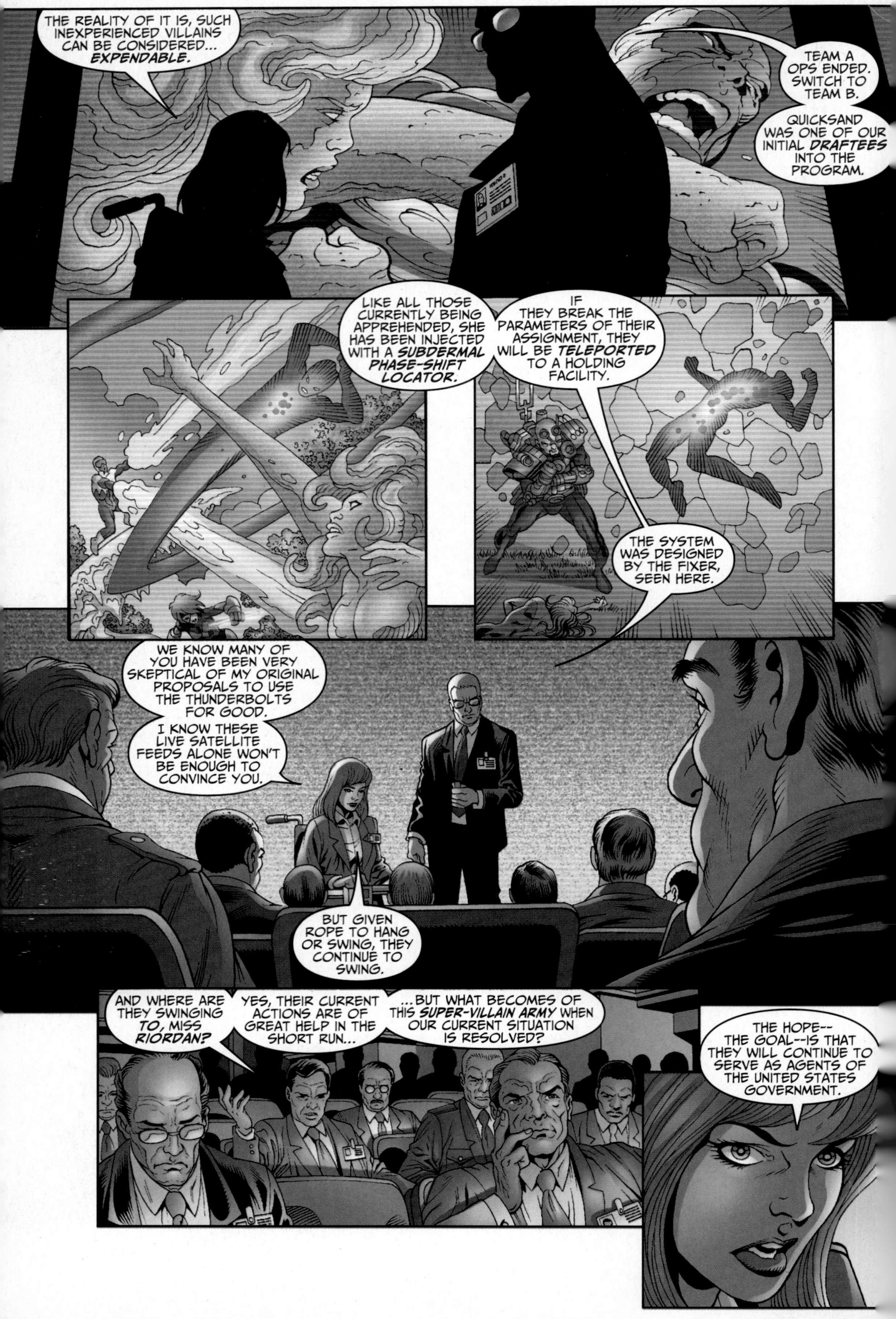
THE REALITY OF IT IS, SUCH INEXPERIENCED VILLAINS CAN BE CONSIDERED... EXPENDABLE.
TEAM A OPS ENDED. SWITCH TO TEAM B.
QUICKSAND WAS ONE OF OUR INITIAL DRAFTEES INTO THE PROGRAM.
LIKE ALL THOSE CURRENTLY BEING APPREHENDED, SHE HAS BEEN INJECTED WITH A SUBDERMAL PHASE-SHIFT LOCATOR.
IF THEY BREAK THE PARAMETERS OF THEIR ASSIGNMENT, THEY WILL BE TELEPORTED TO A HOLDING FACILITY.
THE SYSTEM WAS DESIGNED BY THE FIXER, SEEN HERE.
WE KNOW MANY OF YOU HAVE BEEN VERY SKEPTICAL OF MY ORIGINAL PROPOSALS TO USE THE THUNDERBOLTS FOR GOOD.
I KNOW THESE LIVE SATELLITE FEEDS ALONE WON'T BE ENOUGH TO CONVINCE YOU.
BUT GIVEN ROPE TO HANG OR SWING, THEY CONTINUE TO SWING.
AND WHERE ARE THEY SWINGING TO, MISS RIORDAN?
YES, THEIR CURRENT ACTIONS ARE OF GREAT HELP IN THE SHORT RUN...
...BUT WHAT BECOMES OF THIS SUPER-VILLAIN ARMY WHEN OUR CURRENT SITUATION IS RESOLVED?
THE HOPE-- THE GOAL--IS THAT THEY WILL CONTINUE TO SERVE AS AGENTS OF THE UNITED STATES GOVERNMENT.

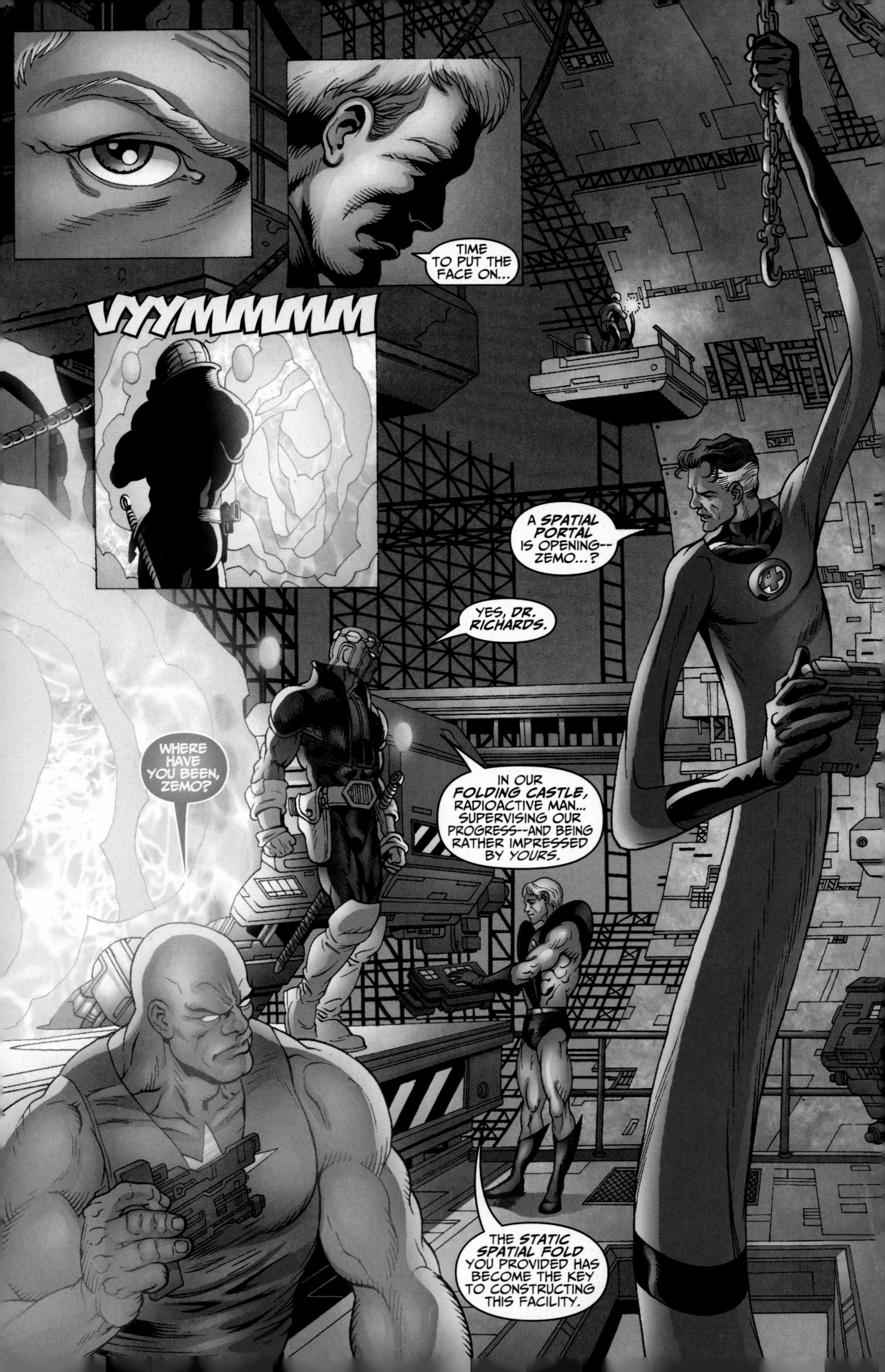
TIME TO PUT THE FACE ON...
VYYMMMMM
A SPATIAL PORTAL IS OPENING-- ZEMO...?
YES, DR. RICHARDS.
WHERE HAVE YOU BEEN, ZEMO?
IN OUR FOLDING CASTLE, RADIOACTIVE MAN... SUPERVISING OUR PROGRESS--AND BEING RATHER IMPRESSED BY YOURS.
THE STATIC SPATIAL FOLD YOU PROVIDED HAS BECOME THE KEY TO CONSTRUCTING THIS FACILITY.

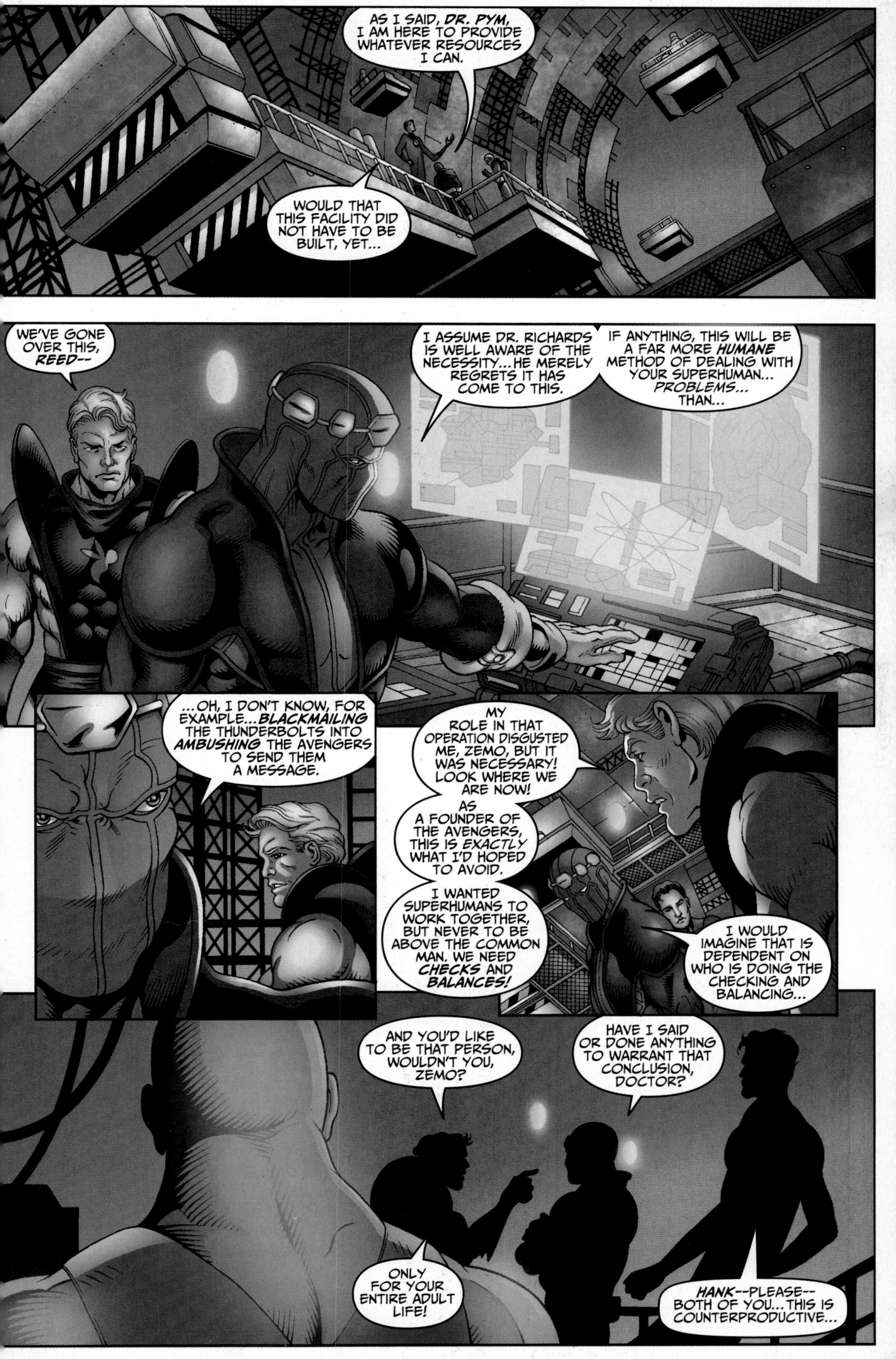
AS I SAID, DR. PYM, I AM HERE TO PROVIDE WHATEVER RESOURCES I CAN.
WOULD THAT THIS FACILITY DID NOT HAVE TO BE BUILT, YET...
WE'VE GONE OVER THIS, REED--
I ASSUME DR. RICHARDS IS WELL AWARE OF THE NECESSITY...HE MERELY REGRETS IT HAS COME TO THIS.
IF ANYTHING, THIS WILL BE A FAR MORE HUMANE METHOD OF DEALING WITH YOUR SUPERHUMAN... PROBLEMS... THAN...
...OH, I DON'T KNOW, FOR EXAMPLE...BLACKMAILING THE THUNDERBOLTS INTO AMBUSHING THE AVENGERS TO SEND THEM A MESSAGE.
MY ROLE IN THAT OPERATION DISGUSTED ME, ZEMO, BUT IT WAS NECESSARY! LOOK WHERE WE ARE NOW!
AS A FOUNDER OF THE AVENGERS, THIS IS EXACTLY WHAT I'D HOPED TO AVOID.
I WANTED SUPERHUMANS TO WORK TOGETHER, BUT NEVER TO BE ABOVE THE COMMON MAN. WE NEED CHECKS AND BALANCES!
I WOULD IMAGINE THAT IS DEPENDENT ON WHO IS DOING THE CHECKING AND BALANCING...
AND YOU'D LIKE TO BE THAT PERSON, WOULDN'T YOU, ZEMO?
HAVE I SAID OR DONE ANYTHING TO WARRANT THAT CONCLUSION, DOCTOR?
ONLY FOR YOUR ENTIRE ADULT LIFE!
HANK--PLEASE--BOTH OF YOU...THIS IS COUNTERPRODUCTIVE...

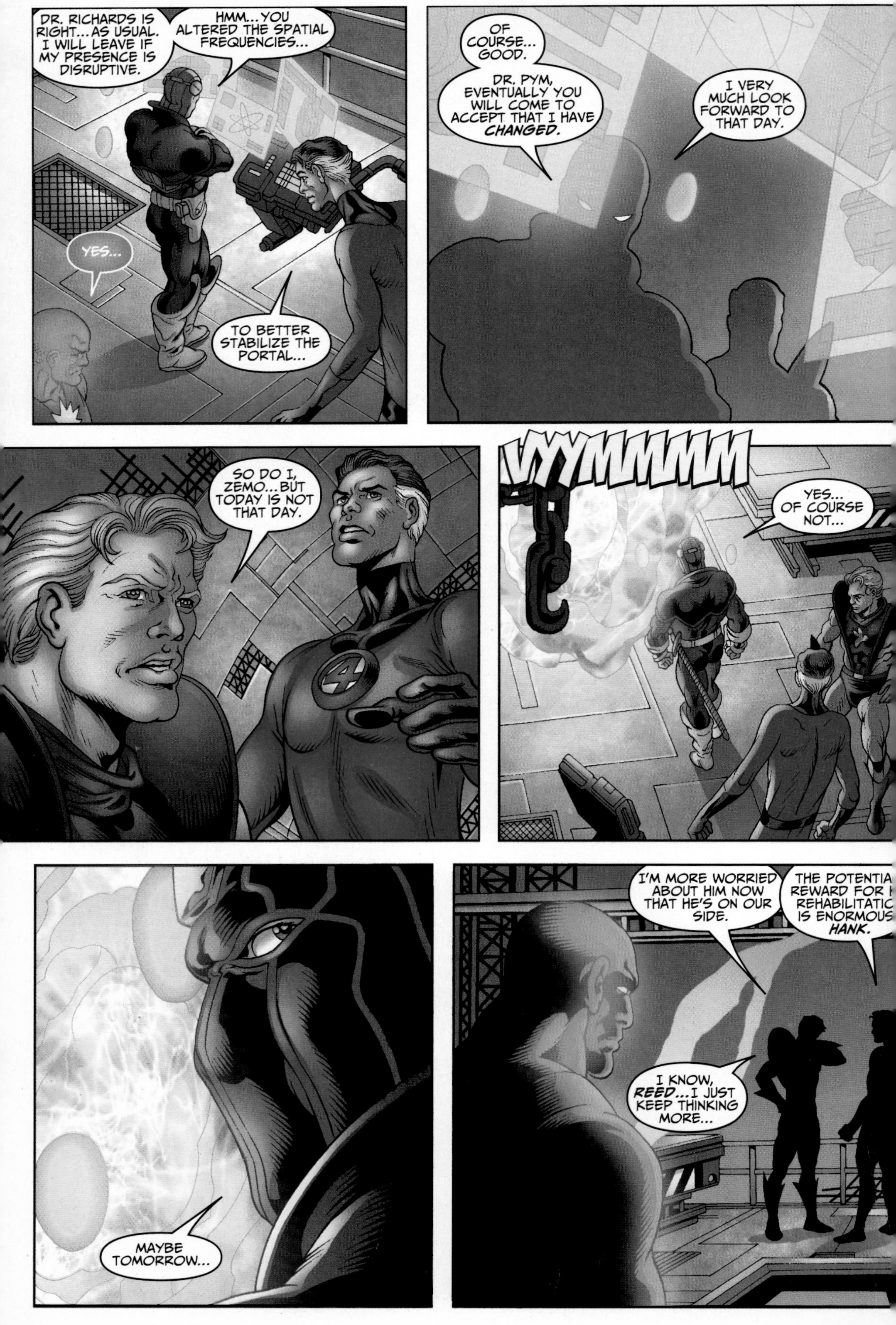
DR. RICHARDS IS RIGHT... AS USUAL. I WILL LEAVE IF MY PRESENCE IS DISRUPTIVE.
HMM... YOU ALTERED THE SPATIAL FREQUENCIES...
YES...
TO BETTER STABILIZE THE PORTAL...
OF COURSE... GOOD.
DR. PYM, EVENTUALLY YOU WILL COME TO ACCEPT THAT I HAVE CHANGED.
I VERY MUCH LOOK FORWARD TO THAT DAY.
SO DO I, ZEMO... BUT TODAY IS NOT THAT DAY.
VYYMMMMM
YES... OF COURSE NOT...
MAYBE TOMORROW...
I'M MORE WORRIED ABOUT HIM NOW THAT HE'S ON OUR SIDE.
THE POTENTIA REWARD FOR H REHABILITATIC IS ENORMOUS HANK.
I KNOW, REED... I JUST KEEP THINKING MORE...

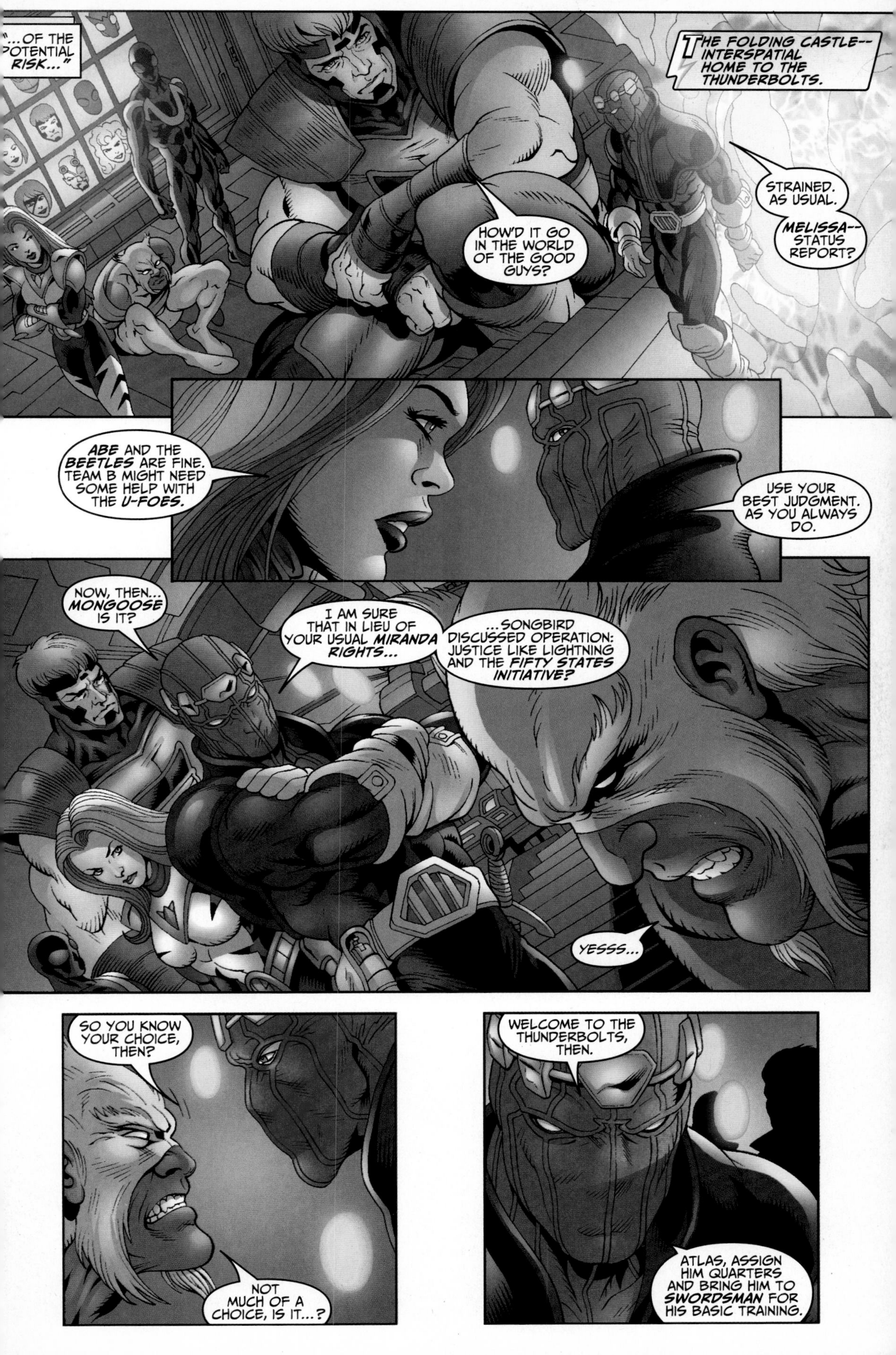
"...OF THE POTENTIAL RISK..."
THE FOLDING CASTLE-- INTERSPATIAL HOME TO THE THUNDERBOLTS.
HOW'D IT GO IN THE WORLD OF THE GOOD GUYS?
STRAINED. AS USUAL.
MELISSA-- STATUS REPORT?
ABE AND THE BEETLES ARE FINE. TEAM B MIGHT NEED SOME HELP WITH THE U-FOES.
USE YOUR BEST JUDGMENT. AS YOU ALWAYS DO.
NOW, THEN... MONGOOSE IS IT?
I AM SURE THAT IN LIEU OF YOUR USUAL MIRANDA RIGHTS...
...SONGBIRD DISCUSSED OPERATION: JUSTICE LIKE LIGHTNING AND THE FIFTY STATES INITIATIVE?
YESSS...
SO YOU KNOW YOUR CHOICE, THEN?
NOT MUCH OF A CHOICE, IS IT...?
WELCOME TO THE THUNDERBOLTS, THEN.
ATLAS, ASSIGN HIM QUARTERS AND BRING HIM TO SWORDSMAN FOR HIS BASIC TRAINING.

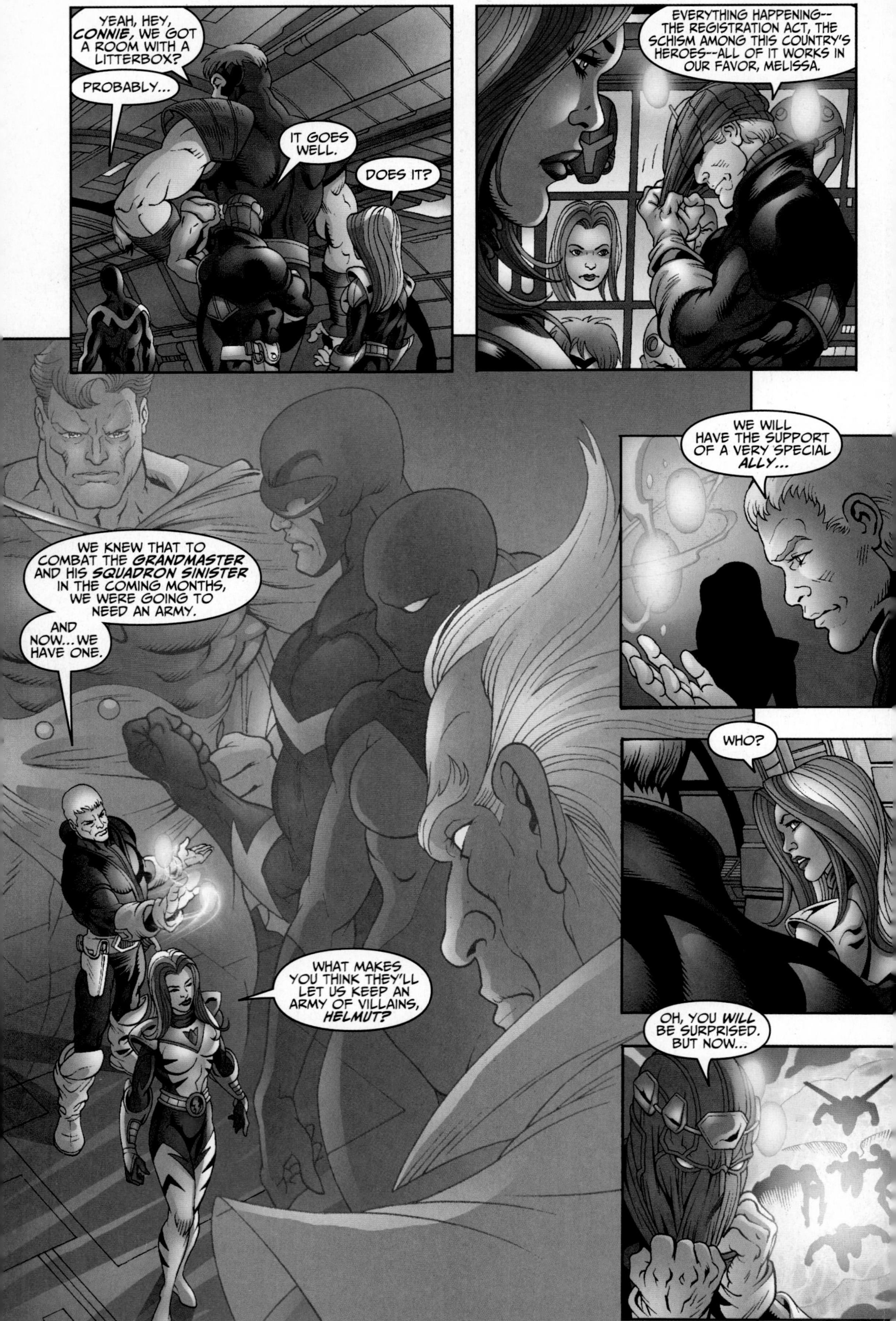

YEAH, HEY, CONNIE, WE GOT A ROOM WITH A LITTERBOX?
PROBABLY...
IT GOES WELL.
DOES IT?
EVERYTHING HAPPENING-- THE REGISTRATION ACT, THE SCHISM AMONG THIS COUNTRY'S HEROES--ALL OF IT WORKS IN OUR FAVOR, MELISSA.
WE KNEW THAT TO COMBAT THE GRANDMASTER AND HIS SQUADRON SINISTER IN THE COMING MONTHS, WE WERE GOING TO NEED AN ARMY.
AND NOW...WE HAVE ONE.
WHAT MAKES YOU THINK THEY'LL LET US KEEP AN ARMY OF VILLAINS, HELMUT?
WE WILL HAVE THE SUPPORT OF A VERY SPECIAL ALLY...
WHO?
OH, YOU WILL BE SURPRISED. BUT NOW...

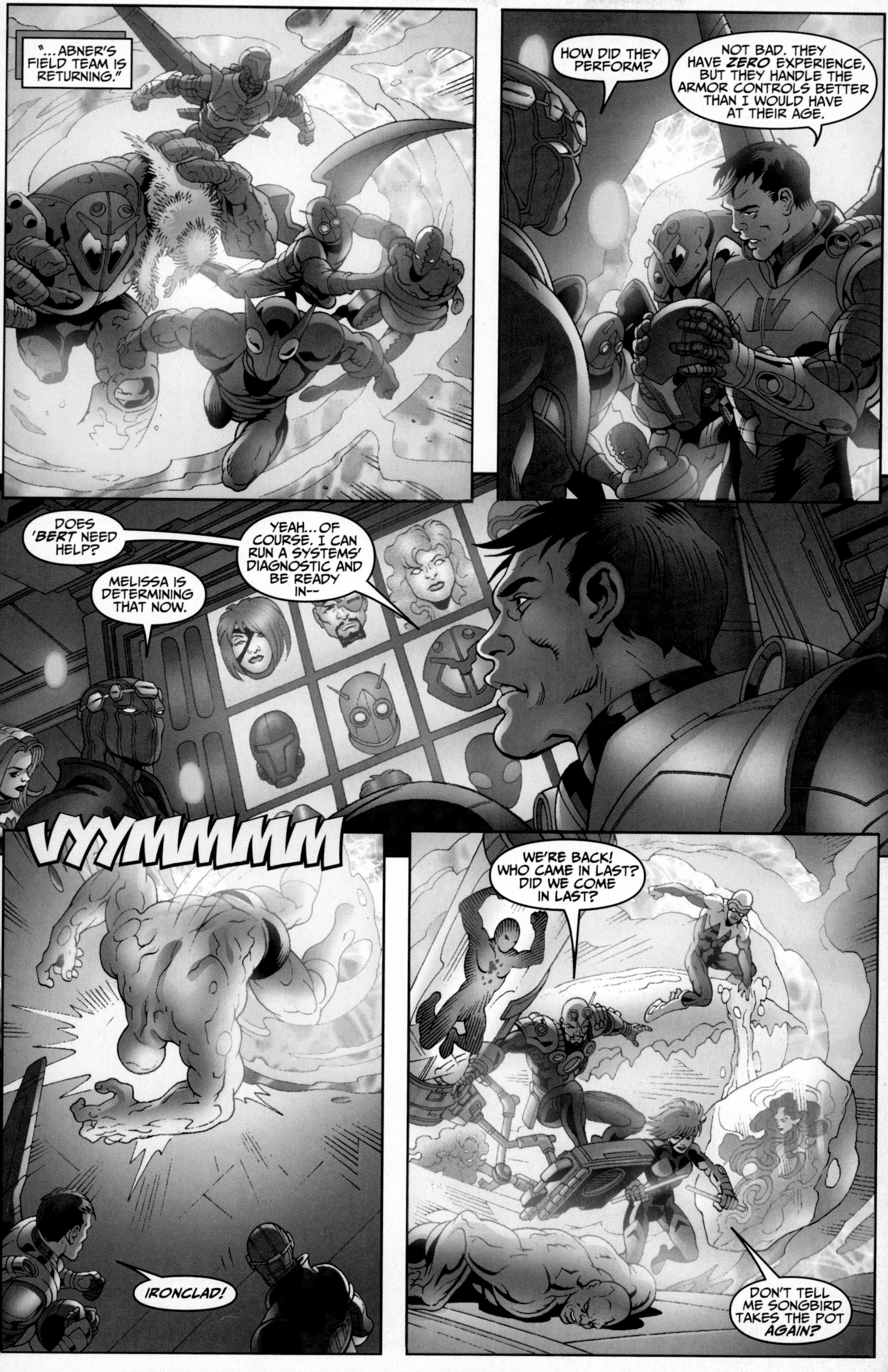
"...ABNER'S FIELD TEAM IS RETURNING."
HOW DID THEY PERFORM?
NOT BAD. THEY HAVE ZERO EXPERIENCE, BUT THEY HANDLE THE ARMOR CONTROLS BETTER THAN I WOULD HAVE AT THEIR AGE.
DOES 'BERT NEED HELP?
YEAH... OF COURSE. I CAN RUN A SYSTEMS' DIAGNOSTIC AND BE READY IN--
MELISSA IS DETERMINING THAT NOW.
VYYMMMMM
IRONCLAD!
WE'RE BACK! WHO CAME IN LAST? DID WE COME IN LAST?
DON'T TELL ME SONGBIRD TAKES THE POT AGAIN?

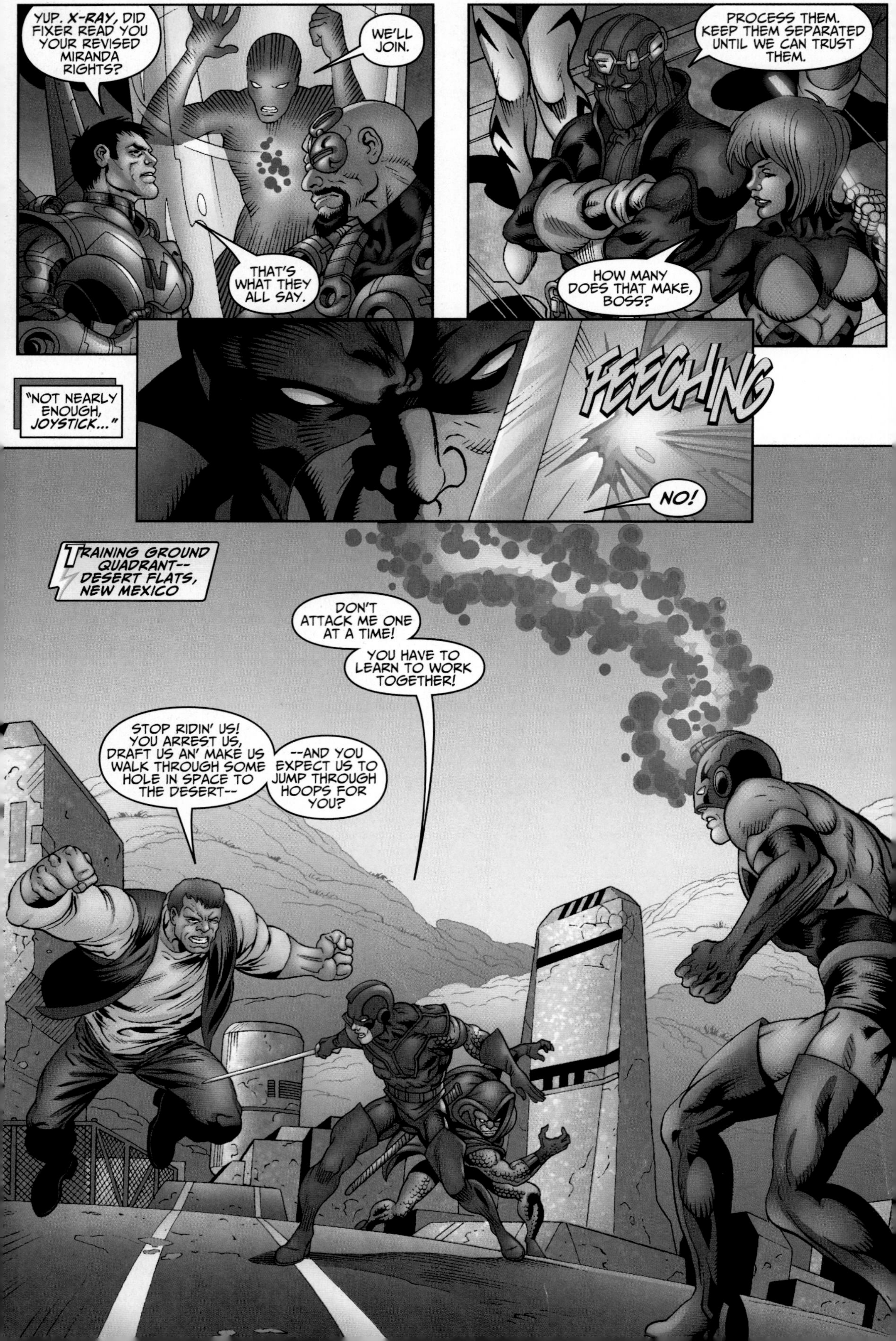
YUP. X-RAY, DID FIXER READ YOU YOUR REVISED MIRANDA RIGHTS?
WE'LL JOIN.
THAT'S WHAT THEY ALL SAY.
PROCESS THEM. KEEP THEM SEPARATED UNTIL WE CAN TRUST THEM.
HOW MANY DOES THAT MAKE, BOSS?
"NOT NEARLY ENOUGH, JOYSTICK..."
FEECHING
NO!
TRAINING GROUND QUADRANT-- DESERT FLATS, NEW MEXICO
DON'T ATTACK ME ONE AT A TIME!
YOU HAVE TO LEARN TO WORK TOGETHER!
STOP RIDIN' US! YOU ARREST US, DRAFT US AN' MAKE US WALK THROUGH SOME HOLE IN SPACE TO THE DESERT--
--AND YOU EXPECT US TO JUMP THROUGH HOOPS FOR YOU?

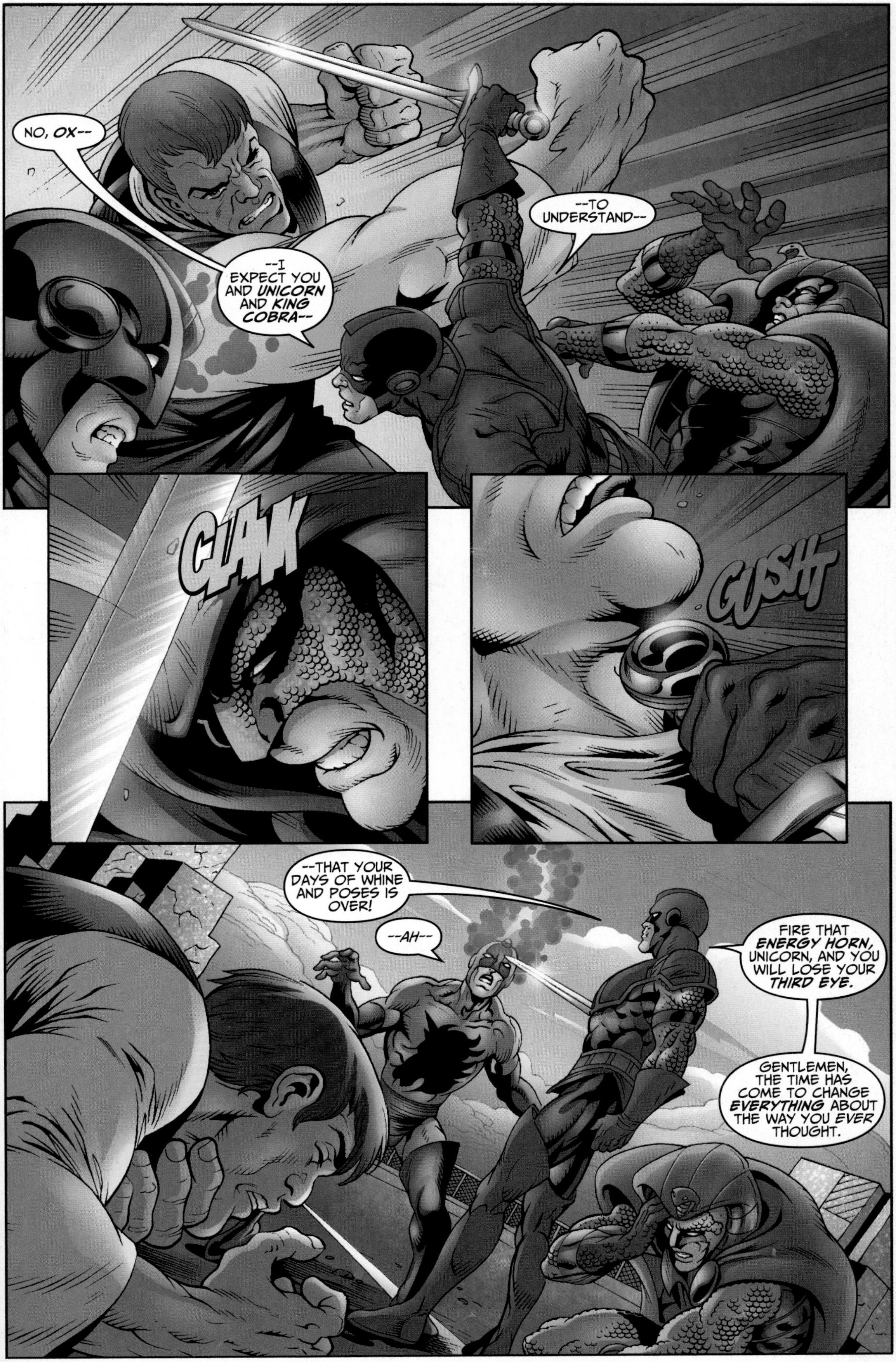

NO, OX--
--I EXPECT YOU AND UNICORN AND KING COBRA--
--TO UNDERSTAND--
CLANK
GUSH
--THAT YOUR DAYS OF WHINE AND POSES IS OVER!
--AH--
FIRE THAT ENERGY HORN, UNICORN, AND YOU WILL LOSE YOUR THIRD EYE.
GENTLEMEN, THE TIME HAS COME TO CHANGE EVERYTHING ABOUT THE WAY YOU EVER THOUGHT.

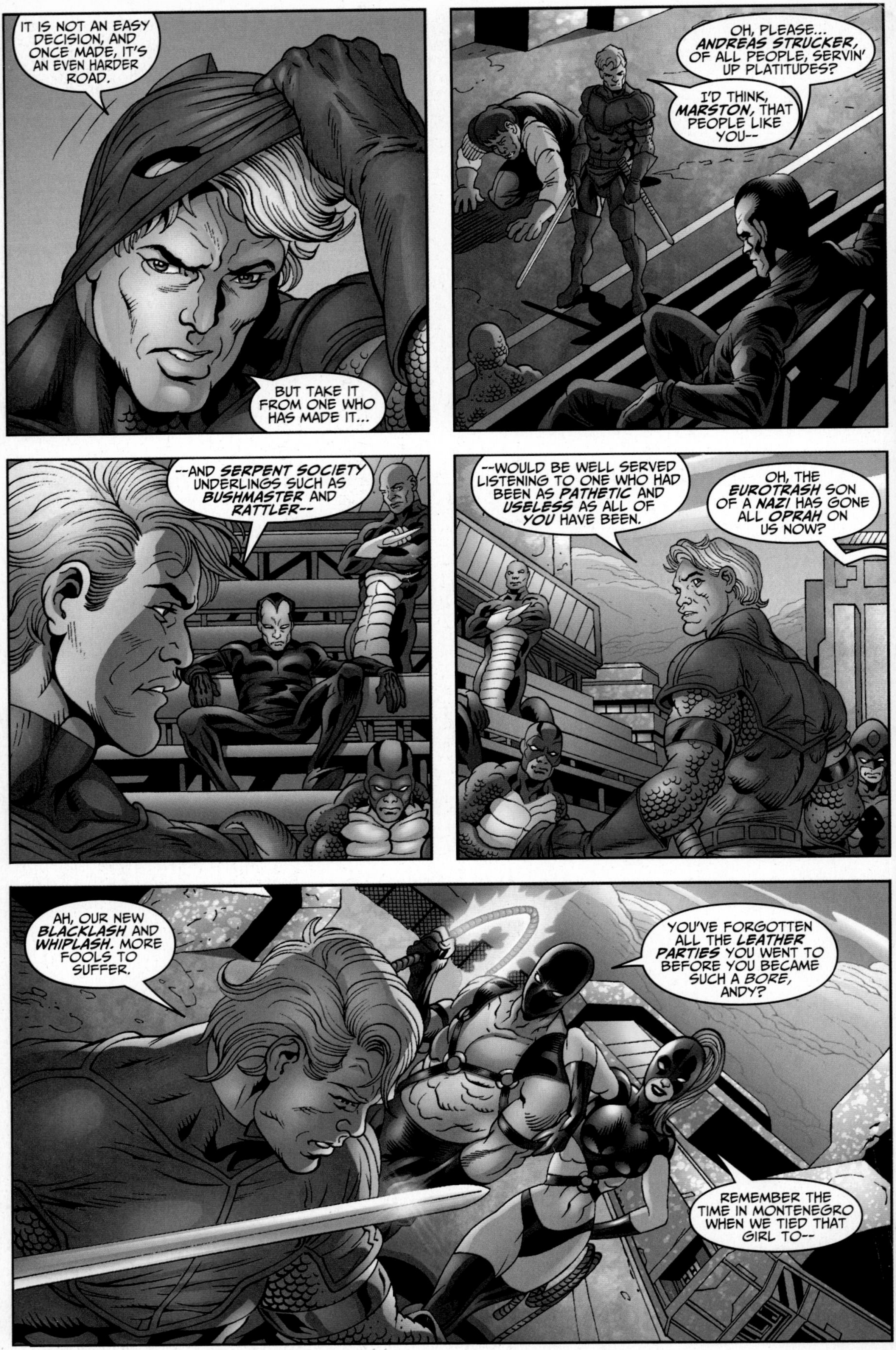
IT IS NOT AN EASY DECISION, AND ONCE MADE, IT'S AN EVEN HARDER ROAD.
BUT TAKE IT FROM ONE WHO HAS MADE IT...
OH, PLEASE... ANDREAS STRUCKER, OF ALL PEOPLE, SERVIN' UP PLATITUDES?
I'D THINK, MARSTON, THAT PEOPLE LIKE YOU--
--AND SERPENT SOCIETY UNDERLINGS SUCH AS BUSHMASTER AND RATTLER--
--WOULD BE WELL SERVED LISTENING TO ONE WHO HAD BEEN AS PATHETIC AND USELESS AS ALL OF YOU HAVE BEEN.
OH, THE EUROTRASH SON OF A NAZI HAS GONE ALL OPRAH ON US NOW?
AH, OUR NEW BLACKLASH AND WHIPLASH. MORE FOOLS TO SUFFER.
YOU'VE FORGOTTEN ALL THE LEATHER PARTIES YOU WENT TO BEFORE YOU BECAME SUCH A BORE, ANDY?
REMEMBER THE TIME IN MONTENEGRO WHEN WE TIED THAT GIRL TO--

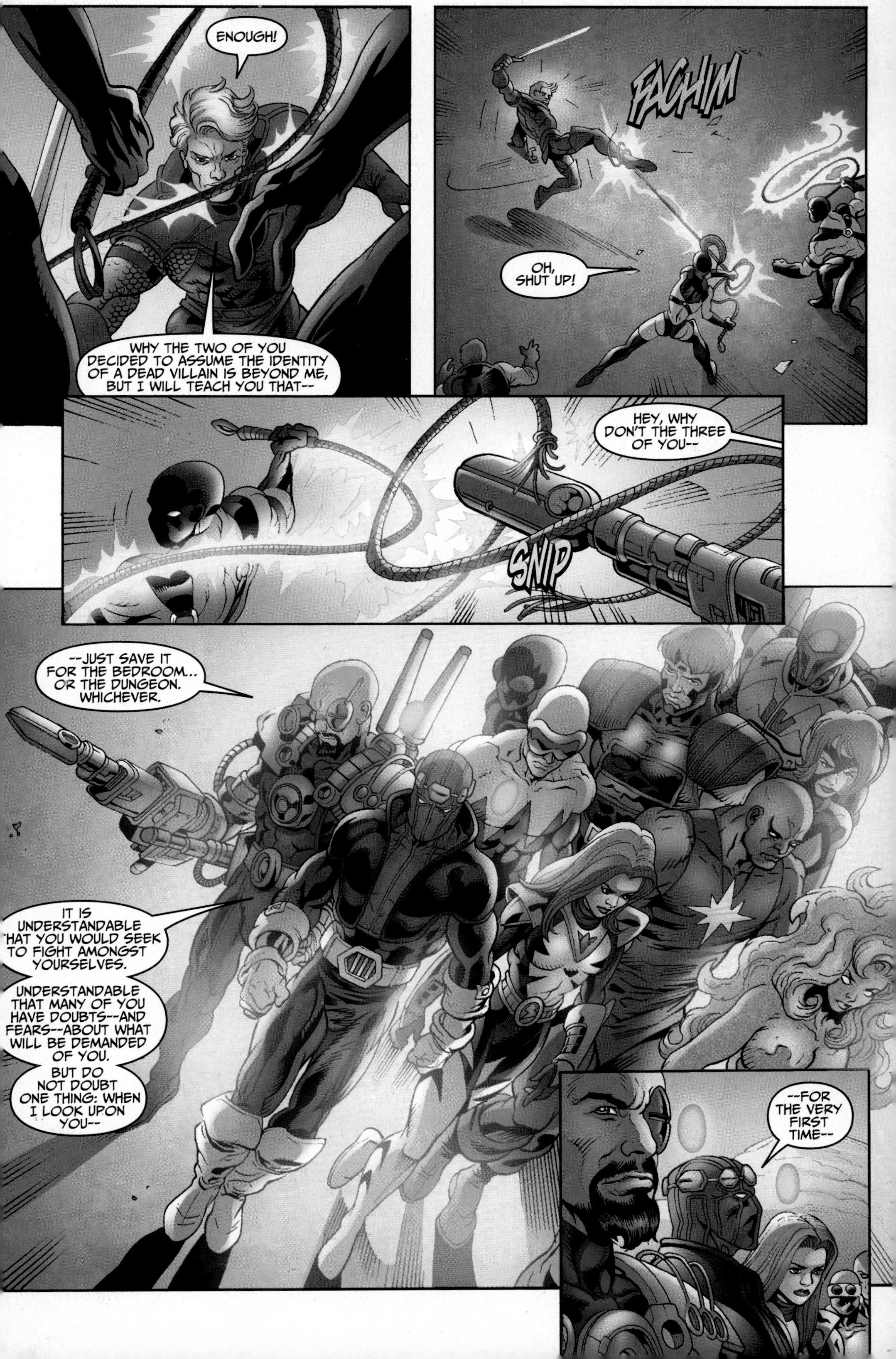
ENOUGH!
WHY THE TWO OF YOU DECIDED TO ASSUME THE IDENTITY OF A DEAD VILLAIN IS BEYOND ME, BUT I WILL TEACH YOU THAT--
FACHIM
OH, SHUT UP!
HEY, WHY DON'T THE THREE OF YOU--
SNIP
--JUST SAVE IT FOR THE BEDROOM... OR THE DUNGEON. WHICHEVER.
IT IS UNDERSTANDABLE THAT YOU WOULD SEEK TO FIGHT AMONGST YOURSELVES.
UNDERSTANDABLE THAT MANY OF YOU HAVE DOUBTS--AND FEARS--ABOUT WHAT WILL BE DEMANDED OF YOU.
BUT DO NOT DOUBT ONE THING: WHEN I LOOK UPON YOU--
--FOR THE VERY FIRST TIME--

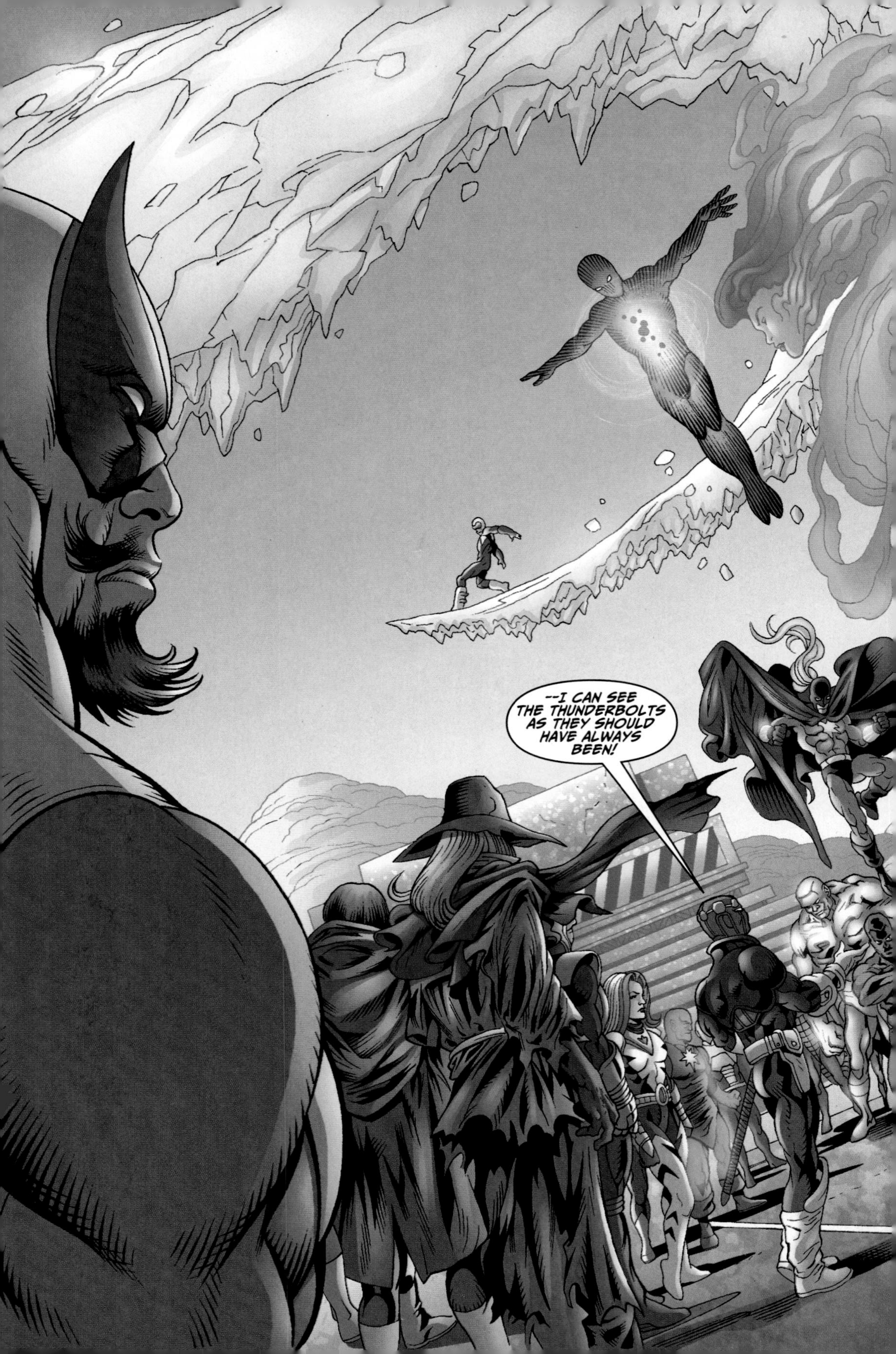
--I CAN SEE THE THUNDERBOLTS AS THEY SHOULD HAVE ALWAYS BEEN!

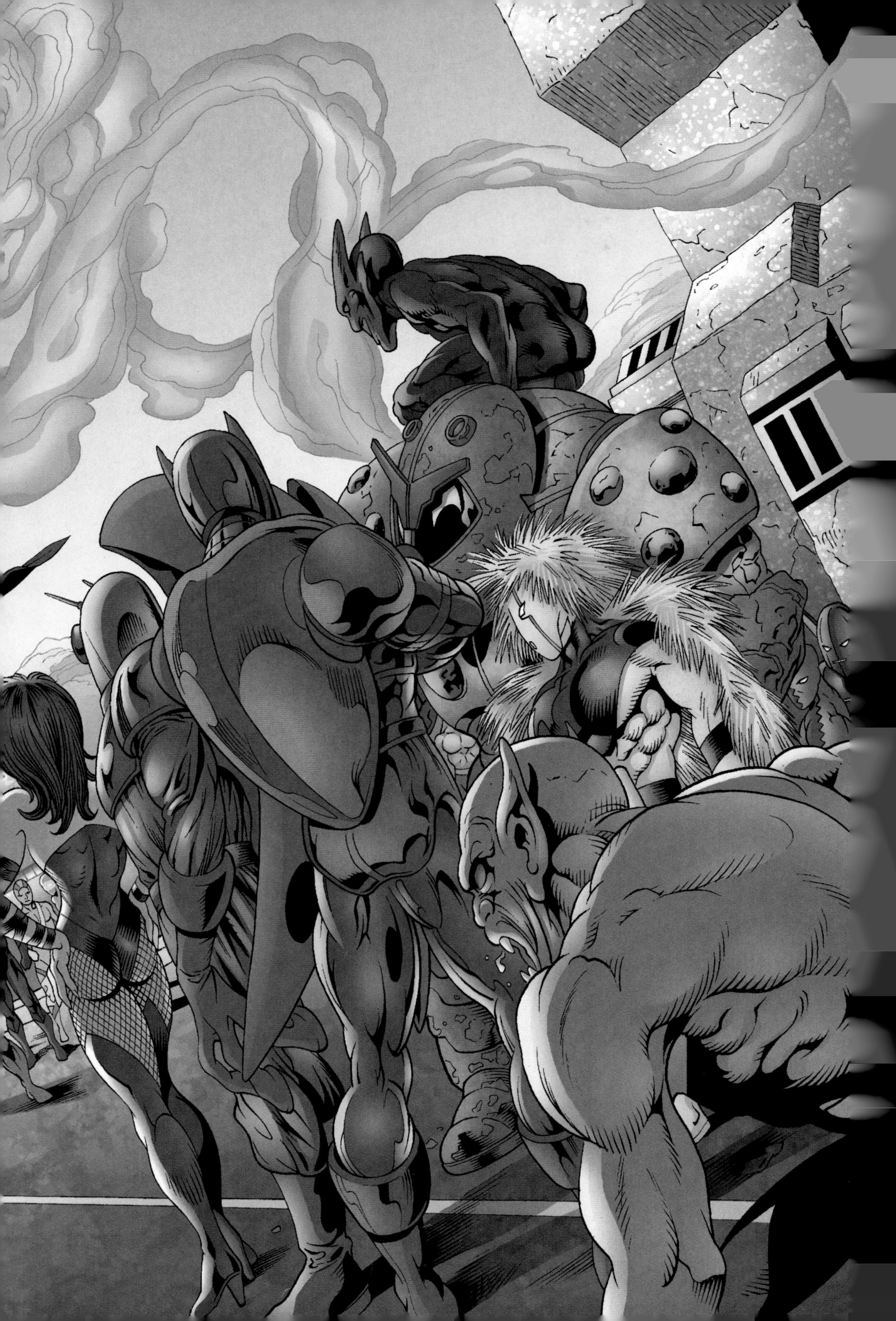

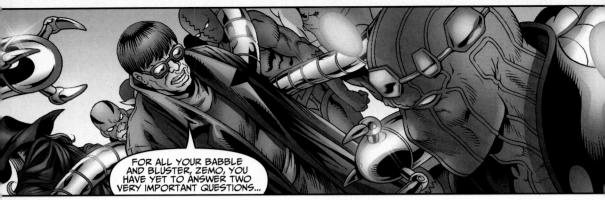

FOR ALL YOUR BABBLE AND BLUSTER, ZEMO, YOU HAVE YET TO ANSWER TWO VERY IMPORTANT QUESTIONS...

WHAT DO WE GET OUT OF THIS--

--AND WHY SHOULD THIS... SITUATION...REMAIN AN OPTION FOR ANY OF US ONCE THE ISSUES OF THIS REGISTRATION ACT ARE SETTLED?

DR. OCTOPUS, FIRST, YOU GET TO EARN REDEMPTION. WHAT THAT IS WORTH TO YOU IS AN INDIVIDUAL DECISION.

AND WITH FREEDOM COMES PERPETUAL OPPORTUNITY TO HUMILIATE THE SUPER HEROES WHO HAVE ALWAYS HUMILIATED YOU.

THE FORMER IS APOCRYPHAL, THE LATTER IS... ACCEPTABLE...

...YET BOTH SEEM TO BE SHORT-TERM PROPOSITIONS.

IN FACT, RIGHT NOW, I LEAVE TO ENSURE THAT BOTH...

VYYMMMMM

...WILL BE VERY, VERY LONG OPTIONS INDEED...

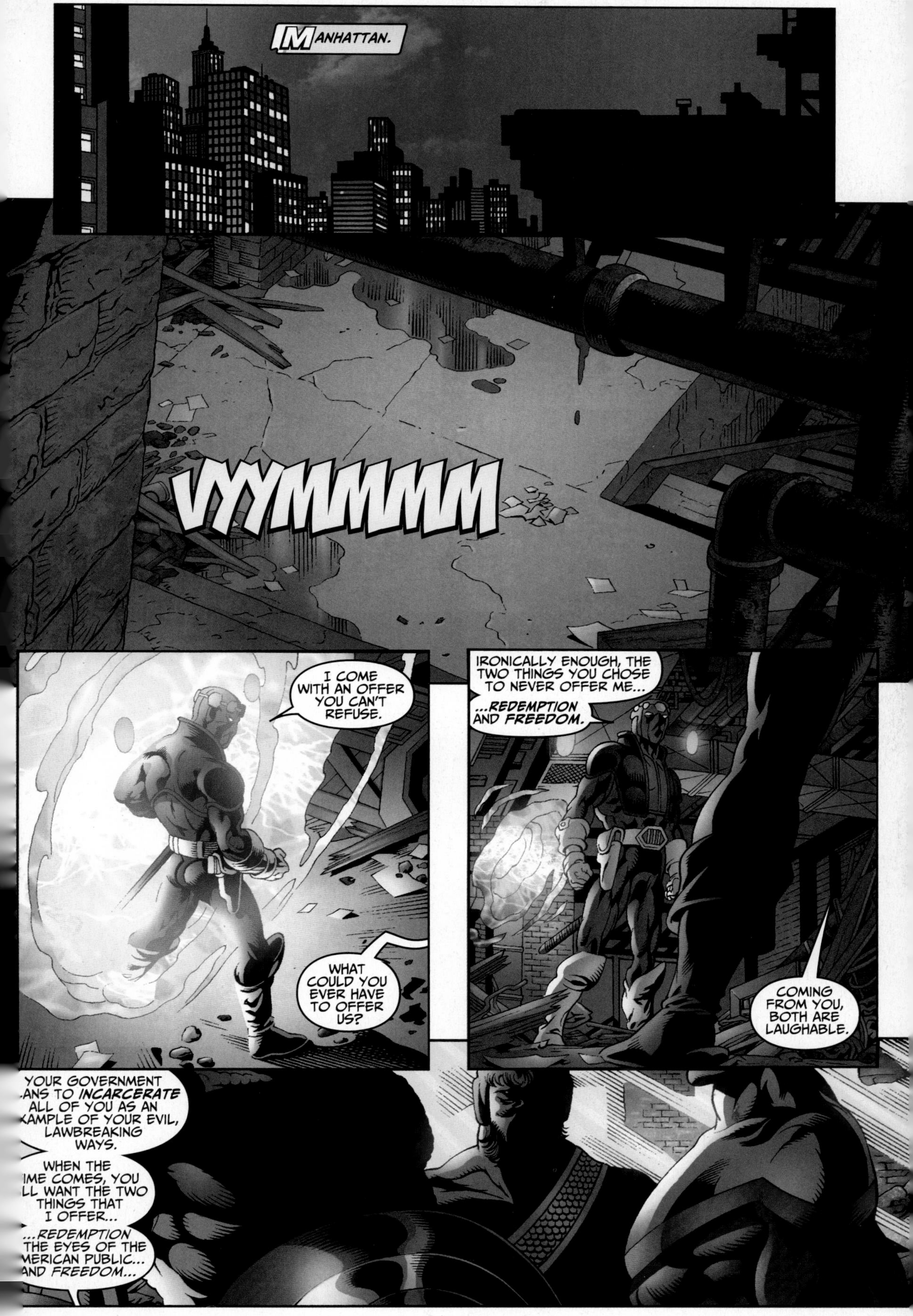
MANHATTAN.
VYYMMMMM
I COME WITH AN OFFER YOU CAN'T REFUSE.
WHAT COULD YOU EVER HAVE TO OFFER US?
IRONICALLY ENOUGH, THE TWO THINGS YOU CHOSE TO NEVER OFFER ME...
...REDEMPTION AND FREEDOM.
COMING FROM YOU, BOTH ARE LAUGHABLE.
YOUR GOVERNMENT ANS TO INCARCERATE ALL OF YOU AS AN AMPLE OF YOUR EVIL, LAWBREAKING WAYS.
WHEN THE IME COMES, YOU LL WANT THE TWO THINGS THAT I OFFER...
...REDEMPTION THE EYES OF THE MERICAN PUBLIC... AND FREEDOM...

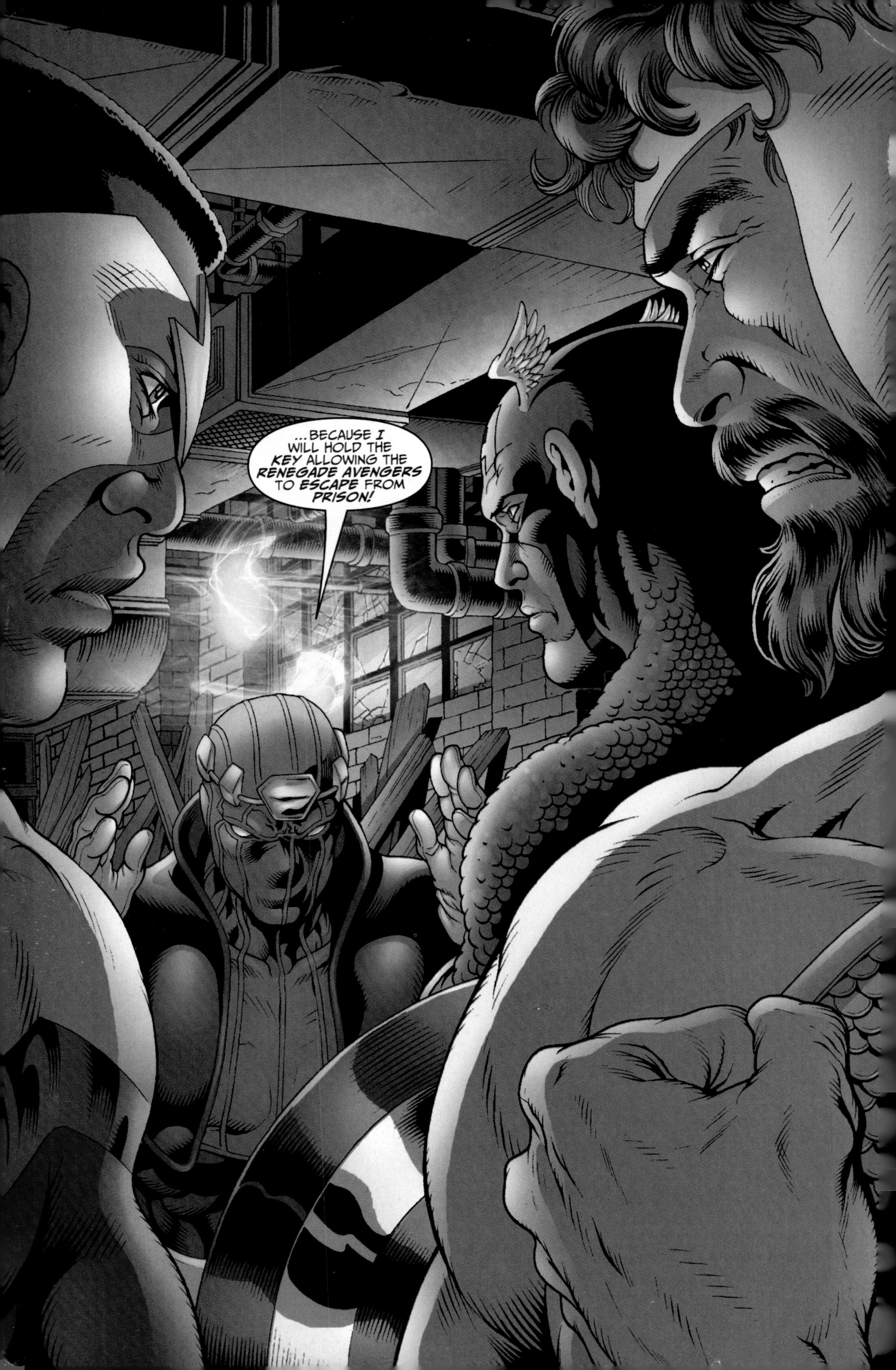
...BECAUSE *I* WILL HOLD THE *KEY* ALLOWING THE *RENEGADE AVENGERS* TO *ESCAPE* FROM *PRISON!*

THUNDERBOLTS
A MARVEL COMICS EVENT

CIVIL
WAR

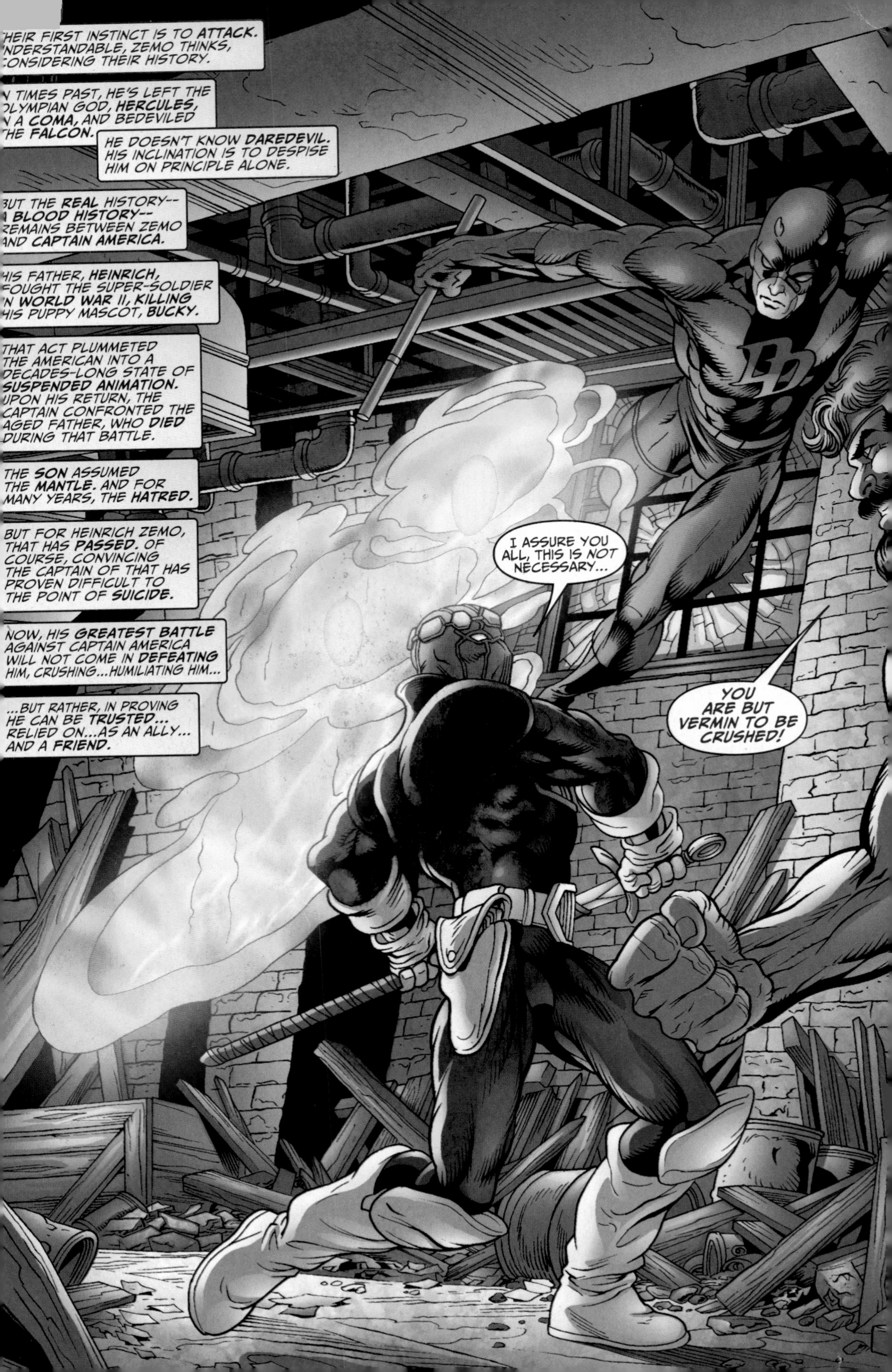
THEIR FIRST INSTINCT IS TO ATTACK. NDERSTANDABLE, ZEMO THINKS, CONSIDERING THEIR HISTORY.
N TIMES PAST, HE'S LEFT THE OLYMPIAN GOD, HERCULES, N A COMA, AND BEDEVILED THE FALCON.
HE DOESN'T KNOW DAREDEVIL. HIS INCLINATION IS TO DESPISE HIM ON PRINCIPLE ALONE.
BUT THE REAL HISTORY-- A BLOOD HISTORY-- REMAINS BETWEEN ZEMO AND CAPTAIN AMERICA.
HIS FATHER, HEINRICH, FOUGHT THE SUPER-SOLDIER N WORLD WAR II, KILLING HIS PUPPY MASCOT, BUCKY.
THAT ACT PLUMMETED THE AMERICAN INTO A DECADES-LONG STATE OF SUSPENDED ANIMATION. UPON HIS RETURN, THE CAPTAIN CONFRONTED THE AGED FATHER, WHO DIED DURING THAT BATTLE.
THE SON ASSUMED THE MANTLE. AND FOR MANY YEARS, THE HATRED.
BUT FOR HEINRICH ZEMO, THAT HAS PASSED. OF COURSE, CONVINCING THE CAPTAIN OF THAT HAS PROVEN DIFFICULT TO THE POINT OF SUICIDE.
NOW, HIS GREATEST BATTLE AGAINST CAPTAIN AMERICA WILL NOT COME IN DEFEATING HIM, CRUSHING...HUMILIATING HIM...
...BUT RATHER, IN PROVING HE CAN BE TRUSTED... RELIED ON...AS AN ALLY... AND A FRIEND.
I ASSURE YOU ALL, THIS IS NOT NECESSARY...
YOU ARE BUT VERMIN TO BE CRUSHED!

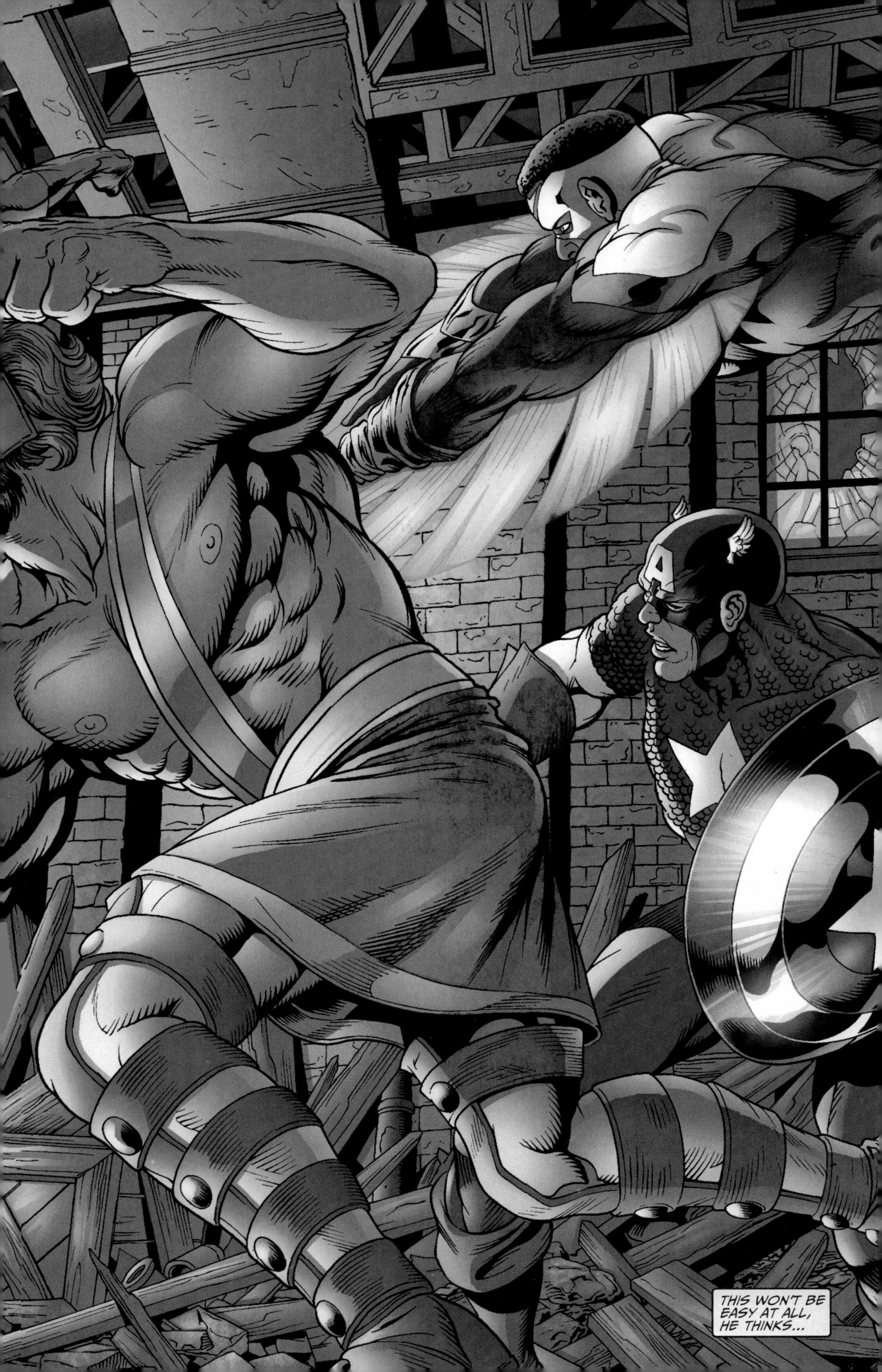
THIS WON'T BE EASY AT ALL, HE THINKS...

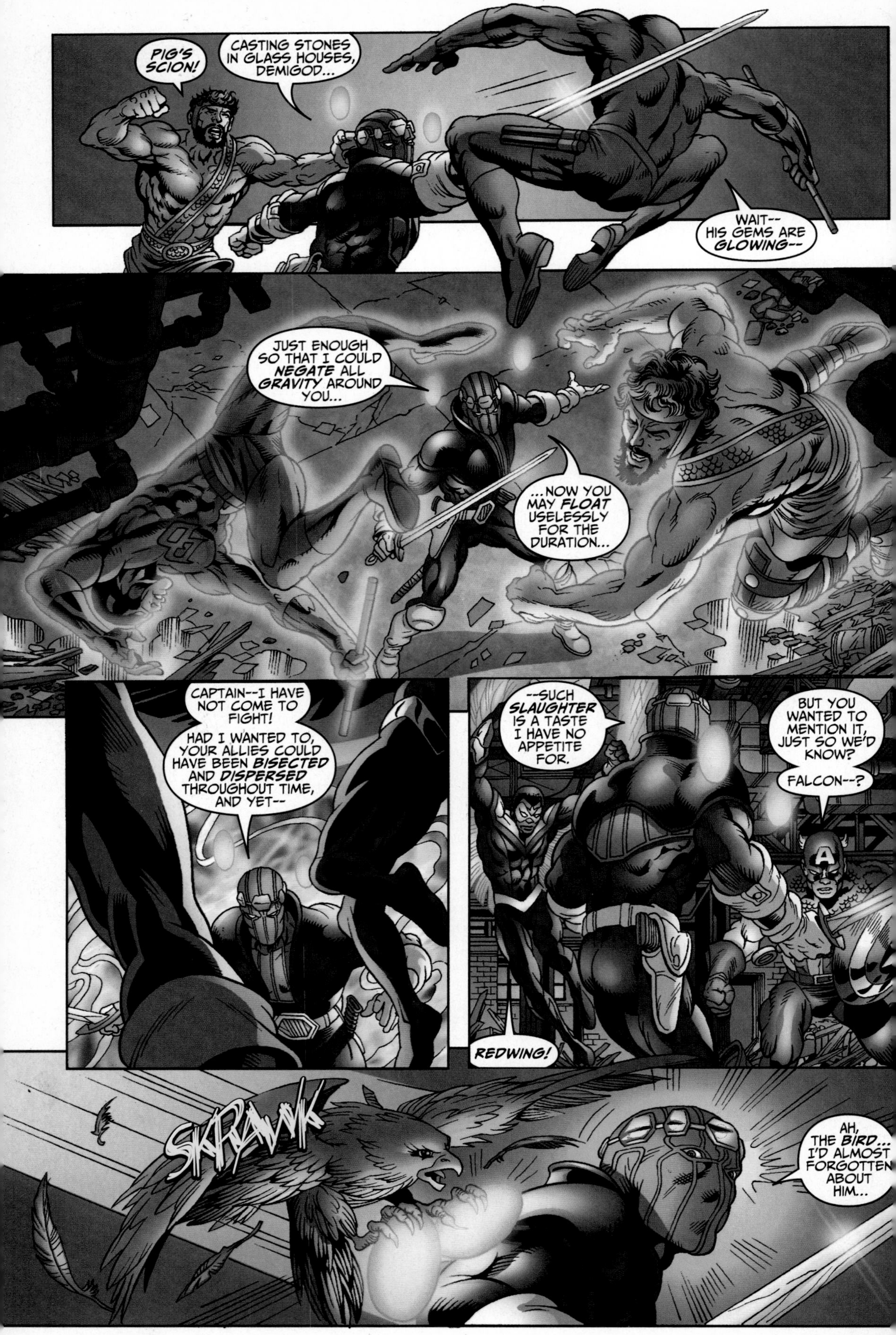
PIG'S SCION!
CASTING STONES IN GLASS HOUSES, DEMIGOD...
WAIT-- HIS GEMS ARE GLOWING--
JUST ENOUGH SO THAT I COULD NEGATE ALL GRAVITY AROUND YOU...
...NOW YOU MAY FLOAT USELESSLY FOR THE DURATION...
CAPTAIN--I HAVE NOT COME TO FIGHT!
HAD I WANTED TO, YOUR ALLIES COULD HAVE BEEN BISECTED AND DISPERSED THROUGHOUT TIME, AND YET--
--SUCH SLAUGHTER IS A TASTE I HAVE NO APPETITE FOR.
BUT YOU WANTED TO MENTION IT, JUST SO WE'D KNOW?
FALCON--?
REDWING!
SKRAWK
AH, THE BIRD... I'D ALMOST FORGOTTEN ABOUT HIM...

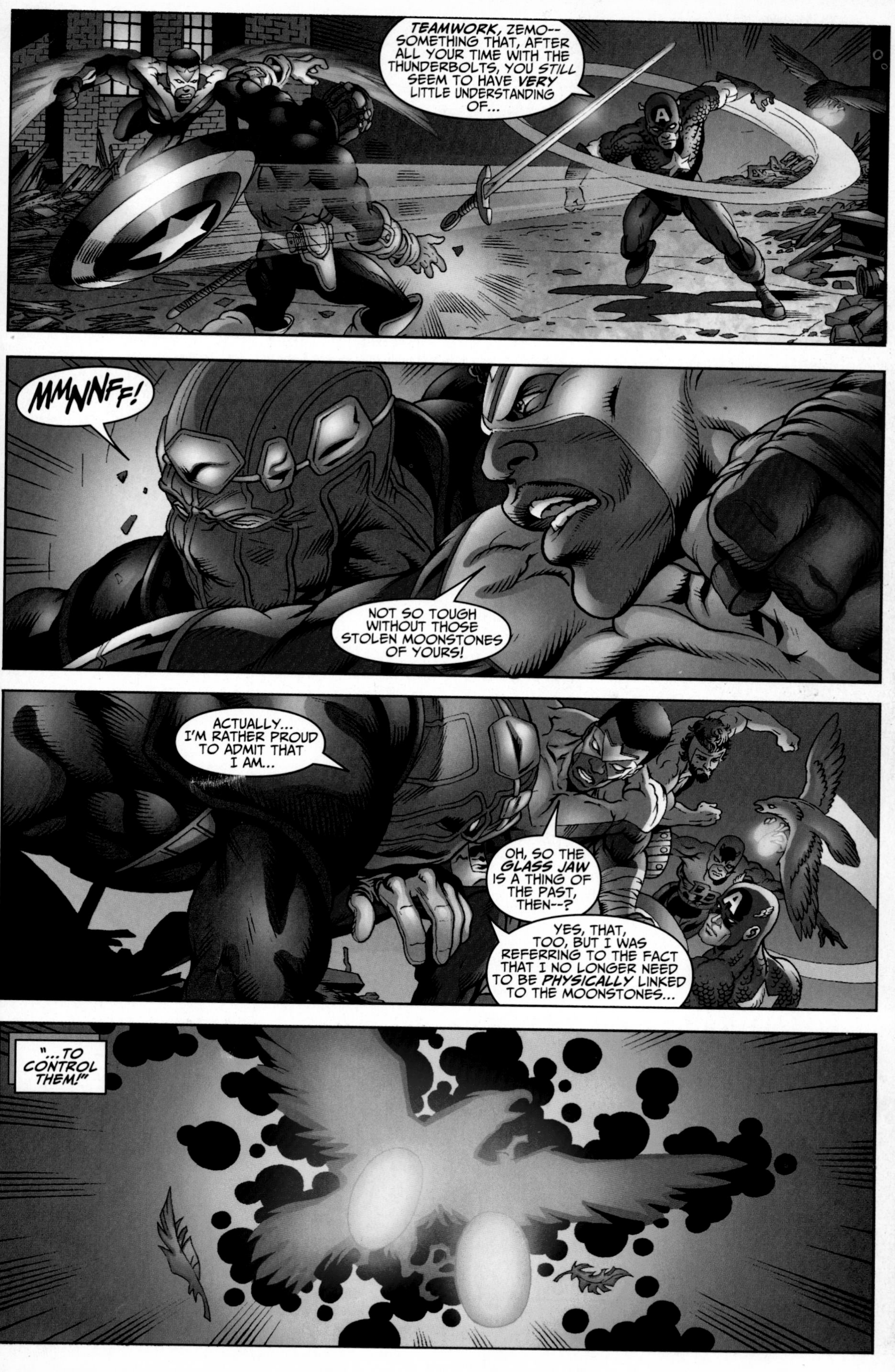
TEAMWORK, ZEMO-- SOMETHING THAT, AFTER ALL YOUR TIME WITH THE THUNDERBOLTS, YOU STILL SEEM TO HAVE VERY LITTLE UNDERSTANDING OF...
MMNNFF!
NOT SO TOUGH WITHOUT THOSE STOLEN MOONSTONES OF YOURS!
ACTUALLY... I'M RATHER PROUD TO ADMIT THAT I AM...
OH, SO THE GLASS JAW IS A THING OF THE PAST, THEN--?
YES, THAT, TOO, BUT I WAS REFERRING TO THE FACT THAT I NO LONGER NEED TO BE PHYSICALLY LINKED TO THE MOONSTONES...
"...TO CONTROL THEM!"

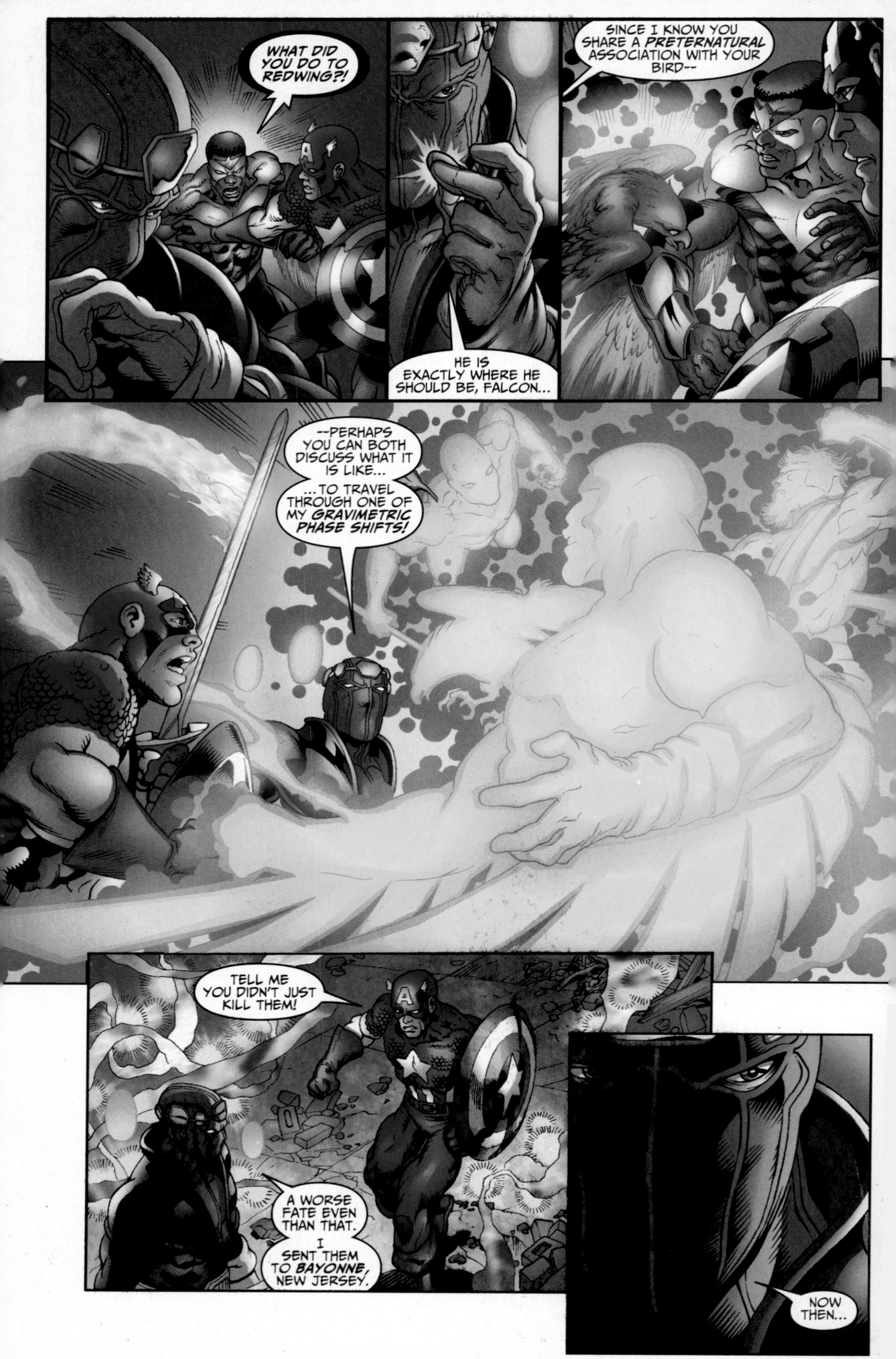
WHAT DID YOU DO TO REDWING?!
HE IS EXACTLY WHERE HE SHOULD BE, FALCON...
SINCE I KNOW YOU SHARE A PRETERNATURAL ASSOCIATION WITH YOUR BIRD--
--PERHAPS YOU CAN BOTH DISCUSS WHAT IT IS LIKE...
...TO TRAVEL THROUGH ONE OF MY GRAVIMETRIC PHASE SHIFTS!
TELL ME YOU DIDN'T JUST KILL THEM!
A WORSE FATE EVEN THAN THAT.
I SENT THEM TO BAYONNE, NEW JERSEY.
NOW THEN...

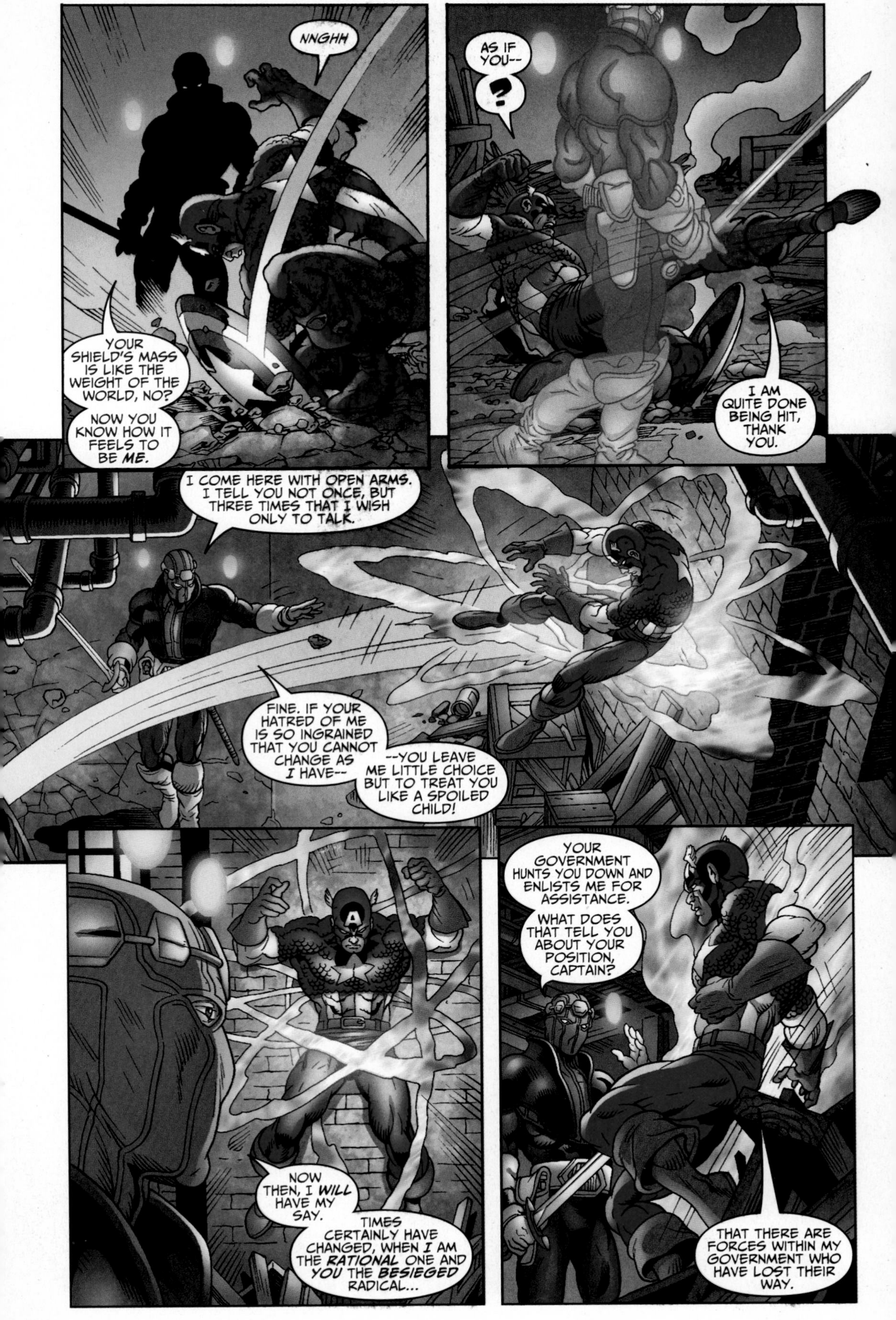
NNGHH
YOUR SHIELD'S MASS IS LIKE THE WEIGHT OF THE WORLD, NO?
NOW YOU KNOW HOW IT FEELS TO BE *ME*.
AS IF YOU--
?
I AM QUITE DONE BEING HIT, THANK YOU.
I COME HERE WITH OPEN *ARMS*. I TELL YOU NOT ONCE, BUT THREE TIMES THAT I WISH ONLY TO TALK.
FINE. IF YOUR HATRED OF ME IS SO INGRAINED THAT YOU CANNOT CHANGE AS *I* HAVE--
--YOU LEAVE ME LITTLE CHOICE BUT TO TREAT YOU LIKE A SPOILED CHILD!
NOW THEN, I *WILL* HAVE MY SAY.
TIMES CERTAINLY HAVE CHANGED, WHEN *I* AM THE *RATIONAL* ONE AND *YOU* THE *BESIEGED* RADICAL...
YOUR GOVERNMENT HUNTS YOU DOWN AND ENLISTS ME FOR ASSISTANCE.
WHAT DOES THAT TELL YOU ABOUT YOUR POSITION, CAPTAIN?
THAT THERE ARE FORCES WITHIN MY GOVERNMENT WHO HAVE LOST THEIR WAY.

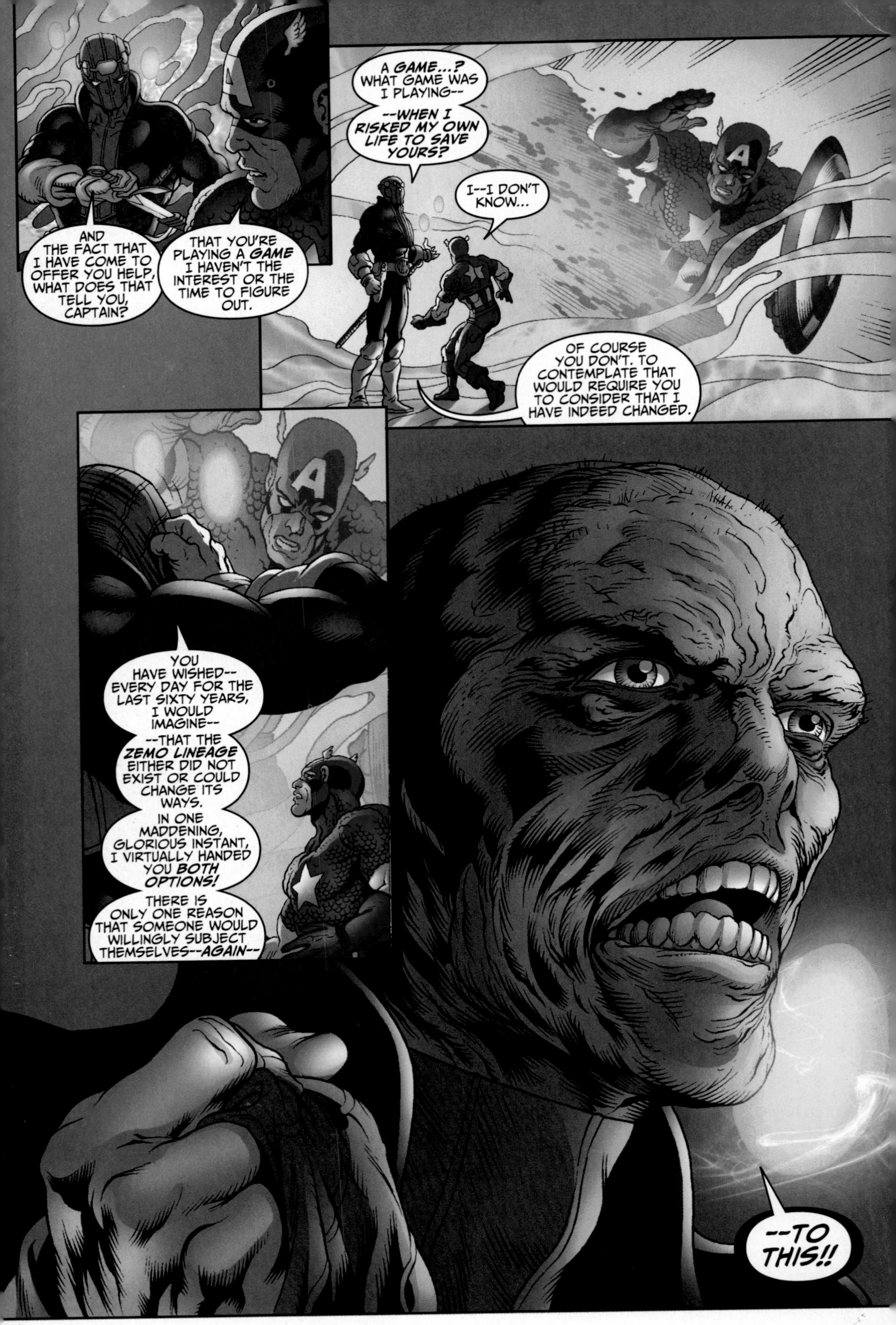
AND THE FACT THAT I HAVE COME TO OFFER YOU HELP, WHAT DOES THAT TELL YOU, CAPTAIN?
THAT YOU'RE PLAYING A *GAME* I HAVEN'T THE INTEREST OR THE TIME TO FIGURE OUT.
A *GAME...?* WHAT GAME WAS I PLAYING--
--WHEN I RISKED MY OWN LIFE TO SAVE YOURS?
I--I DON'T KNOW...
OF COURSE YOU DON'T. TO CONTEMPLATE THAT WOULD REQUIRE YOU TO CONSIDER THAT I HAVE INDEED CHANGED.
YOU HAVE WISHED-- EVERY DAY FOR THE LAST SIXTY YEARS, I WOULD IMAGINE--
--THAT THE *ZEMO LINEAGE* EITHER DID NOT EXIST OR COULD CHANGE ITS WAYS.
IN ONE MADDENING, GLORIOUS INSTANT, I VIRTUALLY HANDED YOU *BOTH OPTIONS!*
THERE IS ONLY ONE REASON THAT SOMEONE WOULD WILLINGLY SUBJECT THEMSELVES--*AGAIN*--
--TO THIS!!

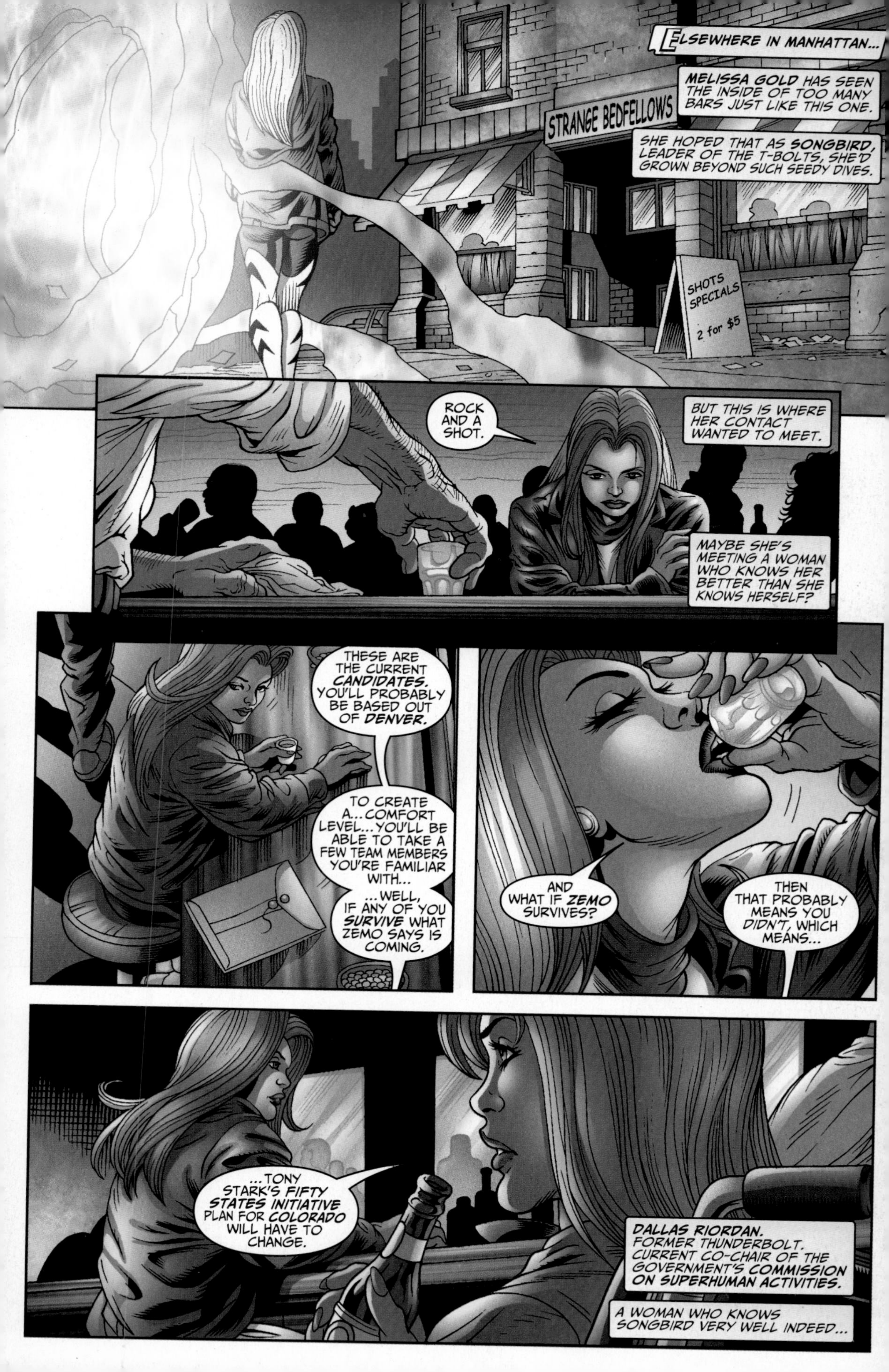
ELSEWHERE IN MANHATTAN...
MELISSA GOLD HAS SEEN THE INSIDE OF TOO MANY BARS JUST LIKE THIS ONE.
STRANGE BEDFELLOWS
SHE HOPED THAT AS SONGBIRD, LEADER OF THE T-BOLTS, SHE'D GROWN BEYOND SUCH SEEDY DIVES.
SHOTS SPECIALS 2 for $5
ROCK AND A SHOT.
BUT THIS IS WHERE HER CONTACT WANTED TO MEET.
MAYBE SHE'S MEETING A WOMAN WHO KNOWS HER BETTER THAN SHE KNOWS HERSELF?
THESE ARE THE CURRENT CANDIDATES. YOU'LL PROBABLY BE BASED OUT OF DENVER.
TO CREATE A...COMFORT LEVEL...YOU'LL BE ABLE TO TAKE A FEW TEAM MEMBERS YOU'RE FAMILIAR WITH...
...WELL, IF ANY OF YOU SURVIVE WHAT ZEMO SAYS IS COMING.
AND WHAT IF ZEMO SURVIVES?
THEN THAT PROBABLY MEANS YOU DIDN'T, WHICH MEANS...
...TONY STARK'S FIFTY STATES INITIATIVE PLAN FOR COLORADO WILL HAVE TO CHANGE.
DALLAS RIORDAN. FORMER THUNDERBOLT. CURRENT CO-CHAIR OF THE GOVERNMENT'S COMMISSION ON SUPERHUMAN ACTIVITIES.
A WOMAN WHO KNOWS SONGBIRD VERY WELL INDEED...

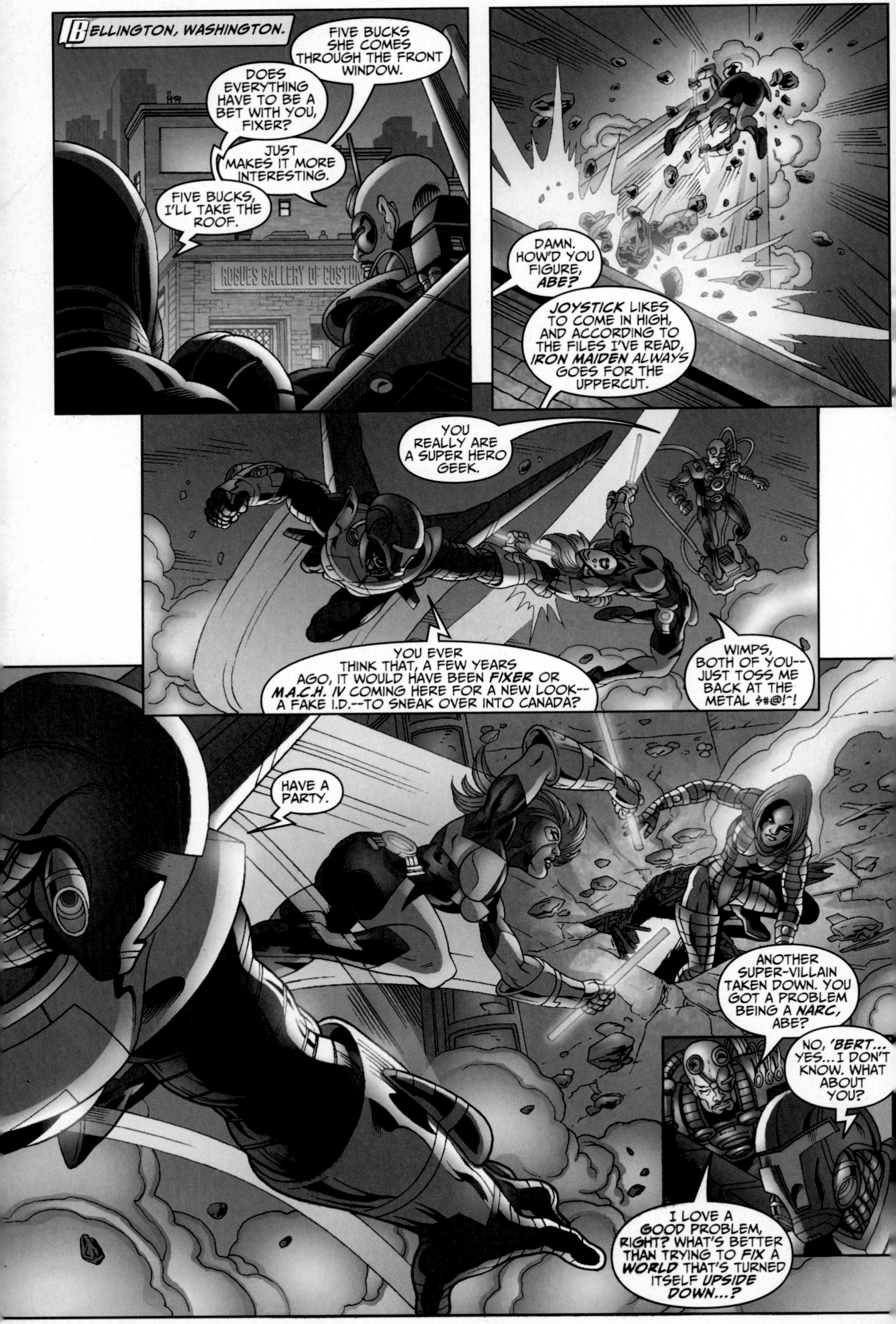
BELLINGTON, WASHINGTON.
FIVE BUCKS SHE COMES THROUGH THE FRONT WINDOW.
DOES EVERYTHING HAVE TO BE A BET WITH YOU, FIXER?
JUST MAKES IT MORE INTERESTING.
FIVE BUCKS, I'LL TAKE THE ROOF.
ROGUES GALLERY OF COSTUM
DAMN. HOW'D YOU FIGURE, ABE?
JOYSTICK LIKES TO COME IN HIGH, AND ACCORDING TO THE FILES I'VE READ, IRON MAIDEN ALWAYS GOES FOR THE UPPERCUT.
YOU REALLY ARE A SUPER HERO GEEK.
YOU EVER THINK THAT, A FEW YEARS AGO, IT WOULD HAVE BEEN FIXER OR M.A.C.H. IV COMING HERE FOR A NEW LOOK--A FAKE I.D.--TO SNEAK OVER INTO CANADA?
WIMPS, BOTH OF YOU--JUST TOSS ME BACK AT THE METAL $#@!~!
HAVE A PARTY.
ANOTHER SUPER-VILLAIN TAKEN DOWN. YOU GOT A PROBLEM BEING A NARC, ABE?
NO, 'BERT... YES...I DON'T KNOW. WHAT ABOUT YOU?
I LOVE A GOOD PROBLEM, RIGHT? WHAT'S BETTER THAN TRYING TO FIX A WORLD THAT'S TURNED ITSELF UPSIDE DOWN...?

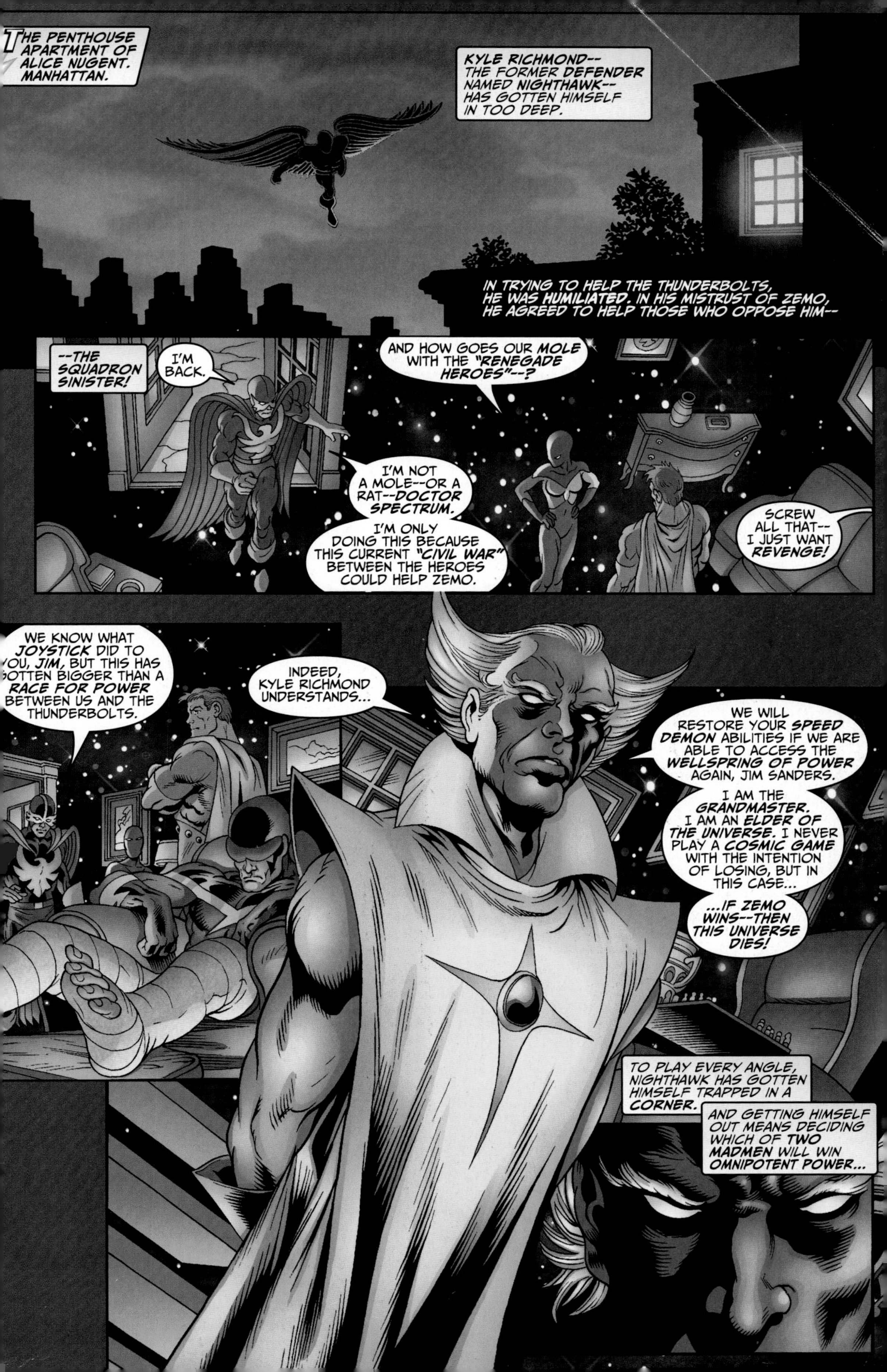
THE PENTHOUSE APARTMENT OF ALICE NUGENT. MANHATTAN.
KYLE RICHMOND-- THE FORMER DEFENDER NAMED NIGHTHAWK-- HAS GOTTEN HIMSELF IN TOO DEEP.
IN TRYING TO HELP THE THUNDERBOLTS, HE WAS HUMILIATED. IN HIS MISTRUST OF ZEMO, HE AGREED TO HELP THOSE WHO OPPOSE HIM--
--THE SQUADRON SINISTER!
I'M BACK.
AND HOW GOES OUR MOLE WITH THE "RENEGADE HEROES"--?
I'M NOT A MOLE--OR A RAT--DOCTOR SPECTRUM.
I'M ONLY DOING THIS BECAUSE THIS CURRENT "CIVIL WAR" BETWEEN THE HEROES COULD HELP ZEMO.
SCREW ALL THAT-- I JUST WANT REVENGE!
WE KNOW WHAT JOYSTICK DID TO YOU, JIM, BUT THIS HAS GOTTEN BIGGER THAN A RACE FOR POWER BETWEEN US AND THE THUNDERBOLTS.
INDEED, KYLE RICHMOND UNDERSTANDS...
WE WILL RESTORE YOUR SPEED DEMON ABILITIES IF WE ARE ABLE TO ACCESS THE WELLSPRING OF POWER AGAIN, JIM SANDERS.
I AM THE GRANDMASTER. I AM AN ELDER OF THE UNIVERSE. I NEVER PLAY A COSMIC GAME WITH THE INTENTION OF LOSING, BUT IN THIS CASE...
...IF ZEMO WINS--THEN THIS UNIVERSE DIES!
TO PLAY EVERY ANGLE, NIGHTHAWK HAS GOTTEN HIMSELF TRAPPED IN A CORNER.
AND GETTING HIMSELF OUT MEANS DECIDING WHICH OF TWO MADMEN WILL WIN OMNIPOTENT POWER...

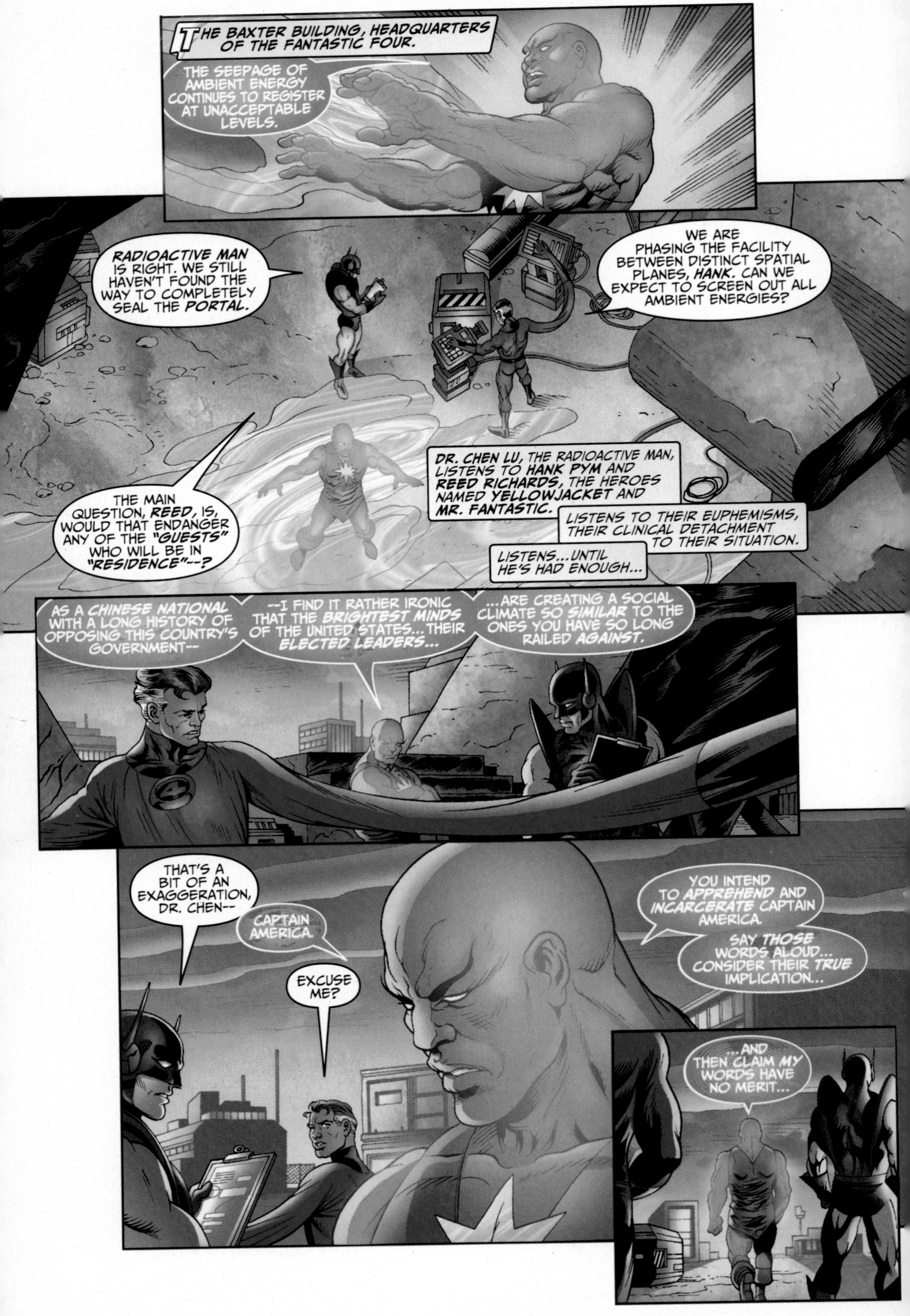
THE BAXTER BUILDING, HEADQUARTERS OF THE FANTASTIC FOUR.
THE SEEPAGE OF AMBIENT ENERGY CONTINUES TO REGISTER AT UNACCEPTABLE LEVELS.
RADIOACTIVE MAN IS RIGHT. WE STILL HAVEN'T FOUND THE WAY TO COMPLETELY SEAL THE PORTAL.
WE ARE PHASING THE FACILITY BETWEEN DISTINCT SPATIAL PLANES, HANK. CAN WE EXPECT TO SCREEN OUT ALL AMBIENT ENERGIES?
THE MAIN QUESTION, REED, IS, WOULD THAT ENDANGER ANY OF THE "GUESTS" WHO WILL BE IN "RESIDENCE"--?
DR. CHEN LU, THE RADIOACTIVE MAN, LISTENS TO HANK PYM AND REED RICHARDS, THE HEROES NAMED YELLOWJACKET AND MR. FANTASTIC.
LISTENS TO THEIR EUPHEMISMS, THEIR CLINICAL DETACHMENT TO THEIR SITUATION.
LISTENS...UNTIL HE'S HAD ENOUGH...
AS A CHINESE NATIONAL WITH A LONG HISTORY OF OPPOSING THIS COUNTRY'S GOVERNMENT--
--I FIND IT RATHER IRONIC THAT THE BRIGHTEST MINDS OF THE UNITED STATES...THEIR ELECTED LEADERS...
...ARE CREATING A SOCIAL CLIMATE SO SIMILAR TO THE ONES YOU HAVE SO LONG RAILED AGAINST.
THAT'S A BIT OF AN EXAGGERATION, DR. CHEN--
CAPTAIN AMERICA.
EXCUSE ME?
YOU INTEND TO APPREHEND AND INCARCERATE CAPTAIN AMERICA.
SAY THOSE WORDS ALOUD... CONSIDER THEIR TRUE IMPLICATION...
...AND THEN CLAIM MY WORDS HAVE NO MERIT...

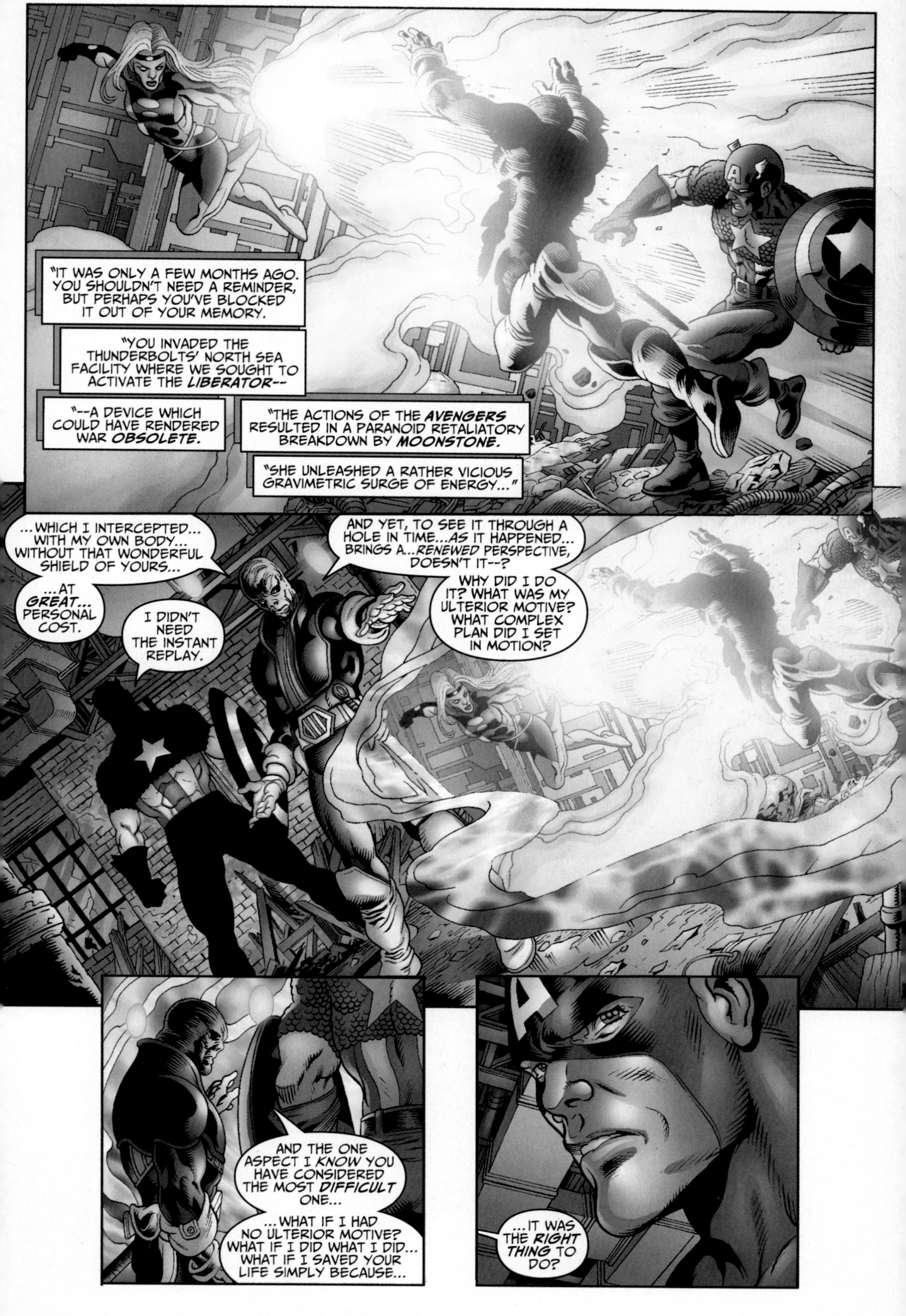
"IT WAS ONLY A FEW MONTHS AGO. YOU SHOULDN'T NEED A REMINDER, BUT PERHAPS YOU'VE BLOCKED IT OUT OF YOUR MEMORY.
"YOU INVADED THE THUNDERBOLTS' NORTH SEA FACILITY WHERE WE SOUGHT TO ACTIVATE THE *LIBERATOR*--
"--A DEVICE WHICH COULD HAVE RENDERED WAR *OBSOLETE.*
"THE ACTIONS OF THE *AVENGERS* RESULTED IN A PARANOID RETALIATORY BREAKDOWN BY *MOONSTONE.*
"SHE UNLEASHED A RATHER VICIOUS GRAVIMETRIC SURGE OF ENERGY..."
...WHICH I INTERCEPTED... WITH MY OWN BODY... WITHOUT THAT WONDERFUL SHIELD OF YOURS...
...AT *GREAT*... PERSONAL COST.
I DIDN'T NEED THE INSTANT REPLAY.
AND YET, TO SEE IT THROUGH A HOLE IN TIME...*AS* IT HAPPENED... BRINGS A...*RENEWED* PERSPECTIVE, DOESN'T IT--?
WHY DID I DO IT? WHAT WAS MY ULTERIOR MOTIVE? WHAT COMPLEX PLAN DID I SET IN MOTION?
AND THE ONE ASPECT I *KNOW* YOU HAVE CONSIDERED THE MOST *DIFFICULT* ONE...
...WHAT IF I HAD NO ULTERIOR MOTIVE? WHAT IF I DID WHAT I DID... WHAT IF I SAVED YOUR LIFE SIMPLY BECAUSE...
...IT WAS THE *RIGHT THING* TO DO?

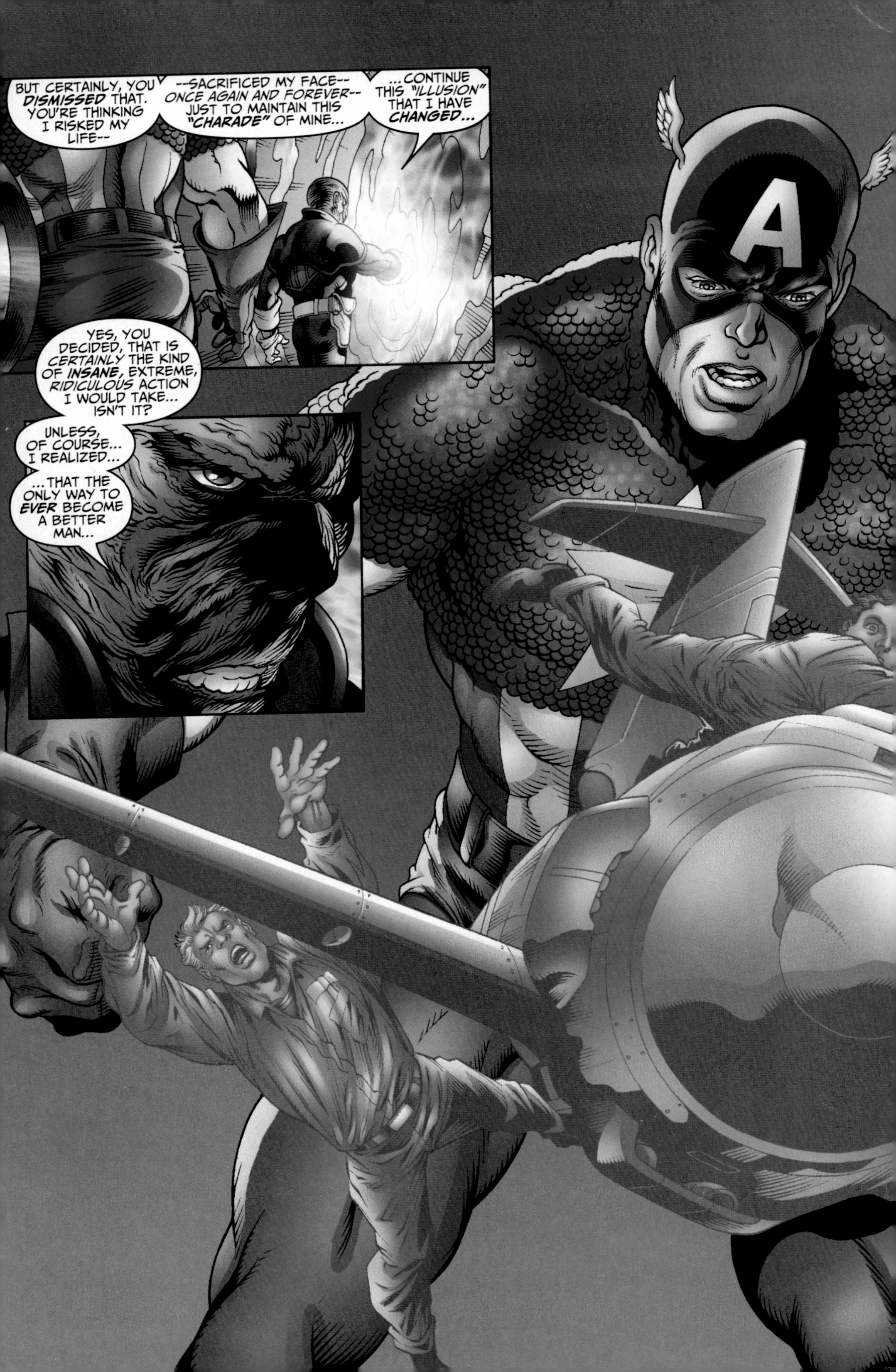
BUT CERTAINLY, YOU DISMISSED THAT. YOU'RE THINKING I RISKED MY LIFE--
--SACRIFICED MY FACE-- ONCE AGAIN AND FOREVER-- JUST TO MAINTAIN THIS "CHARADE" OF MINE...
...CONTINUE THIS "ILLUSION" THAT I HAVE CHANGED...
YES, YOU DECIDED, THAT IS CERTAINLY THE KIND OF INSANE, EXTREME, RIDICULOUS ACTION I WOULD TAKE... ISN'T IT?
UNLESS, OF COURSE... I REALIZED...
...THAT THE ONLY WAY TO EVER BECOME A BETTER MAN...

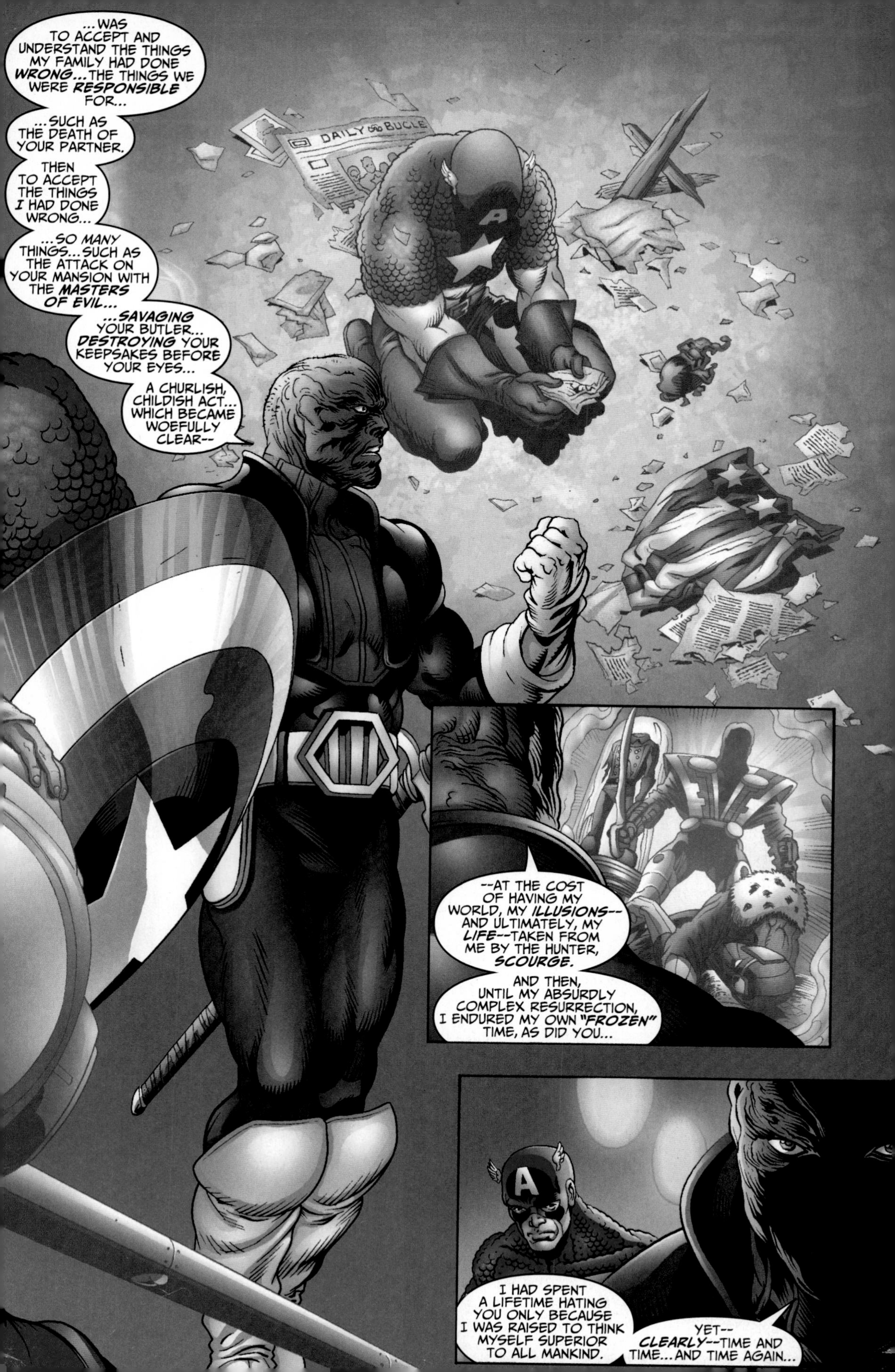
...WAS TO ACCEPT AND UNDERSTAND THE THINGS MY FAMILY HAD DONE WRONG... THE THINGS WE WERE RESPONSIBLE FOR...
...SUCH AS THE DEATH OF YOUR PARTNER.
THEN TO ACCEPT THE THINGS I HAD DONE WRONG...
...SO MANY THINGS... SUCH AS THE ATTACK ON YOUR MANSION WITH THE MASTERS OF EVIL...
...SAVAGING YOUR BUTLER... DESTROYING YOUR KEEPSAKES BEFORE YOUR EYES...
A CHURLISH, CHILDISH ACT... WHICH BECAME WOEFULLY CLEAR--
--AT THE COST OF HAVING MY WORLD, MY ILLUSIONS-- AND ULTIMATELY, MY LIFE--TAKEN FROM ME BY THE HUNTER, SCOURGE.
AND THEN, UNTIL MY ABSURDLY COMPLEX RESURRECTION, I ENDURED MY OWN "FROZEN" TIME, AS DID YOU...
I HAD SPENT A LIFETIME HATING YOU ONLY BECAUSE I WAS RAISED TO THINK MYSELF SUPERIOR TO ALL MANKIND.
YET-- CLEARLY--TIME AND TIME... AND TIME AGAIN...

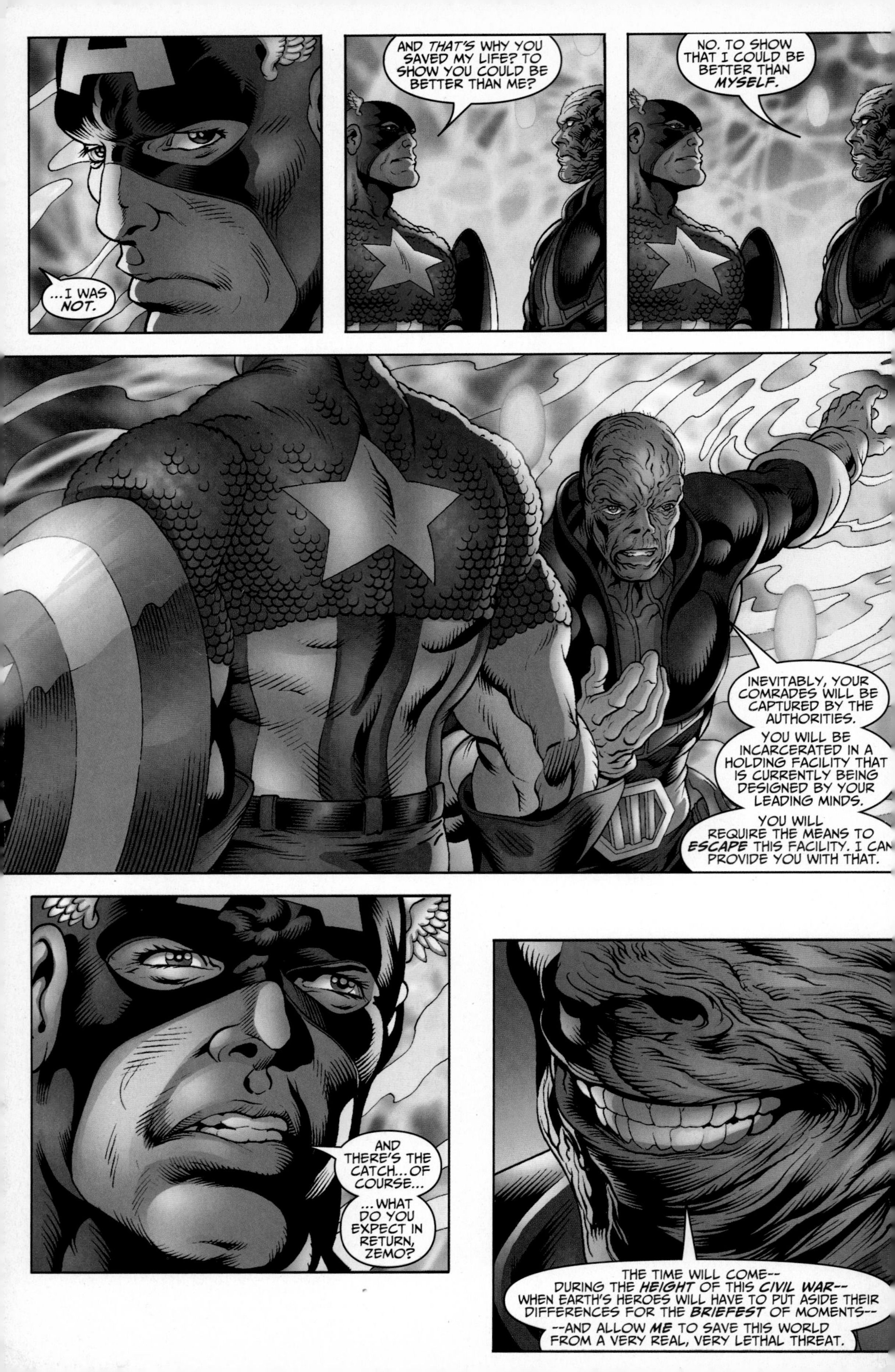

...I WAS NOT.
AND THAT'S WHY YOU SAVED MY LIFE? TO SHOW YOU COULD BE BETTER THAN ME?
NO. TO SHOW THAT I COULD BE BETTER THAN MYSELF.
INEVITABLY, YOUR COMRADES WILL BE CAPTURED BY THE AUTHORITIES.
YOU WILL BE INCARCERATED IN A HOLDING FACILITY THAT IS CURRENTLY BEING DESIGNED BY YOUR LEADING MINDS.
YOU WILL REQUIRE THE MEANS TO ESCAPE THIS FACILITY. I CAN PROVIDE YOU WITH THAT.
AND THERE'S THE CATCH...OF COURSE...
...WHAT DO YOU EXPECT IN RETURN, ZEMO?
THE TIME WILL COME-- DURING THE HEIGHT OF THIS CIVIL WAR-- WHEN EARTH'S HEROES WILL HAVE TO PUT ASIDE THEIR DIFFERENCES FOR THE BRIEFEST OF MOMENTS--
--AND ALLOW ME TO SAVE THIS WORLD FROM A VERY REAL, VERY LETHAL THREAT.

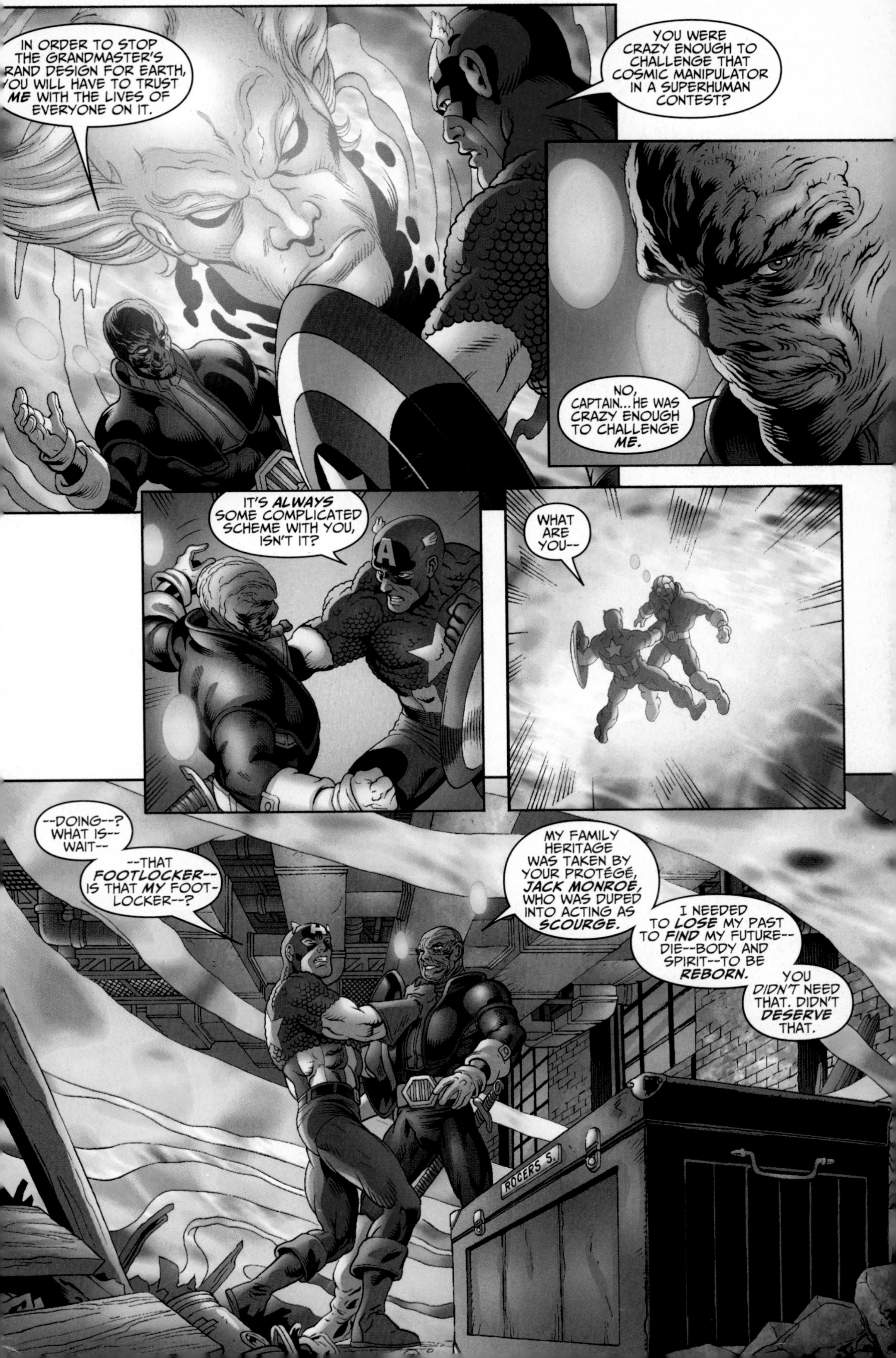
IN ORDER TO STOP THE GRANDMASTER'S GRAND DESIGN FOR EARTH, YOU WILL HAVE TO TRUST ME WITH THE LIVES OF EVERYONE ON IT.
YOU WERE CRAZY ENOUGH TO CHALLENGE THAT COSMIC MANIPULATOR IN A SUPERHUMAN CONTEST?
NO, CAPTAIN... HE WAS CRAZY ENOUGH TO CHALLENGE ME.
IT'S ALWAYS SOME COMPLICATED SCHEME WITH YOU, ISN'T IT?
WHAT ARE YOU--
--DOING--? WHAT IS-- WAIT--
--THAT FOOTLOCKER-- IS THAT MY FOOTLOCKER--?
MY FAMILY HERITAGE WAS TAKEN BY YOUR PROTÉGÉ, JACK MONROE, WHO WAS DUPED INTO ACTING AS SCOURGE.
I NEEDED TO LOSE MY PAST TO FIND MY FUTURE-- DIE--BODY AND SPIRIT--TO BE REBORN.
YOU DIDN'T NEED THAT. DIDN'T DESERVE THAT.
ROGERS S.

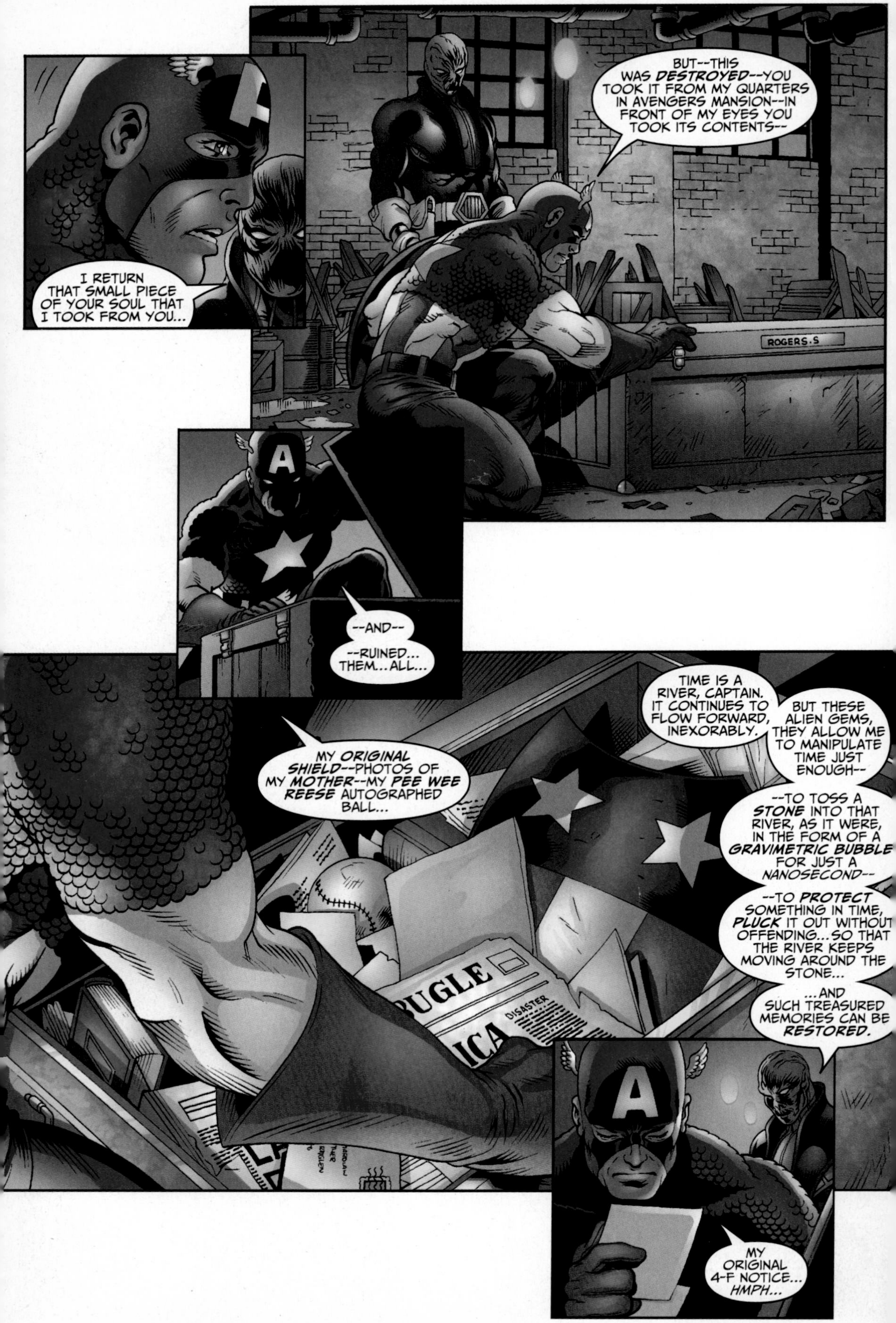
I RETURN THAT SMALL PIECE OF YOUR SOUL THAT I TOOK FROM YOU...
BUT--THIS WAS DESTROYED--YOU TOOK IT FROM MY QUARTERS IN AVENGERS MANSION--IN FRONT OF MY EYES YOU TOOK ITS CONTENTS--
ROGERS.S
--AND--
--RUINED... THEM... ALL...
MY ORIGINAL SHIELD--PHOTOS OF MY MOTHER--MY PEE WEE REESE AUTOGRAPHED BALL...
TIME IS A RIVER, CAPTAIN. IT CONTINUES TO FLOW FORWARD, INEXORABLY.
BUT THESE ALIEN GEMS, THEY ALLOW ME TO MANIPULATE TIME JUST ENOUGH--
--TO TOSS A STONE INTO THAT RIVER, AS IT WERE, IN THE FORM OF A GRAVIMETRIC BUBBLE FOR JUST A NANOSECOND--
--TO PROTECT SOMETHING IN TIME, PLUCK IT OUT WITHOUT OFFENDING... SO THAT THE RIVER KEEPS MOVING AROUND THE STONE...
...AND SUCH TREASURED MEMORIES CAN BE RESTORED.
BUGLE
DISASTER
ICA
MY ORIGINAL 4-F NOTICE... HMPH...

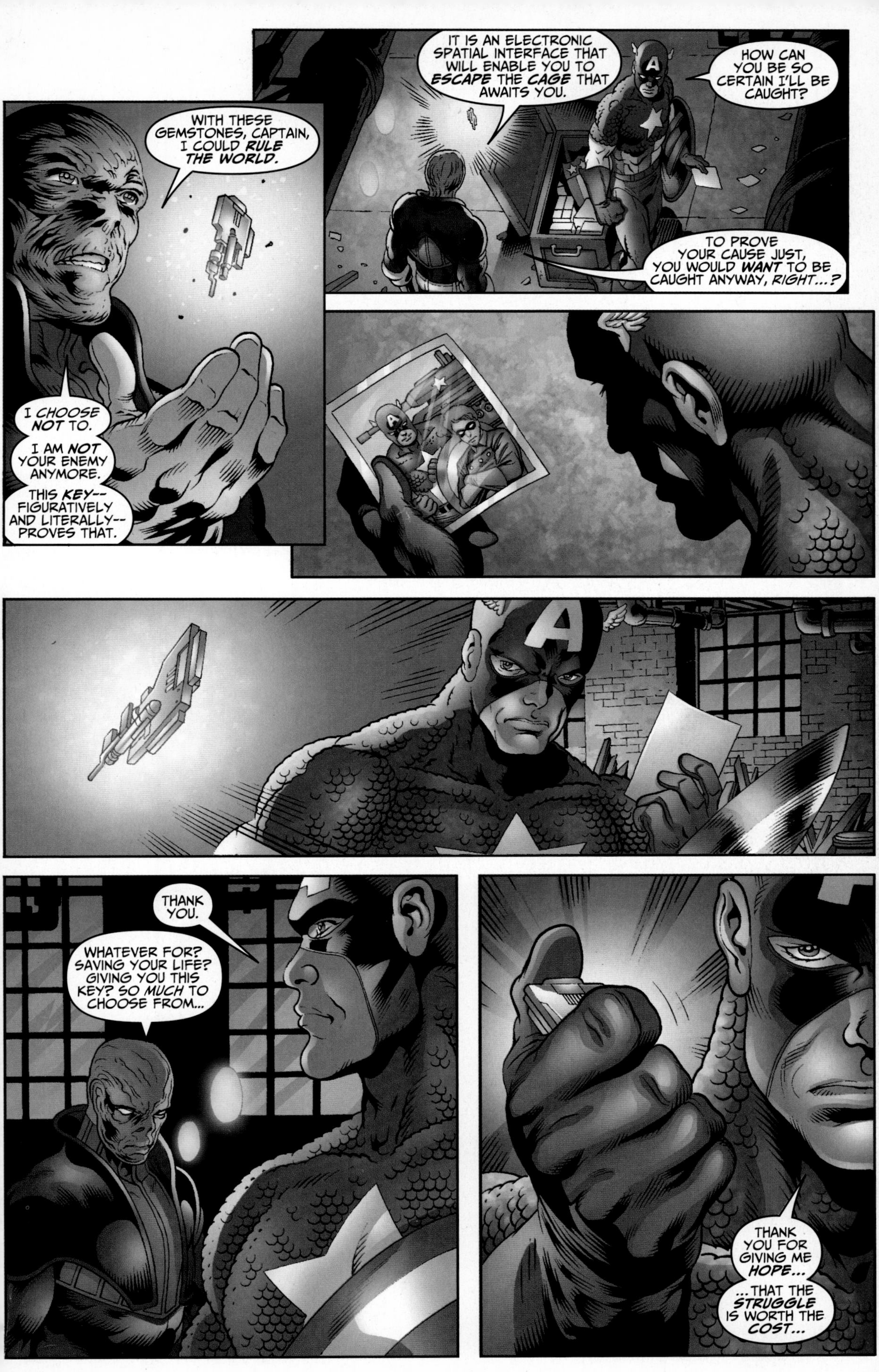

WITH THESE GEMSTONES, CAPTAIN, I COULD RULE THE WORLD.
I CHOOSE NOT TO.
I AM NOT YOUR ENEMY ANYMORE.
THIS KEY-- FIGURATIVELY AND LITERALLY-- PROVES THAT.
IT IS AN ELECTRONIC SPATIAL INTERFACE THAT WILL ENABLE YOU TO ESCAPE THE CAGE THAT AWAITS YOU.
HOW CAN YOU BE SO CERTAIN I'LL BE CAUGHT?
TO PROVE YOUR CAUSE JUST, YOU WOULD WANT TO BE CAUGHT ANYWAY, RIGHT...?
THANK YOU.
WHATEVER FOR? SAVING YOUR LIFE? GIVING YOU THIS KEY? SO MUCH TO CHOOSE FROM...
THANK YOU FOR GIVING ME HOPE...
...THAT THE STRUGGLE IS WORTH THE COST...

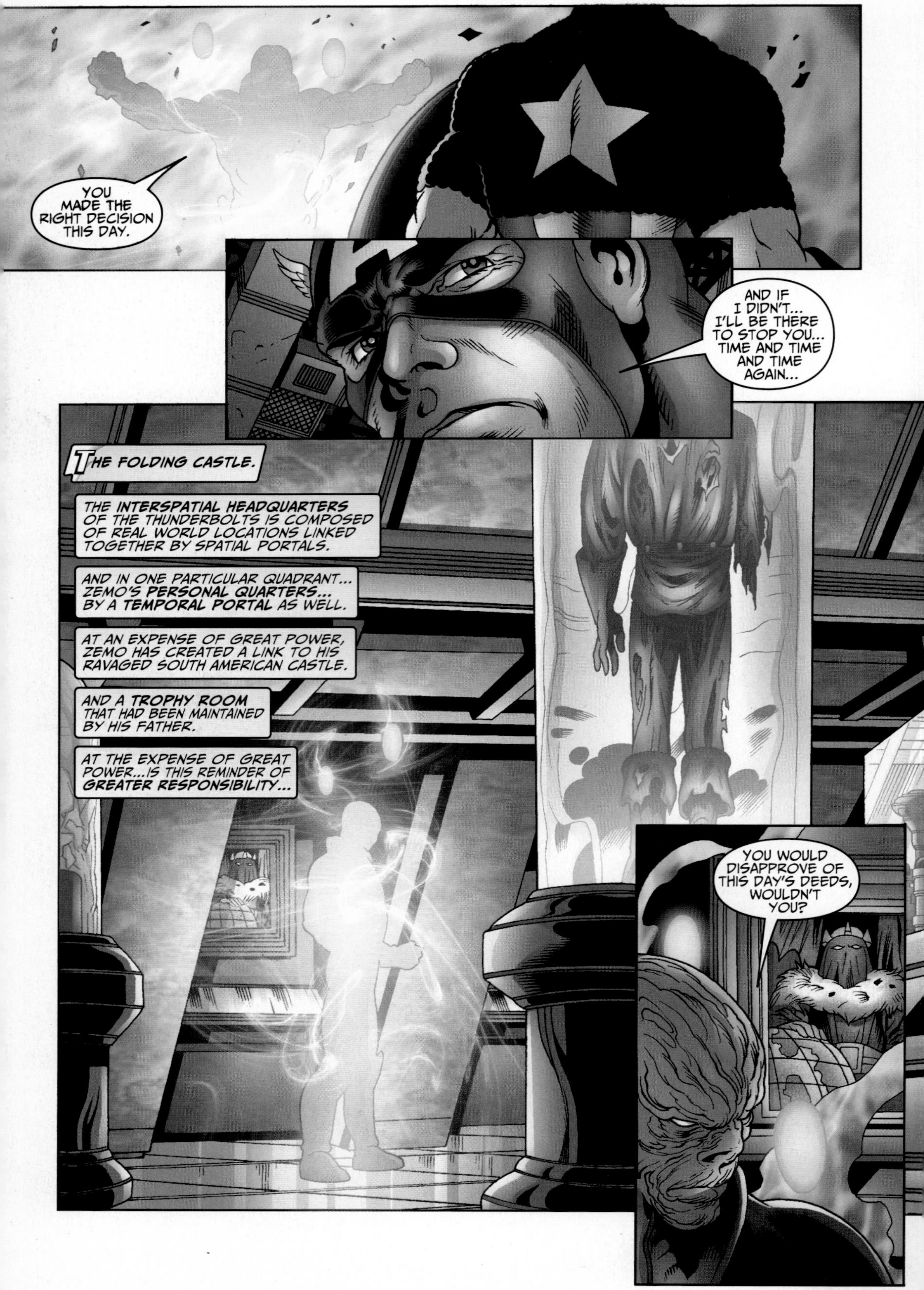
YOU MADE THE RIGHT DECISION THIS DAY.
AND IF I DIDN'T... I'LL BE THERE TO STOP YOU... TIME AND TIME AND TIME AGAIN...
THE FOLDING CASTLE.
THE INTERSPATIAL HEADQUARTERS OF THE THUNDERBOLTS IS COMPOSED OF REAL WORLD LOCATIONS LINKED TOGETHER BY SPATIAL PORTALS.
AND IN ONE PARTICULAR QUADRANT... ZEMO'S PERSONAL QUARTERS... BY A TEMPORAL PORTAL AS WELL.
AT AN EXPENSE OF GREAT POWER, ZEMO HAS CREATED A LINK TO HIS RAVAGED SOUTH AMERICAN CASTLE.
AND A TROPHY ROOM THAT HAD BEEN MAINTAINED BY HIS FATHER.
AT THE EXPENSE OF GREAT POWER...IS THIS REMINDER OF GREATER RESPONSIBILITY...
YOU WOULD DISAPPROVE OF THIS DAY'S DEEDS, WOULDN'T YOU?

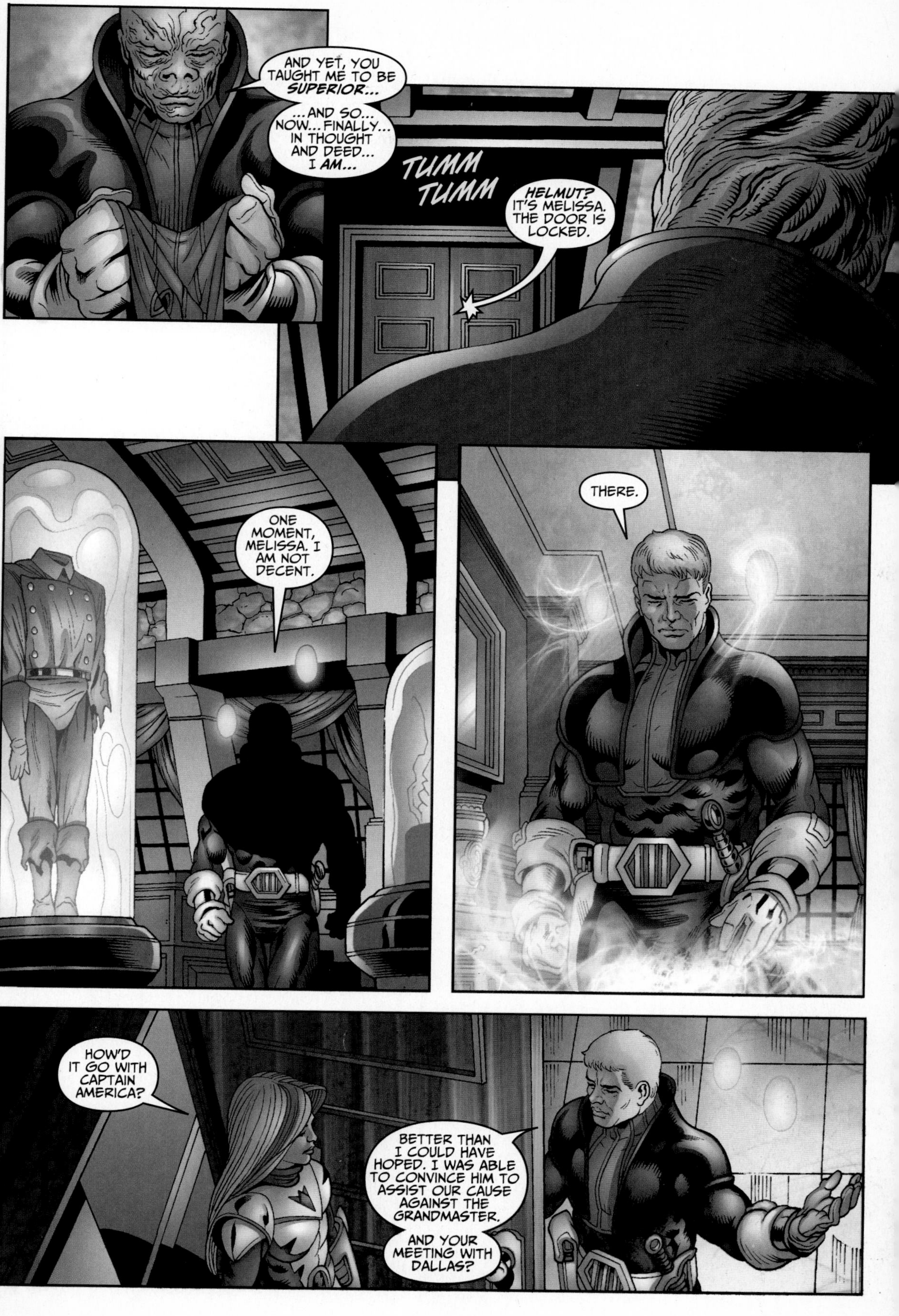
AND YET, YOU TAUGHT ME TO BE SUPERIOR...
...AND SO... NOW... FINALLY... IN THOUGHT AND DEED... I AM...
TUMM TUMM
HELMUT? IT'S MELISSA. THE DOOR IS LOCKED.
ONE MOMENT, MELISSA. I AM NOT DECENT.
THERE.
HOW'D IT GO WITH CAPTAIN AMERICA?
BETTER THAN I COULD HAVE HOPED. I WAS ABLE TO CONVINCE HIM TO ASSIST OUR CAUSE AGAINST THE GRANDMASTER.
AND YOUR MEETING WITH DALLAS?

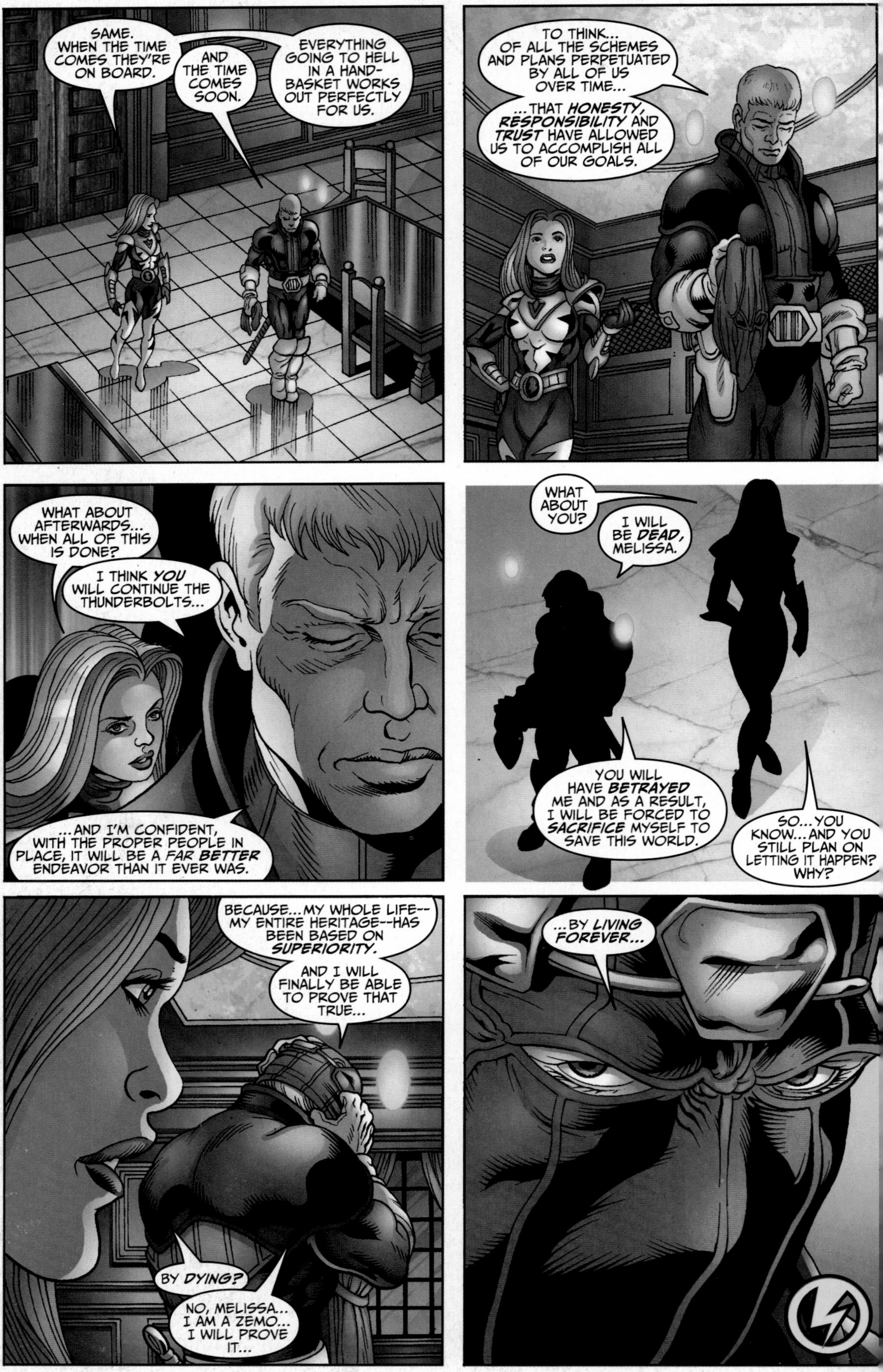
SAME. WHEN THE TIME COMES THEY'RE ON BOARD.
AND THE TIME COMES SOON.
EVERYTHING GOING TO HELL IN A HAND-BASKET WORKS OUT PERFECTLY FOR US.
TO THINK... OF ALL THE SCHEMES AND PLANS PERPETUATED BY ALL OF US OVER TIME...
...THAT HONESTY, RESPONSIBILITY AND TRUST HAVE ALLOWED US TO ACCOMPLISH ALL OF OUR GOALS.
WHAT ABOUT AFTERWARDS... WHEN ALL OF THIS IS DONE?
I THINK YOU WILL CONTINUE THE THUNDERBOLTS...
...AND I'M CONFIDENT, WITH THE PROPER PEOPLE IN PLACE, IT WILL BE A FAR BETTER ENDEAVOR THAN IT EVER WAS.
WHAT ABOUT YOU?
I WILL BE DEAD, MELISSA.
YOU WILL HAVE BETRAYED ME AND AS A RESULT, I WILL BE FORCED TO SACRIFICE MYSELF TO SAVE THIS WORLD.
SO...YOU KNOW...AND YOU STILL PLAN ON LETTING IT HAPPEN? WHY?
BECAUSE...MY WHOLE LIFE--MY ENTIRE HERITAGE--HAS BEEN BASED ON SUPERIORITY.
AND I WILL FINALLY BE ABLE TO PROVE THAT TRUE...
BY DYING?
NO, MELISSA... I AM A ZEMO... I WILL PROVE IT...
...BY LIVING FOREVER...

HISTORY: The Squadron Sinister is a primarily criminal alliance of super-beings assembled in the Earth-616 reality in imitation of the Squadron Supreme, the leading heroes in the alternate Earth-712 reality. Over the years, both Squadrons have had similarly-powered, similarly-costumed members operating under costumed identities which originated with four of the Squadron Supreme's founders: the seemingly extraterrestrial strongman Hyperion (actually the last known survivor of Earth-712's Eternals), the nocturnal vigilante Nighthawk (Earth-712's Kyle Richmond), the super-swift Whizzer (Stan Stewart) and Doctor Spectrum (Joe Ledger), who wielded an energy-manipulating crystal prism given to him by the alien Skrull Skymax (later the Skrullian Skymaster).

Over a decade ago, Earth-712 was visited by reality-616's Grandmaster, an Elder of the Universe and cosmic-powered compulsive gamesman. Grandmaster used Earth-712's Squadron Supreme as his pawns in a game played with that reality's Scarlet Centurion, pitting the Squadron against the Centurion's super-criminal Institute of Evil. The Squadron Supreme triumphed, and an impressed Grandmaster hoped to employ them as his permanent champions, but they were unwilling, and the Grandmaster departed without them.

Later, Grandmaster visited the alternate future kingdom of Kang the Conqueror (a divergent counterpart of the Scarlet Centurion) and challenged him to a contest of champions: the Game of the Galaxies. If Kang won, he would be granted the power over life and death, which he needed to revive his near-dead love Ravonna. If Grandmaster won, Kang and Earth would be destroyed. Seeking champions, Kang recruited his old foes the Avengers, the leading superheroes of Earth-616's modern era. Remembering his success with the Squadron Supreme, Grandmaster decided to create his own Earth-616 version of the Squadron Supreme to battle the Avengers.

Traveling into Earth-616's recent past, the Grandmaster empowered chemist James Sanders and millionaire playboy Kyle Richmond as the new Whizzer and Nighthawk, doing so by tapping into the "Universal Wellspring," a mysterious and seemingly limitless source of alchemical power. Grandmaster also created a new Hyperion, an artificial being who believed himself to be the sole survivor of an atom-sized alien world which had been accidentally destroyed by human scientists, giving him a bitter grudge against humanity. Finally, Grandmaster sought out Krimonn, a treasonous Skrull who had been trapped in the form of a sentient crystal prism and set adrift in space after trying to overthrow the Skrullian emperor; Grandmaster guided the prism to Earth and into the hands of African supremacist Dr. Kinji Obatu, the influential, ruthless and power-hungry economics minister of an oil-rich emerging African nation. Forming a symbiotic bond with each other which allowed them to channel vast energies through the prism, Obatu and Krimonn became the new Dr. Spectrum under Grandmaster's guidance. Together, these new incarnations of Dr. Spectrum, Hyperion, Nighthawk and Whizzer formed the Squadron Sinister, serving the Grandmaster in exchange for their powers.

As participants in the Game of the Galaxies, the Squadron Sinister fought Avengers at the sites of various celebrated monuments. Captain America thwarted Nighthawk's attempt to steal or destroy the Statue of Liberty; Iron Man (Tony Stark) defeated Dr. Spectrum at the Taj Mahal after discovering that Spectrum's power prism was vulnerable to ultraviolet radiation, which existed on a wavelength beyond the prism's range of energy manipulation; Thor shrunk Hyperion down to tiny size and trapped him in a glass bubble outside the Sphinx; and Goliath (Clint Barton) battled Whizzer below the Big Ben clock tower in London until local hero Black Knight (Dane Whitman) intervened, taking down Whizzer by surprise. The Avengers had won, but Black Knight's interference led to that round of the game being declared a draw; in a second round, the Avengers defeated Grandmaster's backup pawns, Earth-616's World War II heroes the Invaders (1940s incarnations of Captain America,

CURRENT MEMBERS: Doctor Spectrum (Alice Nugent), Hyperion (Zhib Ran), Nighthawk (Kyle Richmond), Speed Demon (James Sanders)
FORMER MEMBERS: Doctor Spectrum (Kinji Obatu), Doctor Spectrum (Billy Roberts), Hyperion construct
BASE OF OPERATIONS: Manhattan penthouse apartment; formerly Nugent Technologies, Old Tappan, New Jersey; Crayton Observatory
FIRST APPEARANCE: Avengers #69 (1969)

Human Torch and Sub-Mariner). Kang won the Game, but was awarded only a partial victory due to the Knight spoiling the first round, forcing him to choose between the power of life or death rather than receiving both. His hatred for the Avengers outweighing his love for Ravonna, Kang opted for the power of death and would have killed the Avengers had he not been felled by the Black Knight. The Grandmaster departed, taking Kang's fleeting power with him, and released the Squadron Sinister from his service.

Resuming his Dr. Spectrum identity, Obatu came into further conflict with Iron Man, but Spectrum was hindered by a near-constant struggle for dominance between the rival personalities of Obatu and Krimonn. At one point, the prism deserted Obatu and took possession of Iron Man (actually Iron Man stand-in Eddie March), but the prism-possessed March was overpowered by Thor and gravely injured. The prism then re-bonded with Obatu, but Spectrum was defeated by the real Iron Man (Stark), who smashed the prism to bits. Obatu boasted that his influential

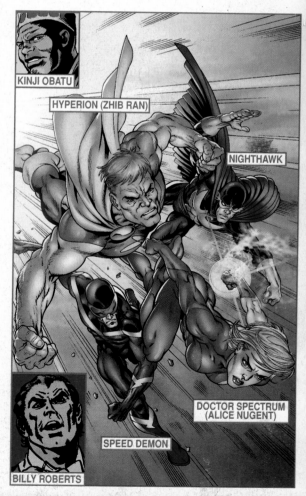

KINJI OBATU

HYPERION (ZHIB RAN)

NIGHTHAWK

DOCTOR SPECTRUM (ALICE NUGENT)

SPEED DEMON

BILLY ROBERTS

foreign position would prevent him from facing any punishment for Spectrum's crimes, but his country's tyrannical president locked him up upon his return to Africa. Meanwhile, the power prism's fragments slowly reintegrated until the gem was whole again. Detroit sanitation worker Bob Farmer found it, but the good-hearted Farmer was apparently immune to its corrupting influence. He donated the gem to celebrity evangelist Billy Roberts, who quickly bonded with the prism and became the new Dr. Spectrum.

Meanwhile, Grandmaster's departure from Earth had somehow swept the shrunken Hyperion up into outer space, where he was eventually rescued and restored to normal by alien prospector Nebulon. Seeing a chance for revenge, Hyperion offered to sell Nebulon the Earth for mining purposes, even though Nebulon insisted Earth would have to be flooded for his people to function there. Whizzer and Spectrum (who credited Nebulon with helping him render Krimonn's consciousness within the prism largely dormant) agreed to assist in this project, confident that Nebulon could transport them to other suitable worlds if Earth became unlivable. Regrouping in secret at Crayton Observatory, the Squadron coerced their reluctant fourth member, Nighthawk, into aiding in the construction of a giant laser cannon that would melt the polar icecaps and flood the Earth. Nighthawk helped the heroic Defenders ruin the Squadron's scheme, which seemingly destroyed Nebulon and the Squadron when their cannon exploded. A reformed Nighthawk became a longtime member of the Defenders thereafter.

Nebulon and the Squadron were actually hurled into the other-dimensional realm of Zaar, home of the enlightened Ludberdites, whose advanced technology enabled Nebulon to send the Squadron back to Earth when they decided not to stay in this new world. Regrouping at Crayton Observatory with an energy-draining weapon derived from Ludberdite technology, the Squadron were unexpectedly attacked by the Defenders, who had tracked them down after mistakenly theorizing that the Squadron were responsible for the recent near-murder of Nighthawk; the true culprit in that crime had actually been criminal scientist Egghead, who was quickly apprehended by his old foe Yellowjacket (Hank Pym). The Squadron captured the Defenders after their Ludberdite weapon reduced the Hulk to human form, but Yellowjacket soon freed the heroes, who arrived in time to save the hospitalized Nighthawk from an actual Squadron attempt on his life. The Defenders defeated the Squadron Sinister, and Spectrum's prism shattered again during the battle.

Since the Squadron were not wanted criminals and could not be jailed by the authorities, Defenders leader Doctor Strange magically erased the three Squadron members' memories of their special powers and criminal careers, allowing them to pursue various civilian roles. Roberts returned to his evangelism, Sanders found work as a chemist, and Hyperion worked at a health club as "Mister Kant." Meanwhile, Obatu escaped prison and partnered with witch doctor W'Sulli, who controlled a vampiric zombie he called his zuvembie. Aided by the zuvembie, Obatu returned to America, where he abducted the African warrior monarch Black Panther (T'Challa) and various prominent African Americans, bringing them back to his native country as a peace offering to its president. The scheme was foiled through the combined efforts of Brother Voodoo, the Thing and Black Panther; the zuvembie seemingly slew W'Sulli and Obatu after they lost control of it during the conflict.

When Hank Pym restored the seemingly inert power prism as a gift for his wife the Wasp, Krimonn's consciousness possessed Wasp through the gem and attacked the Avengers as Dr. Spectrum. To treat her condition, the Avengers sought out previous prism host Roberts, though doing so meant breaking Strange's spell and restoring all of the Squadron's lost memories. Hyperion attacked the Avengers and Ms. Marvel alongside his new friend Thundra until Vision talked Hyperion into reconsidering his vendetta against humanity and ceasing hostilities. Meanwhile, Whizzer

also attacked the Avengers, who swiftly defeated him. As for Roberts, he claimed he had been an unwilling pawn of the prism and offered to help the Avengers cure Wasp, but he really wanted the prism for himself. Re-bonding with the gem, Roberts attacked the Avengers as Dr. Spectrum, but the prism abandoned him for Thor, whom Krimonn had long sought as a host body. Merging with Thor's hammer Mjolnir and controlling him through it, the prism continued attacking the Avengers until Thor was separated from his hammer, which soon transformed into the walking stick of Thor's mortal alter ego due to Odin's then-active enchantment. As a result of this transformation, the prism faded away into nothingness, taking Krimonn's consciousness with it.

For years thereafter, the Squadron remained disbanded. Nighthawk continued fighting crime; Whizzer continued his criminal career in a new guise as Speed Demon, eventually joining the team of reformed villains known as the Thunderbolts, albeit as one of their less reformed members; and Hyperion died battling his Earth-712 counterpart. Recently, however, there has been new activity relating to the Universal Wellspring that first empowered the Squadron Sinister. The Church of the Universal Wellspring, a super-powered cult devoted to its worship and protection, has been sighted tapping pockets of Wellspring energy around the world. A newly formed power prism also mysteriously appeared, bonding with divorced Des Moines factory worker Martha Gomes, who used it to become the latest criminal Dr. Spectrum. After battling the Thunderbolts as a pawn of the mind-controlling Purple Man, the new Spectrum fought them again when they interfered with her own robbery spree; however, the prism apparently rejected Gomes during the battle, going dormant and allowing her to be captured. Gomes was taken into custody for examination by the CSA (Commission on Superhuman Activities), who called in brilliant telecommunications specialist Alice Nugent to help them attempt communication with the new power prism. Both a lab assistant and an employer to Hank Pym in the past, Nugent had long coveted super-powers for herself, and the prism soon bonded with her as the newest Dr. Spectrum, a process Nugent later attributed to the Grandmaster. Around the same time, a new Hyperion (Zhib Ran) appeared on Earth, allegedly the sole survivor of a "Microverse" world unwittingly destroyed by cosmic-powered Thunderbolts member Photon (Genis-Vell). Meanwhile, the Wellspring-empowered Nighthawk and Speed Demon found their powers increasing significantly.

Claiming he must master the Wellspring for the sake of the world and the universe, and predicting that this gambit would bring his forces into conflict with the Thunderbolts, the Grandmaster convinced Nugent and the new Hyperion to help him reassemble the Squadron Sinister to this end. Nighthawk and Speed Demon refused to rejoin at first, and fought off the Squadron's attempts at forcible recruitment with the aid of the Thunderbolts; however, Speed Demon soon reconsidered, rejoining the Squadron after the Thunderbolts fired him for misconduct. Nighthawk briefly joined the Thunderbolts himself as Speed Demon's replacement, but he quit the team in part because he did not trust their new leader, infamous ex-criminal mastermind Baron Zemo. Regarding Grandmaster as the lesser of two evils in the battle for control of the Wellspring, Nighthawk reluctantly rejoined the Squadron for the duration of the conflict, which ended with the Squadron's defeat and the seeming demise of the Grandmaster.

FURTHER READING: More details regarding the individual exploits of Earth-616's Kyle Richmond, James Sanders and the various Hyperions can be found in the Handbook profiles for Nighthawk, Speed Demon and Hyperion.

NOTE: Aspiring to become the future benevolent rulers of the planet, Nugent and Hyperion prefer to call their alliance Supreme Power, though most others continue referring to the group as the Squadron Sinister.